Disney Historical Highlights

The Walt and Roy Disney Years
1954-1972

Jim Korkis

Theme Park Press
The Happiest Books on Earth
www.ThemeParkPress.com

Editor: Bob McLain
Layout: Artisanal Text

ISBN 979-8-89609-014-4
Printed in the United States of America

Theme Park Press | www.ThemeParkPress.com
Address queries to ben@themeparkpress.com

Contents

Introduction

Even people who think they know everything about the early history of Disneyland and have studied it for decades, still don't really know everything. So much was going on at the Park every year that information was never properly documented or overshadowed by major events.

How many people realize that actress Annette Funicello got dressed up as an Indian princess and signed autographs in the Indian Village one weekend in 1959 or that in February of that same year Disneyland hosted a Western Weekend with Warner Brothers television westerns stars like Ty Hardin as Bronco Lane and Will Hutchins as Sugarfoot showing up in costume to meet guests?

So many other larger things were taking place that same year like the introduction of the Monorail, the Matterhorn and the Submarine Voyage that these interesting trivia tidbits simply slipped away when 1959 was being discussed and examined.

Over the years, I have been contacted by several different authors who wanted to write a book with each chapter covering a different year in Disneyland's existence. I wished them well and offered to help when I could.

None of them ever got beyond writing a chapter or two before realizing what a daunting task it would be and I never heard from any of them ever again.

Some years at Disneyland were obviously more exciting and filled with interesting things while other years seemed to have nothing much to list and required extensive research to find and verify any information at all.

Much contradictory information exists about the earliest years of Disneyland so it was important not to rely on just one source, even if it were supplied by the Walt Disney Company itself.

Even nomenclature was flexible with Bill Elliot's musical group going by at least fourteen different names in the early years on Disney signage, documents and advertisements. Generally, people refer to them as Bill Elliot and his Date Niters.

Many of the people I have interviewed over the decades who worked at Disneyland in its first fifteen years under Walt and Roy had faulty memories especially when it came to dates, names events and more or confused things with their time during the earliest years of Walt Disney World.

The only person who actually finished a book about Disneyland's year-to-year evolution was my good friend Sam Gennawey with *The Story of Disneyland* (2014) but even he had to mash several years together into single chapters and because of space limitations had to leave many interesting things out.

Over the last several years, I have been a guest on the Sweep Spot podcast to promote my latest books. It is a show hosted by two former Disneyland custodians, Lynn Barron and Ken Pellman, and primarily focused on Disneyland and its history.

They asked each year if I could do an hour or so on a particular year of Disneyland's past related to the current year. So in 2019, I would talk about Disneyland in 1959 or 1969.

Some years were so packed with things it was difficult to squeeze everything into an hour and other years were transitional years with little if anything happening at the Park so it was difficult to find enough interesting material to fill an hour.

However, that experience inspired me that I might be able to write a book about Disneyland year-by-year at least for the earliest years of the Happiest Place on Earth that really interested me. Once again, that task turned out to be, as it had for other authors, to be much more challenging than I initially imagined even hoping that the research I had previously done would give me a good foundation.

Each chapter in this book is devoted to a single year in Disneyland's early history when either Walt Disney or his brother Roy or both were at the helm of the park. After their deaths, everyone that I have interviewed over the decades has indicated that the spirit of Disneyland changed significantly and not always necessarily for the better.

The book is entitled "Historical Highlights" because it was not possible to squeeze everything into a single chapter so I made the choice to focus on some of the highlights that hadn't been previously documented as well as the major changes.

It is not meant to be comprehensive but an entertaining and informative glimpse into the past like peeking through a hole in a fence. Many things are seen but just as many are missed.

However, I did try to include something on every page that would be surprising to even the most dedicated Disneyland scholar. As with all of my previous books, I wrote this book so that I would have a reference of everything I knew that I could use and trust.

Some attractions have lasted for decades and been changed many times. I tried to restrict myself to just the year the attraction opened and how it appeared at the time of its debut with a few exceptions.

The information about attendance, number of cast members and payroll came from an official document released by the Walt Disney Company in 1980 to the media to celebrate Disneyland's 25th anniversary. The company has never released another update since that time and, in fact, has tightened restrictions considerably on revealing any similar information.

Supposedly, it was meant to show the growth of the Park over the years. It listed that total Disney capital expenditures soared from seventeen million in 1955 to a hundred and forty million in 1972. Total Local Expenditures by Disneyland rose from five million in 1955 to forty million dollars in 1972. This included goods, services, and payroll to local residents. In those early years, Disneyland had a policy of buying and hiring locally whenever possible.

So much went on at Disneyland, even during the slower years, that this book can only be just a quick snapshot of the Walt and Roy years of Disneyland with things missing, including some things that may have been particularly memorable for you or others.

I hope this time traveling trip will give Disneyland afficionados a better perspective and appreciation of the park that Walt built and he ran with his brother Roy.

I hope that it gives those who were there during those years some fond memories and for those who weren't even born during those years some sense of why the Park was so magical for those of us who did get a chance to briefly experience it in its earliest years.

I grew up going to Disneyland a kid with my parents and two brothers and as I wrote some of these chapters I could clearly remember what things looked like and felt like. I continued to visit the park as a teenager with my friends and later as an adult. Every time I felt better for having been in the Park and my spirit uplifted.

Disneyland has changed greatly in the last half century and yet has somehow remained very much the same. Let's never forget that it all started with two brothers who made something that had never previously existed and continues to delight the entire world.

Welcome to the Disneyland that will always be a source of joy and inspiration for all the world. Disneyland will always be truly your land of hopes and dreams.

Jim Korkis
Disney Historian
February 2022

1954

Walt told an interviewer for *LOOK* magazine (November 2, 1954):"In Disneyland, clocks and watches will lose all meaning, for there is no present. There are only yesterday, tomorrow and the timeless land of fantasy. Disneyland is based on the dreams and hard facts that have created America.

"I want this to be a place for parents and children to spend pleasant times together: and for teachers and pupils to discover greater ways of understanding and education."

The Canadian Broadcasting Corporation (CBC) introduced *Telescope* in 1963 as a 30-minute television program that would "examine, reflect and project the Canadian image" and for ten years this half-hour documentary series covered a wide range of subjects pertaining to Canadians.

Generally, the show featured a personality profile of a Canadian (national figure, international celebrity, or notable unknown citizen). Since Walt's father, Elias, was born in Canada, Walt was invited to be interviewed by host Fletcher Markle on September 25, 1963.

During that interview, Walt famously shared the story of the birth of Disneyland:

"Well it came about when my daughters were very young and Saturday was always Daddy's day with the two daughters. So we'd start out and try to go someplace, you know, different things, and I'd take them to the merry-go-round and I took them different places and as I'd sit while they rode the merry-go-round and did all these things... sit on a bench, you know, eating peanuts. I felt that there should be something built, some kind of an amusement enterprise built, where the parents and the children could have fun together.

"So that's how Disneyland started. Well, it took many years. It was a period of maybe fifteen years developing. I started with many ideas, threw them away, started all over again. And, eventually, it evolved into what you see today at Disneyland. But it all started from a Daddy with two daughters wondering where he could take them where he could have a little fun with them too."

As a teenager, Walt first announced his interest in building a different kind of amusement park. It was a dream that he kept coming back to several times during his life, even occasionally making tentative planning attempts over the years before Disneyland opened in 1955.

The Burbank City Council rejected in 1952 Walt's proposal for building a Mickey Mouse Park across the street from the Disney Studio but that only motivated Walt to think bigger and continue to focus on new ideas.

He visited with amusement park owners and with people who made rides and bombarded them with a seemingly endless stream of questions. His curiosity seemed insatiable.

Imagineer Harper Goff recalled that during the summer and fall of 1954, "Walt sent us all around to every amusement park in the country. We would take pictures and come back and tell Walt all about what they were doing. One of the things we tried to get was their 'gate'...how much they charged, how many people came through, and how much they made. Also what kinds of operating problems they had, such as dishonesty."

All of these reports helped Walt formulate what he wanted and what he did not want in his park.

When Disney stockholders disagreed with Walt's plans, he made an impassioned and tearful plea to them: "You say we are not in the amusement park business. No, we're not. But we are in the entertainment business. And amusement parks are entertainment.

"I know it is difficult for you to envision Disneyland the way I can. This kind of thing has never been done before. There's nothing like it in the entire world. I know, because I've looked. That's why it can be great because it will be unique. A new concept in entertainment, and I think...I KNOW...it can be a success!"

Retlaw—"Walter" spelled backward—had been incorporated on April 6, 1953. The company would provide Walt with a way to generate income to fund the development of Disneyland as well as provide financial protection for his family if he lost all his money.

He negotiated the following deal: in return for licensing his name to Walt Disney Productions, he would receive either a five-percent royalty from every merchandising transaction, or he would take a share of up to fifteen percent in every Disney project.

Since the Walt Disney name appeared on virtually everything, the agreement was especially lucrative over the years. In addition, the company could continue to use Walt's name after his death and that provided income for his family.

"I borrowed on the insurance I'd been paying on for thirty years, and sold my house in Palm Springs to get Disneyland to a point where I could show people what it would be," Walt said justifying the reason for the creation of Retlaw. "My wife complained that if anything happened to me, I would have spent all the family money."

Walt's used that money to finance his own separate design company, WED Enterprises (now known as Walt Disney Imagineering) that was an acronym for the initials of Walter Elias Disney.

WED Enterprises was a separate business entity from the Disney Studio but utilized some of the same employees and its function was to create Disneyland. All of those employees were paid by Walt not the Disney Studio even though some costs were getting charged back to the studio.

For years, people assumed the company must have something to do with weddings. In 1965, Walt Disney Productions purchased WED and its assets. It was rechristened as Walt Disney Imagineering in 1987.

On the morning of August 8, 1953, Walt reviewed the site map for Disneyland that Imagineer Marvin Davis was currently working on and picked up a No. 1 carbon pencil and drew a triangle around the plot of land to indicate where he wanted his railroad to run.

"I just want it to look like nothing else in the world," said Walt. "And it should be surrounded by a train."

For two years, Davis worked on more than a hundred different versions of the master plan for Disneyland.

As Davis told an interviewer, "Walt wanted to see every idea that you could possibly have before he settled on something."

In order to get investors interested in the project, Walt developed a "pitch kit" for his older brother Roy that contained an eight-page single-space document filled with ideas for different rides and themed areas entitled the "Disneyland Prospectus".

It was written by Bill Walsh who was working at the studio from Walt's ideas. It stated: "Walt Disney sometime—in 1955—will present for the people of the world—and to children of all ages—a new experience in entertainment. In these pages is proffered a glimpse into this great adventure...a preview of what the visitor will find in...... Disneyland."

"Like Alice stepping through the Looking Glass, to step through the portals of Disneyland will be like entering another world.

"Disneyland will be the essence of America as we know it...the nostalgia of the past, the exciting glimpses into the future. It will give meaning to the pleasure of the children—and pleasure to the experience of adults. It will focus a new interest upon Southern California through the mediums of television and other exploitation. It will be a place for California to be at home, to bring its guests, to demonstrate its faith in the future...

"And mostly as stated at the beginning—it will be a place for people to find happiness and knowledge."

It also included a drawing of what it would look like. On Saturday morning on September 26, 1953 former Disney artist Herb Ryman received an urgent call from Walt to come to the Disney Studio. When he arrived, Walt launched into a dramatic presentation of what he wanted Disneyland to be.

Walt finished by saying, "My brother Roy is going to New York on Monday to arrange for financing. You know bankers. They have no imagination. They just can't visualize it when you tell them so I am going to show them with a big sketch of the park."

An excited Herb asked, "I would love to see it. Where is it?"

Without a pause, Walt answered, "You're going to do it."

For the next forty-two hours the two men remained in the building. They went over some of the preliminary work done by others and Walt's vivid verbal descriptions enhanced how the final vision should look. Marvin Davis' elevation diagram was added to the lower right hand of the final drawing for reference to understand the layout.

Later in 1953 and 1954, other similar booklets were produced along with large presentation portfolios of artwork on stiff paper backing for use on an easel during meetings with nervous investors and sponsors of concessions or attractions. These later booklets included photographs of little model buildings, painted and lighted to look remarkably real.

All of this was done to help people see the vision that Walt saw that this was not another amusement park or carnival but something very different.

Despite all the research and initial planning, it was not until the ABC television network signed on as an investor that Walt got the cash and credit-line needed for going ahead with actually building Disneyland.

By 1954, Disneyland Inc. was a jointly owned venture of Walt Disney Productions, Western Publishing, Walt Disney himself and the American Broadcasting Company (ABC) to build and manage the Disneyland theme park in Anaheim, California.

The investment pool consisted of 34.485% by ABC (at a cost of $500,000 and guaranteeing up to $4,500,000 in bank loans), 34.48% by Walt Disney Productions ($500,000), 13.8% by Western Printing and Lithography Company ($200,000), and 17.5% by Walt Disney ($250,000).

As a provision for the joint ownership, Walt Disney Productions had the option to repurchase the shares of the other investors within seven years. With the initial success of the park, the company was able to buy back early the shares held by Walt Disney and Western Publishing in 1957.

Between 1955 and 1960 Dell produced ten giant-sized Disneyland comic books containing hundreds of pages of new, original content as well as coloring books, story books, and activity books that all focused on the park.

Walt Disney said on July 17, 1965 at a gathering of Disneyland employees at the Disneyland Hotel in celebration of Disneyland tenth anniversary:

"I remember that we were dealing with all three networks ... they wanted our television show. And I kept insisting I wanted this amusement park.

"And everybody said, 'What the hell's he want that damn amusement park for?'

"And I couldn't think of a good reason except ... I don't know ... I wanted it. (laughter)

"ABC needed the television show so damned bad (loud laughter from the audience) that they bought the amusement park."

Walt had always had an interest in television but as he told an interviewer, "I saw that if I was ever going to have my park, here at last was a way to tell millions of people about it...with TV. TV was the start of Disneyland."

While ABC was eager to make the deal even if they had to invest in what they referred to as "Walt's fairground", it still took many long meetings to hammer out the agreement.

The first rumors of the deal came in March 1954 with an official announcement on April 2, 1954 when the papers had been signed by both sides.

Within a month, Walt and his team had come up with the concept of an anthology series so that different teams could be working on different segments at the same time. The show would be split each week into segments that aligned with the themed lands of Disneyland so that Disneyland the Park and Disneyland the Show would be the same.

For a $500,000 investment in Disneyland plus guaranteeing up to $4.5 million dollars in potential bank loans, and receiving all profits for ten years from the park's food concessions, ABC owned 34.485% of the park, had a commitment for a weekly television show produced by Disney as well as first refusal on all future Disney television projects.

Interest in running the food concessions reflected UPT's previous experience in American cinemas, where most of the profit often came from retailing drinks, popcorn, candy and other items rather than from ticket sales.

On October 27, 1954, ABC aired the first weekly *Disneyland* television show, on Wednesday night, 7:30 to 8:30 pm. The first episode was titled *The Disneyland Story*. The episode explained what to expect on the new television show as well as what to expect of the new theme park. Approximately 30.8 million American viewers watched the show and the show received critical acclaim.

Walt got a weekly platform to build anticipation for his new theme park and invest audiences into wanting to come since they saw the behind-the-scenes construction progress and felt they were included in the process. In addition, the show was able to define the new entertainment enterprise as a national attraction rather than a local one.

The contract with ABC also resulted in ABC doing the largest live remote television broadcast up to that time on July 17, 1955 when it aired the show *Dateline: Disneyland* featuring the celebrity-studded opening of Disneyland the theme park.

On July 2, 1959 Disney filed a lawsuit against ABC, asking the court to invalidate the contracts between the two companies under provisions of the federal antitrust laws. Roy felt strongly that it was a "breach of faith" for ABC to claim ownership of two Disney shows that aired on the network, *Zorro* and the *Mickey Mouse Club*.

Finally, arrangements were made to settle out of court with one of the provisions being Disney buying back the ABC shares in Disneyland for $7.5 million dollars.

The amount was not arrived at by any complicated mathematical process. It was pulled out of the air by Roy himself who felt that all the publicity about the financial success of Disneyland had created an inflated idea of the value of the shares.

He also hoped it would be attractive enough that ABC, in need of money for expansion, would not argue. Roy was vocal in wanting to be rid of the deal even if it were financially unattractive for WDP.

Disney had to borrow from Prudential in order to have the cash to pay ABC. About ABC, Roy later said, "They were not likeable, workable people."

The deal was completed in June 1960 giving WDP complete ownership. In May 1961, Disneyland, Inc. was merged into the parent company of Walt Disney Productions and the weekly Disney television show was moved to NBC where it aired in "living color" for the first time.

"My brother figured we better buy those guys out," said Walt in 1965. "They had a third interest. They only had a half-million dollars invested in the park.

"But my brother figured, 'If we don't buy 'em out now, we're going to be paying a lot more later.' And it was a smart move that he did it then."

The price for purchasing the land in Anaheim would be relatively inexpensive at an average of $4,500 per acre. The total cost for just the land was $879,000. The purchase of the land by Disney would not be announced officially until May 1954.

Unfortunately, the original public groundbreaking ceremony that was scheduled had to be cancelled because of the threat of a protest demonstration by a handful of local residents led by two Garden Grove businessmen that might have stalled the annexation of the land Disneyland was on.

According to Disney, construction on Disneyland officially began July 21, 1954 approximately one year before the park opened.

Ron Dominguez started working at Disneyland in 1955 when he was nineteen years old and later became the vice president of the park. In 1954, he was living with his mother on a section of land that Disney purchased.

In a 1985 interview, he remembered, "The two real estate men who put the deal together were personal friends of our family. Ed Wagner and Frank Miller. They assured my mother that she was selling to a quality organization.

"There was a man who was caretaker for one of the orange groves and Walt hired him for about a year to keep the trees watered until they decided what they needed to keep. The man lived in one of the houses that had been moved. Most of the land was cleared by August and some of the trees on our property ended up in the Jungle Cruise jungle.

"I can remember the bulldozers uprooting the nearby orchards starting in July 1954 and we didn't pack up until August because our new house wasn't ready yet. When we left, we were stepping around ditches and holes because work was already being done.

"They took our house and a house from the Callens estate and put the two together for the Administration building. Another Callens house was used as the personnel office on West Street for the first three years or so.

"Before we moved out, we met Earl Shelton who was the Disney coordinator of construction and I later contacted him to set up an interview for a job. He had been always gently pushing us to get out of the house so his construction crew could start some work there.

"I'm glad my parents decided to sell. Business was always slow at the fruit stand anyway.

"There's something from my old orange grove, from that original property, that is still at Disneyland, a palm tree (over by the Indiana Jones Fast Pass the fat tall tree that punches through the boathouse). For a long time it was in the queue for the Jungle Cruise.

"Walt agreed to save it as part of the deal for buying our property. He was a sentimental guy like my mom and he saw how important it was to her. Besides he needed all the trees he could get."

When construction started, the city of Anaheim had five small hotels and two motels for a total of 87 rooms. There were 34 restaurants in the city and 42 policemen. The jail only had two cells.

There were 4,000 orange trees on the property that Walt had purchased and less than 20 houses. Some of those were saved and moved elsewhere to serve as offices for Disneyland. Others were torn down or burned to the ground.

Construction included:

- 3.5 million board feet of lumber

- 1 million square feet of asphalt

- 5,000 cubic yards of concrete (roughly 32,000 sacks)

- Over 35,000 cubic yards of dirt was moved

- 8,467 feet of clay pipe for the sewer system

- 4,000 feet of gas line

- 7,000 feet of water line

- 2,000 lineal feet of storm draining piping

There were1,200 full size trees and 9,000 shrubs planted that cost Walt approximately $400,000 and "depleting nurseries from Santa Barbara to San Diego" according to newspaper columnist Hedda Hopper. However, the land still included much open land, native brush, bare river banks and unpaved access roads that could be seen by guests from the train. There was approximately five million square feet of pavement.

As Imagineer Ken Anderson recalled, "They hadn't even finished the freeway to Disneyland. Six miles of it from Buena Park and Tustin wasn't finished. It was just dirt. They had contracted to finish that thing that year but when we opened Disneyland, you still sometimes had to take all these detours down dirt roads. Still, people came and we were astounded."

Imagineer Bill Martin remembered, "In 1954 we got the go-ahead to build Disneyland but we didn't know what we couldn't do in those days. We had nothing to go on because nothing had ever been built like Disneyland before. We toured amusement parks as they were around the country in those days but they had little creative impetus to offer us, so we went to work on something entirely new using the Disney movies, of course, for the way to tell the story."

1955

On January 5, 1955, the Disneyland plot of land officially became part of the City of Anaheim so had access to all of the necessary infrastructure from sewage to garbage collection and more.

ABC aired "A Progress Report" on the weekly *Disneyland* television show on February 9, 1955. A helicopter trip to Anaheim shows stop-motion photography of construction being done on the park, a model of Main Street and a car ride through the dry riverbed of the Jungle Cruise.

There were twenty-one days of rain during the spring construction period, the wettest spring in Los Angeles in twenty years that slowed construction. Then when Disneyland opened, the rain stopped but there were ten days of one hundred plus degree temperatures.

The dollar cost for excavation, utilities, nuts, bolts, nails, concrete, wood, plaster, everything from the ground up was estimated by McNeil Construction Company that was awarded the contract by Disney. McNeil used sixty subcontractors with materials purchased from several hundred sources in Southern California. During the last weeks, crews worked in shifts twenty-four hours a day, every day of the week.

Van France, the creator of Disneyland University, said, "Today's visitor would have a difficult time visualizing what it was like. The Santa Ana Freeway was far from complete. There were still many signal lights. The local roads were all two lane. And, we were in the country. Sidewalks, curbings and gutters were to come later."

By May 1955, TWA advertised that a person could soon buy a ticket from New York City direct to Disneyland, with the last leg of the flight completed by helicopter. Those Disneyland flights were managed by Los Angeles Airways, a company that offered helicopter service to nearly a dozen southland locations, including Los Angeles International Airport and Long Beach.

In 1955, a helicopter flight to Disneyland cost roughly four dollars a person each way. There were four flights daily from Los Angeles International Airport to Disneyland carrying seven to nine passengers.

The helicopter pad, itself, was located just outside Tomorrowland, on a little strip of asphalt not far from where the skyway station would be built. Thousands of guests utilized this service but private and military helicopters also landed in the heliport transporting high profile celebrity and political figures.

Public transportation to the park also included a variety of busses including Metropolitan Coach Lines, Tanner Gray Line Motor Tours, Pacific Greyhound Lines and Orange County and Long Beach bus systems.

On July 13, 1955 ABC aired the weekly Disneyland television show episode "A Further Report on Disneyland". Walt introduced an update to the soon to open park and took a look at the many details necessary to ensure the park was ready to debut.

He turned the show over to Winston Hibler who told how the studio technicians went about designing and building the attractions. Speeded-up construction by the use of stop-motion photography was used to show the frantic pace to complete the park.

"The Plaza or the Hub is the heart of Disneyland," explained Walt. "Shooting out from here like the four cardinal points of the compass, Disneyland is divided into four cardinal realms...Adventureland, Tomorrowland, Fantasyland and Frontierland."

Those four lands had been selected because they represented the four most popular movie genres of the mid-1950s.

Of course, never officially called a land was Main Street U.S.A. Main Street U.S.A. was the only "land" that every single visitor to Disneyland had to visit to get in and out of the park. It acted as a transition from reality to fantasy and an easy corridor to get guests to the hub and then to other lands.

One of the things that made Disneyland a different experience was that it was like a movie set with the guests being immersed in it as if they were actors, one of the reasons people behave differently at Disneyland.

The famous plaque that hangs about the entrance tunnel to Main Street U.S.A. was not installed on opening day because Walt had made some significant changes to the wording.

Originally, the plaque stated: "Disneyland...Where You Leave Today...And Visit the World of Fantasy, Yesterday And Tomorrow". On June 22, 1955 Walt edited those thirteen words to its current version: "Disneyland...Here You Leave Today...And Enter the World of Yesterday, Tomorrow And Fantasy."

On Friday July 15, 1955, the Los Angeles City Council in a colorful certificate proclaimed that day as "Disneyland Day" in honor of Walt's past achievements and to congratulate him on the creation of a "new era" of family entertainment with the opening of Disneyland. Unfortunately, the debut two days later was memorable for all the wrong reasons.

July 17,1955 was forever known as "Black Sunday" in Disney history because of the disastrous press preview that day when the park opened without being fully operational.

"They planned for 11,000 people. Our official records indicate that there were 28,154 guests in the Park that day, and I'm not one to tamper with somebody's estimates" noted Disney Legend Van Arsdale France.

An accurate count of the number of people in the park was challenging since the turnstile clickers had not been turned on and some people climbed over a back fence to get inside. One reason for the sizeable increase was that a large number of tickets had been counterfeited and those who were invited brought more guests than expected.

Dateline: Disneyland was the largest live remote broadcast ever attempted up to that time. The press preview and dedication of Disneyland was aired on ABC-TV and over ninety of its affiliates starting at 4:30 p.m. PST (7:30 p.m. EST).

It was a ninety minute special hosted by Art Linkletter, Bob Cummings and Ronald Reagan. On the East Coast, the show aired opposite *Private Secretary* (a sitcom starring Ann Sothern), *Studio 57* (an anthology show) and *Toast of the Town* (a variety show with musical star Ethel Merman substituting as host for a vacationing Ed Sullivan.)

Linkletter recalled, "The four (counting Walt Disney) of us showed up with no rehearsal of course. We had kind of a rough working script - and it was all live. And I was perched in various places overlooking various parts of the park, and they were around and we'd hop and jump all over.

"ABC had a lot of cameras! And since we didn't have any chance to rehearse, and we didn't have time to move cameras around because the park was so big, we just had to have that many."

Twenty-nine cameras were used. ABC did not have enough so four were borrowed from NBC, two from CBS, two from KTTV, and two from KCOP among other stations including the local KABC outlet. Twelve Zoomar lenses were used allowing the camera man to go from a wide shot to a close-up and vice-versa with relative ease.

Thirteen hydraulic fork lifts were equipped with special camera platforms in the front so that filming could take place over the heads of the crowds and other obstacles as well as making the cameras more mobile. Some of the fork lifts sunk into the freshly laid asphalt.

Because Anaheim was experiencing a heat wave, the cameras would overheat and lose picture. This problem was solved by holding a basket of dry ice under the blower of each camera.

The production included seven directors (including John Rich and Stuart Phelps), five assistant directors and twelve stage managers. ABC hired eighty crowd control people to keep guests away from the cameras and other equipment. The over-all producer coordinating everything was Sherman Marks who the other directors resented because he was not respecting their authority nor sharing information.

The interest in the opening was so great that by the end of March, ABC had sold all the advertising slots which is one of the reasons that Walt was locked into the July 17th date. ABC had taken out $40,000 worth of full page newspaper advertisements to publicize the live telecast that would result in an audience of over ninety million viewers.

Of course, while most assume July 17 was the official opening of Disneyland, Walt considered it an invited-only preview. It was not open to a paying general public.

A Disneyland advertisement in the *Los Angeles Times* newspaper on Friday, July 15, 1955, had this information: "OPENING—Disneyland, Walt Disney's Magic Kingdom, will officially open on Monday, July 18th, and remain open every day during the summer from 10 a.m. to 10 p.m. Beginning in the Fall, Disneyland will be closed on Mondays."

On Sunday, July 17, 1955, a *Los Angeles Times* article entitled "Dream Comes True in Orange Grove: Disneyland, Multimillion Dollar Magic Kingdom, to Open Tomorrow" started its article with this sentence: "A dream comes true tomorrow—Disneyland opens." Of course, the "tomorrow" is referring to July 18th and this may be one of the first times that Disneyland was referred to as the "Magic Kingdom".

In the press packet put together by Eddie Meck the head of Public Relations for Disneyland Inc. given to the media before the press preview, there is a fact sheet and at the top, just under the address, it states: "Opening: July 18, 1955 at 10 a.m."

The first issue of *The Disneyland News* sold by newsboys in the park declared in its lead story: "More than 50,000 visitors were attracted to Disneyland on Monday, July 18, when the Park officially opened its gates."

Roy O. Disney always considered July 18 as the opening day because that is when people paid to get into Disneyland and paid to ride the attractions.

It wasn't until Disneyland's 25th anniversary in 1980 that Disneyland's opening was officially declared forever as July 17 with a special 25 hour party that began at 12:01 AM PST at Disneyland on July 17 and ending the following morning on July 18.

The press preview and the public opening day in July 1955 were disastrous.

Newspaper writer Charles Ridgway said, "Everything you heard was true. They ran out of food. Rides broke down faster than they could fix them. I recall a chunk of window from the *Mark Twain* steamboat crashed on the head of an invited guest who happened to be a state senator.

"Painters still painting. Carpenters still sawing. The waiting lines were all mixed up and criss-crossing each other. The line from Autopia would end up at the Space Bar and vice versa. There was a plumbers' strike and very few toilet facilities were ready and absolutely no drinking fountains.

"I saw people get into fist fights to get a ride on the Jungle Cruise. I watched as Walt Disney messed up over and over in rehearsals as he prepared for live television coverage of the opening later that afternoon.

"After the Opening Day fiasco, the press had told people to stay away. Walt began a campaign of inviting all the press to come back, a few at a time to really see the Park. Many were taken on personal tours by Walt himself. To control crowds at the rides, Walt came up with roped aisles that weaved back and forth where people could still see the ride based on similar queues Walt said he had seen at London theaters."

Newspaper columnist James Bacon stated, "I was a writer for the Associated Press and got invited to the opening on that hot day in July. It really was chaos.

"Walt was flabbergasted the next day when he saw the adverse media reaction to his opening. Headlines like 'Disneyland Premiere is Disaster' or 'Walt's Dream a Nightmare' are hard to take after what Walt went through to get his park built.

"He told me, 'I probably opened it before it was ready. I'm making a list of all the complaints, especially the lack of water fountains, and the next time people come back, you'll see everything fixed. I take all this criticism as constructive criticism. And I'll learn from it'. That was Walt."

Disney Legend Dick Nunis remembered, "During the summer of 1955 the fate of Disneyland was very questionable. Facilities for guests and personnel were primitive compared to today. Money was in short supply. We received complaints about attraction break-downs...lack of drinking fountains...long lines...food...high prices... you name it.

"In August, the temperatures were the hottest they'd ever been... and the humidity! Temperatures were in the 100s with humidity as much as 90%. Attendance went down to next to nothing. You could literally fire a cannon down Main Street on Saturday night – in the summer – and not hit a soul.

"But Walt believed in it. Walt had hocked everything he had to get it open. He wanted to make sure we gave the guest a good show. The compliments far overshadowed the complaints...compliments for the friendliness of our people and the cleanliness of the Park."

Ticket Books

When Disneyland opened to paying customers on July 18, 1955, general admission was $1.00 for adults and 50¢ for children. There were special rates for groups and conventions if they contacted the Customer Relations manager ahead of their visit. In addition, students, servicemen and clergy could get an admission ticket for seventy-five cents.

Attraction tickets were individually priced. An "A" ticket was ten cents. A "B" ticket was twenty-five cents. A "C" ticket was good for any attraction priced at thirty-five cents. Each attraction required a ticket. There were ticket kiosks in each land so cash could be exchanged for a ticket. No cash was accepted at the entrance of any attraction. Shows like the Golden Horseshoe Revue and sponsored exhibits were free.

Those first Disneyland admission and ride tickets were "stubs" on a roll like the kind of ticket a person might purchase at a movie theater or a carnival and not as artistically impressive as the later tickets. That's why the small tickets had a round hole in them, to go through the sprocket that dispensed tickets.

The back of the ticket had the disclaimer "The person using this ticket assumes all risk of personal injury and loss of property. Management reserves the right to revoke the license granted by this ticket". That's because this was the standard "boiler plate" waiver on all generic tickets produced by the Globe Ticket Company who were later responsible for the more elaborate A-E tickets in the famous coupon books.

The first tickets to Disneyland were sold on July 18, 1955. While the cost of an adult ticket was a dollar, nine cents of that price went to a Federal tax which was later abolished in 1956.

There were no ticket books at first, but that changed on October 11, 1955.

"We had major price increase resistance in 1955," recalled Van France. "The rumor was that it cost $40 to visit Disneyland. This was impossible unless a person splurged wildly with purchases everywhere!

"To combat that rumor, Ed Ettinger, head of public relations, came up with the idea of a ticket book. Then we could advertise, 'Admission and eight rides for $2.50'. Ed worried and said, 'I'll either be a goat or a hero'. He was a hero."

The optional "A Day at Disneyland" ticket books were originally just an experimental promotion scheduled only through Thanksgiving 1955. It was advertised as "Have more fun for less money with Disneyland ticket books!"

Unlike the stubs, these tickets, called "coupons" by Disney were larger, more colorful and substantial. Each level was printed on different colored paper. In fact, the term "coupon" later was imprinted on the individual slips rather than the word "ride".

Priced at $2.50 for adults, $2.00 for junior and senior high school students (with ID), and $1.50 for children under twelve years old, each book had a general admission ticket and eight attraction tickets—three "A" coupons, two "B" coupons, and three "C" coupons that was a great bargain since it allowed the guests to pay less than face value.

One of the advantages of the ticket books was to spread the guests throughout the entire park and not have them congregate at just the most popular attractions. Having a variety of tickets also allowed guests to experience several attractions that they might not normally have selected because they were already paid for in their minds.

The primary goal was to have the guests pay only once and not have to constantly keep reaching into their wallets for each attraction. Often, guests would return home with unused, but paid for, tickets and many households still have that surplus today. They are still valid to be exchanged for face value.

Opening Facts

Employees were officially known as Disneylanders. The term "cast member" did not come until the 1960s and was created by Van France.

At its opening Disneyland had approximately 850 employees (600 or so were paid by Disneyland Inc. and the others employed by various companies operating businesses in the park) representing 106 crafts, trades and professions. However, the number quickly grew during that first summer.

Forty-five Security Officers were employed on a full-time basis at Disneyland in 1955 with eight others on call to protect the Park and its guests. In the early months, they were kept busy looking for "stolen" vehicles, which were merely misplaced in the Disneyland parking lot.

By the end of the first summer, there had been visitors from 61 different countries.

Walt banned beer though the suds makers made him some mighty tempting offers. "I could have got most of my costs back with beer concessions alone," Walt told reporter Florabel Muir for an article in the July 10, 1955 edition of the *Daily News*. "A lot of adults will come here, but Disneyland is primarily for children and I don't think kids and liquor mix."

Walt Disney was 53 years old and a grandfather when Disneyland opened.

Disneyland Training

The first Disneyland orientation training program was themed to "We Create Happiness". The orientation book was entitled *A Guide for Hosts and Hostesses* and the following was on page six: "Meet the King of our Magic Kingdom. The most important person in Disneyland is a guest. A guest is a person who enters Disneyland seeking entertainment. A guest may be white, black, brown or yellow...Christian, Jew, Buddhist or Hindu...Republican or Democrat...

"Showoff or wallflower, big shot or small...Rich or poor, healthy or unhealthy...But, from the moment his car turns into the Disneyland parking area until he leaves, he is a guest of Disneyland. How we greet him, how we look, the big and little things, are all vitally important to the enjoyment of his day at Disneyland. A Disneyland guest is to us a King in our Magic Kingdom."

Name Badges

In 1955, only employees of Disneyland, Inc. were issued brass badges stamped with their employee numbers. It wasn't until 1962 that their names were inscribed on them although some high ranking WED employees had their names inscribed rather than a number in the late 1950s.

The badges were an oval shape approximately 1 3/4" tall by 2 1/2" wide. The Disney Company never kept a record of those numbers and who they belonged to but it is known that badge number one was assigned to Walt Disney and that the numbers eventually went into four digits. The badges were produced by the Los Angeles Stamp and Stationery Company with a brooch pin on the back attached to the badge with metal riveting.

The First Children

The Schwartner family had no intention of visiting Disneyland on July 18, 1955. Bill and Mildred Schwartner had different plans for their seven year old son Michael. They drove their family Buick from Bakersfield on July 17 for a trip to Mexico and stopped in North Hollywood to briefly say "hello" to Bill's sister, Carol Vess, who had two children, Christine who was five and Donna who was eleven.

Michael was able to convince his cousins to plead with their parents to go to Disneyland instead the next day, the official public opening of Disneyland. When they arrived at eight o'clock in the morning, there were more than 15,000 people who had been standing in line since six hours earlier.

While her husband and sister-in-law went to buy admission tickets, Mildred went to a wooden awning near the entrance to wait because it was already so hot and there was no shade. Michael was so excited that he engaged in horseplay like doing backflips by the turnstiles and his cousin Christine was running around so wildly that she tripped and scrapped her knee and started crying uncontrollably. In the famous photo, it is clear that there are two bandaids below the knee of her right leg.

It caught the attention of a female Disneyland employee nearby and Mildred thought they were all going to be thrown out. Instead, the employee asked if she could take the children to meet Walt Disney.

Michael remembers spending almost forty-five minutes with Walt. "I was just a kid but he talked to me like a real person," he told *Orange County Register* reporter Joesph Pimentel in 2015. "He asked me if I could wiggle my ears. I said, 'No, can you?' He said, 'Nope, but I can wiggle my nose'. And he did, mustache and all."

Fifteen minutes before the park opened at 10:00 a.m., Walt walked to the front entrance with Michael and Christine and knelt down and greeted them as the first boy and girl to officially set foot in Disneyland. The families did not have to pay for admission and Walt personally took them around the park aboard the train where he explained about the different areas and what they could go see.

They were given a free pass to all of the rides and for all of the food and drink they wanted. They didn't have to wait in line for any ride. They all stayed until the park closed. Michael and Christine were given lifetime passes.

The Disneyland Marquee Sign

For most people, the huge Disneyland Marquee sign on Harbor Boulevard was a significant landmark. However, from 1955 to 1958, the sign didn't exist. Herb Ryman had done a sketch for a sign in 1954 that featured two turrets reminiscent of Sleepy Beauty Castle and a curved ribbon banner stating "Disneyland Entrance" but it was never built. Bill Cottrell said, "We were so anxious just to get the park opened that we didn't have the time, or probably the funds, to put much of a display out on Harbor Boulevard."

Billboards along the Santa Ana Freeway (a huge pink colored sign with yellow lettering that stated "Right Turn. ¼ Mile at Harbor Blvd. Walt Disney's Magic Kingdom Disneyland") directed drivers to the correct exit, but, after that, just the park itself was the only indicator. The Disneyland Hotel erected a big marquee sign in front of its administration building soon after it opened in fall 1955. Each letter of the words "Disneyland Hotel" was on an individual panel, with yellow panels for the "D" and "H". It seems to have been the inspiration for the Disneyland sign put up in 1958 that lasted for thirty years.

One Millionth Visitor

On September 8, 1955 at 2:31 p.m., four year old Elsa Marquez became the one millionth guest to Disneyland. Her mother Bertha was not intending to go to Disneyland that day but with her younger sister Alicia visiting in town from El Paso, Texas and all the kids wanting to go to the new park, the families went.

When they arrived at the gates, the children made a dash for the turnstiles. Raul (Elsa's seven year old brother) was first, followed by Elsa and then Manny (Elsa's four year old cousin). Manny pulled Elsa back so he could get ahead of her. When Elsa finally made it through, balloons came down and music played.

"I was terrified," Elsa remembered in an interview with Joesph Pimentel that appeared in the *Orange County Register* July 17, 2015. "My mom picked me up and a (Disneyland employee dressed as a) sheriff came over and was trying to explain something to her but my mom didn't speak English. So he grabbed me from my mom. Walt Disney bent down and shook my hands. He had a warm presence. He was a very kind person and sweet man. They put some type of crown or headdress on my head. I remember just feeling like a princess."

During this, officials were able to explain to Mrs. Marquez and the rest of the family what was happening. Elsa received a wicker basket that included a stuffed doll of Lady from *Lady and the Tramp,* a deed to Disneyland, a sealed pouch of dirt from Disneyland's groundbreaking and also a lifetime pass. She and her brother rode with the conductor on the train around the park. She led the Disneyland band with a baton. The native Indian dancers performed around her.

When Walt Disney passed away in 1966, she was told her lifetime pass was no longer valid and it took over twenty years for that situation to be rectified.

The First Christmas December 1955

A large, live, decorated Christmas tree stood proudly to the left side of the entrance to Sleeping Beauty Castle to celebrate the Christmas Festival which began November 24, 1955. Another Christmas tree adorned the forward deck of the Mark Twain.

Twelve costumed Dickens Christmas carolers from the University of Southern California under the direction of Dr. Charles Hirt (who would later create the Candlelight Processional) wandered throughout the park warbling Christmas songs and encouraging the Guests to sing along. Besides these carolers, local school bands and youth choral groups also performed usually at the bandstand.

"I trained the Disneyland carolers," said Hirt in a 1993 interview. "This included teaching the singers how to respond to people in the Park. For example, if a little girl walked up to one of the singers, that caroler would sing directly to that child."

A flyer states that "thousands of lights and marvelous festive decorations of every conceivable kind" make Disneyland "a glittering fairyland of fun and thrills".

Parking Lot

Just like the park itself, the parking lot was carefully planned and charged a nominal all-day fee of twenty-five cents.

"A 100-acre parking lot provides space for 12,175 cars – a potential load of about 50,000 adults and kids – and an 'elephant train' takes guests from the parking lot to the main gate," stated the *Hollywood Reporter* July 18, 1955

At roughly 100 acres, the parking lot covered much more land than the park it served. WED studied every somewhat similar venue they could to try to estimate parking needs and determined that the closest example was Forest Lawn Memorial Park.

WED correctly assumed that 92% of the people visiting would arrive by car with the rest coming by bus. At the different venues they studied like Knott's Berry Farm, they learned that each car averaged 3.7 persons and that daily attendance would ebb and flow with a large crowd when the park opened in the morning (and then many departing in the afternoon) and then a second wave in the afternoon staying until the park closed.

Taking the number of potential guests and the number of cars necessary to bring those guests to Disneyland, WED calculated roughly the size of the parking lot. Disneyland was considered primarily a daytime activity originally so no adjustment was made for any nighttime arrivals.

In 1955, the parking lot extended from the Disneyland ticket booths back to roughly where the Tower of Terror in Disney's California Adventure once was but only a couple of sections nearest the entrance were paved. The other parking spots were on dirt which was not uncommon for venues like carnivals and circuses. It was only in later years that the parking lot was paved out to West Katella Avenue. By 1957, management was already debating about raising the price to thirty-five cents.

Closed Mondays

At the end of that first summer, Disneyland started to close on Mondays to take care of maintenance. It was a policy that continued until 1985. Later the park would also close on Tuesdays during the off season. That first Monday the park was closed was September 12. It did open on Monday December 26 and January 2 for the Christmas Festival. For guests unaware of the Monday closings, Knott's Berry Farm remained open on that day, just as Disneyland was open on the day in the middle of the week that Knott's closed.

Who Was That Masked Man?

Walt's friend, Jack Wrather, who was building the Disneyland Hotel also owned the rights to characters like the Lone Ranger and Sgt. Preston of the Yukon. Clayton Moore who was portraying the masked rider of the plains appeared several times in full costume at Disneyland, usually by the Mark Twain or elsewhere in Frontierland, including an appearance on September 13.

Main Street U.S.A.

"Described by Walt Disney as the 'heart line of America', Main Street U.S.A. is an exact replica of a small town main street in that happy era from 1890 to 1910. Complete in every detail, from the horse-drawn streetcars which trundle up Main Street to the fire department's turn-of-the century hose and chemical wagon 'powered' by real fire horses.

"You'll see and visit all of the 1900 period business enterprises on Main Street, the photographer's shop, ice cream parlor, bakery, meat market and grocery, bank, music shop, drug store and many others -- all operating exactly as they did 50 years ago." (1955 Guide Map)

City Hall

- First Aid Station
- Lost Children
- Police, Lost and Found

Food and Refreshments

- Carnation Ice Cream Parlor
- Coca-Cola Refreshment Corner
- Maxwell House Coffee House
- Plaza Pavilion Restaurant
- Red Wagon Inn (Swift)
- Puffin Bake Shop (General Mills) (Manager George Means)

Rides and Amusements

- Fire Wagon (horse drawn hose and chemical wagon) (A ticket)
- Santa Fe & Disneyland Railroad Passenger Train (C ticket)
- Horse Drawn Street Car Trolley (A Ticket)
- 1905 Horseless Carriage (A Ticket)
- Main Street Arcade
- Penny Arcade and Shooting Gallery
- Main Street Cinema (A Ticket)

Shops and Exhibits

- Bank of America (Manager Leo Wagman)
- Bandstand (Plaza Hub)
- Book and Candle Shop (Manager Pat St. George for Disneyland Inc.)
- Blue Bird Shoes for Children
- Candy Palace (Manager Vera Connel for A.R.B. Corporation)
- Emporium Department Store (Managers Earl Phillips and Bob Erickson for Emporium of Orange County)
- Gibson Greeting Cards (Manager Dorothy Tierney for John McInnis for Gibson Art. Co.) (Shared space with Stamp, Coin and Pen Shop/East Center Street entrance)
- Global Van and Bekins Storage (storage lockers cost twenty cents)
- Grandma's Baby Shop (closes in September 1955)
- Hollywood Maxwell's Intimate Apparel Shop

- Jewelry Store (Manager Dwight Long)
- (Eastman) Kodak Camera Center (Manager Herb Reich)
- Print Shop (Managers Joe and Ray Amendt for Castle Services)
- Ruggles China and Glass Shop (Manager Phil Papel)
- Silhouette Studio (Managers Alex De Conslar and Nemo Markey)
- Sunny-View Farms Jams & Jellies (Manager Don Wehrli)
- Swift Market House (Manager Myrt Westering)
- Fine Tobacco Shop (Manager Howard Rogo for Random Parts, Inc.)
- Town Square Realty (Manager Wally Pifer)
- Upjohn Pharmacy (Manager Leo Austin)
- U.S. Time (Timex) Watches and Clocks (Manager Vera Hanson)
- Wonderland Music Store (Manager Mildred Maley for Disneyland Inc.)
- Wurlitzer Music Hall (Victorian and Modern Displays)
- Ellen's Gifts (Wynegar)
- Yale & Towne Lock Shop (Manager Jan Williams)

Shows

- Main St. Cinema

Additional

- Opera House (not open to the public). Plaza Hotel/Plaza Apartments (INA Carefree Corner in September 1956) located at 222 Main Street. During the first year, more than 900,000 people signed the Disneyland Guest Register, located at the Plaza Apartments giving their home towns and addresses.
- There was no post office in Disneyland but there were mail boxes throughout the park for the convenience of guests. The mail was picked up on a regular basis and then delivered to the Anaheim Post Office.

Adventureland

"Those romantic, tropical far-away places that all of us yearn to see, await your visit in Adventureland. A Tahitian trading post provides an exotic threshold for this wonder-world of Nature's own design. Here you'll marvel at the display of tropical flowers, birds, fish and native handicraft gathered from all latitudes. An adventurous cruise in an explorer's boat, over the tropical rivers of the world is a highlight of Adventureland.

"On this exciting trip, you'll thrill to the life-like wild animals, reptiles, birds, monkeys and even native savages. Your boat ventures under a real waterfall as you admire the tropical plants and foliage gathered from all over the world. Truly, an adventure to remember is Adventureland." (1955 Guide Map)

Rides and Amusements

- Explorer's Boat Ride/ Jungle River Boat Ride (C Ticket)

Restaurants and Refreshments

- Pavilion Restaurant
- Tropical Bar

Shops

- The Bazaar (The bazaar was operated by Lawson Engineering and sub-leased to a variety of individual vendors including Lee Brothers Enterprises, Hawaiian Shop, Island Trade Store, Guatemalan Weavers, Curio Hut, Tiki Tropical Traders, Here and There Imports)
- Jack Schrecengoal was the manager of the Bazaar. Individual managers included Berncie De Gonslar (Curio Hut), Ed Jeffries and Marta Cordon (Guatemalan Weavers), Waltah Clark (Hawaiian Shop), Eli Hedley (Island Trade Store), Leal Brenner (Her and There Imports), Bill Wong (Lee Brothers Enterprises Inc. imported Chinese novelty items, china and clothing), Merlen Poemocoah (Tiki's Tropical Traders), Vern Croft (Giftware Stand for Disneyland Inc.)

Frontierland

"Frontierland is where you'll actually 'live' America's colorful and historic past. You'll enter Frontierland through the gates of an old log fort -- past leather stockinged frontiersmen and Indians of many tribes, gathered at the entrance. All the stores and buildings, reminiscent of this period, line the board walk of the town. At the blacksmith shop, you'll watch ponies being shod -- next door you'll see the harness maker at work and across the street the ever-famous general store.

"How about 'hopping' a freight train? At the Frontierland station, you can board a scaled down version of an old-time Santa Fe and Disneyland 'iron horse', and ride in the freight car (comfortably provided with special seat) for an exciting ride around the perimeter of the park. You can board a buckboard, Conestoga Wagon or Concord Stage to ride by the Marshal's office, the jail, assay office and other frontier enterprises, including an exciting trip through the Painted Desert,. The Golden Horseshoe, 'longest little bar with the tallest glassful of pop', faces a river dock in Frontierland. From here you can board a 105 foot paddle-wheeler steamboat for a cruise on the rivers of America." (1955 Guide Map)

Exhibits

- Davy Crockett Museum

Shops

- Assay Office (Jemrocks) (Manager Darcey Hines)
- Bone Kraft (Manager Richard Swenson)
- Pendleton Woolen Mills Dry Goods Store (Sportswear and Saddlery)
- Frontier Trading Post (Manager Eve McFadden)

Shows

- Golden Horseshoe Revue
- Indian Village

Food and Refreshments

- Aunt Jemima's Pancake House (Quaker Oats)
- Casa de Fritos (Mexican Food from Frito Lay)
- Golden Horseshoe (Pepsi Cola)
- Swift's Chicken Plantation Restaurant
- UPT Concessions Food and Beverage Stands

Rides and Amusements

- Conestoga Wagon Ride (B ticket)
- Mark Twain River Boat Ride (C ticket)

- Mike Fink Keel Boats (C ticket)
- Mule Pack Ride (C Ticket)
- Santa Fe & Disneyland Railroad Freight Train (C ticket)
- Shooting Gallery
- Stagecoach (C Ticket)
- Surrey Rides (A ticket)
- Yellowstone Coach Rides (C ticket)

Fantasyland

"A world of imagination -- come to life. You'll cross a drawbridge to enter Fantasyland through the portals of a medieval castle with towers and parapets rising dizzily above you. In Fantasyland you'll take the Peter Pan ride aboard a pirate galleon that soars over moonlit London to Never Land, home of Mermaids, Buccaneers, Indians and Lost Boys, and flit through the Darling home, take the Snow White ride and meet the Seven Dwarfs, the Wicked Witch who will offer you a poisoned apple and all the other characters of this immortal classic.

"Mr. Toad's Wild Ride runs through a series of misadventures in a 1903 vintage automobile, knocking over a cow and crashing into a barn, you travel through the 'Pearly Gates' to the sounds of heavenly music. Other gay, novel amusements of Fantasyland are based on cartoon or story book characters that Walt Disney has brought to screen life. Dumbo, the Flying Elephant, a breath-taking aerial ride, the Mad Tea Party, King Arthur Carousel with 72 gorgeous steeds, the Casey Jr. circus train, Canal Boats of America, England, France and fabulous attractions." (1955 Guide Map)

Food and Refreshments
- Pirate Ship (Van Camp Chicken of the Sea)
- Welch's Grape Juice Stand (adjoining the Mickey Mouse Club Theater)
- UPT Concessions Food and Beverage Stands

Rides
- Canal Boats of the World (B ticket)
- Casey Jr. Circus Train (B ticket)
- Dumbo, the Flying Elephant (B ticket)
- King Arthur's Carrousel (A ticket)
- Mad Hatter's Tea Party (B ticket)

- Mr. Toad's Wild Ride (C ticket)
- Peter Pan Fly-Thru (C ticket)
- Snow White Ride-Thru (C ticket)

Shops

- Merlin's Magic Shop (Managers Bud and Merv Taylor for Taylor and Hume Inc.)
- Toy Shop (Manager Bob Erickson)
- Don Frank's Fantasy of Disneyland (children's clothing)

Show

- Mickey Mouse Club Theater (B ticket)

Tomorrowland

"The daring land of dreams and hopes, upon which the future rests. You'll see the giant pylon-like TWA space rocket, visit buildings of advanced architectural design, participate in American industries' imaginative and exciting exhibits -- all demonstrating what the future holds for everyone.

"Among Tomorrowland's exhibits will be an advance motion picture development, Circarama, consisting of continuous images focused on a 360 degree screen, the three billion year story of the universe from the time the earth was a flaming globe whirling endlessly through space, and a story on oil production with a 40 foot diorama of the Long Beach area for the setting. You'll see an enormous kaleidoscope of color, a gigantic aluminum telescope, a futuristic conception of American home appliances and installations.

"A court of Honor will grace the center of Tomorrowland, flying flags of each state and the American flag. Tape recordings will be used instead of the customary register to identify guests. The Jules Verne Exhibit ('20,000 Leagues Under the Sea') will also be an attraction in Tomorrowland.

"Here young drivers-to-be will learn future driving techniques on freeways of the future and enjoy speedboat excursions through an island-dotted waterway. From Tomorrowland you may have an aerial view of America by boarding a space station which, theoretically, travels in an orbit 500 miles above the earth's surface, or you may be a passenger in a TWA Rocket making a round trip to the moon.

"In short, all of man's dreams of the future are realities in Tomorrowland at Disneyland." (1955 Guide Map)

Exhibits

- Circarama (American Motors)
- Clock of the World (Timex)
- Kaiser Aluminum: "Aluminum Hall of Fame"
- Monsanto: "Hall of Chemistry"
- Richfield Oil: "The World Beneath Us"
- Art Corner

Restaurants and Refreshments

- Space Bar
- Yacht Club

Rides

- Autopia (Richfield) (C ticket)
- Rocket to the Moon (TWA) (C Ticket)
- Space Station X-1 (A ticket)
- Phantom Boats (B ticket)

Shows

- 20,000 Leagues Under the Sea (A ticket)
- Hobbyland Flight Circle

1956

- Attendance: 3.8 million
- Employment: 2,190
- Payroll: $7.8 million
- Highlights:
  - Thirteen new attractions added
  - "Fantasy in the Sky" fireworks display debuts
  - Disneyland welcomes its five millionth visitor
  - "D" Ticket added in June
  - On April first, Disneyland held its first Easter Parade.
  - On Thursday January 26, Disneyland unexpectedly closes for the first time because of a storm described as the second worst in all of Southern California's history.

At the beginning of Disneyland's second year, Walt Disney stated, "Disneyland has become a Southern California institution and a worldwide attraction. In keeping with our pledge, Disneyland will continue to grow, adding new attractions – new enjoyment to provide a place where people can find happiness and knowledge."

Disney Legend Jack Lindquist who started in the Disneyland marketing department recalled, "In January and February we made the first attempt to try to identify markets outside the Los Angeles-Orange County area that could provide real time data of the depth of the 'one-day drive market' for people coming to visit Disneyland.

"We went to the prominent Green Frog Market in Bakersfield, California. This promotion included bringing Disneyland's Autopia cars to give free rides to children on a course set up in the parking lot. Plus, there were appearances by Annette, Jimmie Dodd, Roy Williams and others from the *Mickey Mouse Club* television show. The successful Green Frog experience gave us the rationalization and confidence to expand our marketing territorial boundaries to include Las Vegas, Phoenix, Fresno, Santa Barbara, San Diego and of course, Bakersfield."

Additions

"In its second year of operation, Disneyland saw the opening of more than a dozen new attractions -- the most to be added in a single year in the Park's entire history," wrote Disney Archivist Dave Smith.

In an expansion program that cost over a million and a half dollars, new attractions were opened and existing ones renovated.

"In January, after we opened, we had a hell of a storm," said Disney Legend Joe Fowler to author Bob Thomas. "We (Walt and Fowler) had come down on a Saturday with Dick Irvine. And, of course, the roads were flooded. Walt said to Dick, 'Fine, we'll just spend the time right here'. I think that weekend cost Roy millions because that was the weekend when Walt planned the Skyway and a lot of other things.

"Walt was planning new things right along. His theory was to have new things and keep them fresh and attractive. By that same token, there were certain things that we subsequently took out. The Phantom Boats was one of them."

A Disneyland press release stated, "With the opening of Rainbow Caverns, Walt Disney has brought to a close his Magic Wonderland's first major expansion program only days from the completion of the Park's first year. The program fulfills Walt's promise for this summer season of 'More room, more rides for fun!'"

Attractions That Opened

- Astro Jets (March 24)
- The Crane Company Bathroom of Tomorrow (April 5)
- Red Horseless Carriage (May 12)
- Storybook Land Canal Boats (June 16)
- Tom Sawyer Island Rafts (June 16)
- Skyway to Tomorrowland (June 23)
- Skyway to Fantasyland (June 23)
- Rainbow Ridge Pack Mules (June 26) renamed
- Rainbow Mountain Stage Coach (June 26) renamed
- Rainbow Caverns Mine Train (July 2)
- Indian Village (July) new location
- Indian War Canoes (July 4)
- Junior Autopia (July 23)
- Main Street Omnibus #1 (August)
- Yellow Horseless Carriage (December)

The Disneyland Omnibus was inspired by the tour buses of New York's Fifth Avenue during the 1920s and the open-topped vintage vehicles of Travel Town at Griffith Park in Los Angeles. The Disneyland Omnibus provided guests one of the most leisurely (and elevated) ways to experience Main Street U.S.A. A second bus was added in 1957.

Closures

Davy Crockett Frontier Museum, Phantom Boats, Disneyland Bandstand (Plaza Gardens), Grandma's Baby Shop, Mickey Mouse Club Circus, Intimate Apparel Shop.

Tom Sawyer Island

"When you go to Frontierland, make sure that Walt takes you to Tom Sawyer's Island," said Imagineer Dick Irvine to a *Reader's Digest* reporter in 1960. "Walt was brought up in Missouri—Mark Twain country—and that island is all his. He didn't let anybody help him design it."

Imagineer Marvin Davis stated, "The general shape of the island, the way it curves and so forth, was Walt's idea. The idea for Pirate's Cove on Tom Sawyer Island was also Walt's." It was Walt who came up with all the names for the places on the island.

Vic Greene, the original art director for Frontierland, worked with Imagineers Herb Ryman and Claude Coats to produce the first designs for the Island based on Walt's ideas, including the barrel bridge that appeared in 1957. Sam McKim did some finished renderings for the Old Mill and Fort Wilderness as well as the tree house. Bill Evans did the landscaping. Emil Kuri located some "second hand" animals at a museum to install on the remote end of the island.

During the second week of June 1956, Southern California newspapers featured an advertisement of a raft with a pirate skull-and-crossbones flag making its way to Tom Sawyer Island. It proclaimed:

"Now Open at Disneyland! Another NEW attraction! Tom Sawyer's Island! Cross the river on A RAFT...explore INJUN JOE'S CAVE... with the SUSPENSION BRIDGE...visit FORT WILDERNESS...see the BURNING SETTLER'S CABIN. Relive exciting days out of America's lusty past. Explore all the magical mysteries of an island built just for FUN! Whatever you want to do, you will find fun and excitement for the whole family at this newest Disneyland attraction...Tom Sawyer's Island."

A billboard during the construction announced that the island would open June 1. It didn't. Opening ceremonies were held at noon on Saturday June 16, 1956 at the raft landing on the island. Two young guests were on hand in costume as Tom Sawyer and Becky Thatcher, and appeared in many newspaper and magazine photos with Walt.

The two children from Hannibal, Missouri, Perva Lou Smith and Chris Winkler, had won the very first of the now-annual "Tom Sawyer and Becky Thatcher" contests in Hannibal.

Perva Lou and Chris carried with them from Hannibal water from the Mississippi River and earth from Jackson's Island (the model for the island frequented by Tom and Huck in Twain's novels).

With Walt's help, the two kids christened the raft with a jug of Mississippi River water and planted a box of soil from Jackson's Island near the foot of the landing pier. The island was "officially" made a part of Missouri although as Disney Archivist Dave Smith would clarify decades later this was just for publicity purposes.

After the dedication, there was a tour of the island, including Injun Joe's Cave (actually an above-ground building covered with earth and landscaping to give the illusion of descending into a cave), Huckleberry Finn's Fishing Pier (the area was stocked with 15,000 catfish, perch and bluegill for guests to catch with a bamboo pole and a worm, and Walt caught a fish for the press that day but it got away before he could land it), Fort Wilderness, and other points of interest.

The fishing was soon eliminated because it became quite a challenge for guests to walk around Disneyland the rest of the day with their increasingly pungent catch that soon ended up discarded in some unusual locations.

In the summer of 1957, Castle Rock Ridge, the Pontoon Bridge and Tom and Huck's Treehouse (that for many years was "the highest point in Disneyland") were added for guests to enjoy. Originally, there were only two rafts *Tom* and *Huck* but this expansion prompted the addition of two new rafts, *Becky Thatcher* and *Injun Joe*.

Each of these free floating rafts carried up to 45 guests. There were two landings on the island and there were even occasions when the *Mark Twain* was being refurbished that the rafts would carry guests all the way around the island.

"D" Tickets

The "D" ticket worth forty cents was introduced along with the opening of the Rainbow Ridge Cavern Mine Train ride in 1956. The "C" ticket dropped to thirty cents. Over the years, the costs of each individual ticket fluctuated and attractions were sometimes moved to different levels. For instance, the Jungle Cruise started as a "C" ticket, jumped to being a "D" ticket and finally an "E" Ticket where it remained. What an individual ride "cost" depended upon its popularity, expenses that needed to be recovered, maintenance and other variables.

C.V. Wood

C.V. Wood, vice-president and general manager and a controversial figure in Disneyland history, resigned January 9.

Cornelius Vanderbilt Wood Jr., usually just referred to as C.V. Wood or "Woody", was a controversial and important part of the development of Disneyland. This extroverted salesman was the vice-president and general manager of Disneyland and was responsible for bringing in corporate lessees like Swift and TWA to sponsor things at the park. Wood and his team managed the daily logistics including park hours, employment, policies and more.

Under circumstances that are still somewhat unclear including the implication of money mismanagement like kickbacks from some of the smaller lessees, Wood was asked to resign in January 1956.

Most people assumed it was primarily because he took too much public credit for the creation of Disneyland. Wood billed himself as "The Master Planner (or Builder) of Disneyland" until a lawsuit by Disney in May 1960 for "misrepresentation" stopped him from doing so.

Primarily the legal action wished to stop Wood and his company from representing themselves as having "conceived the idea for Disneyland or designed, engineered or constructed" the park.

In the May 23, 1960 issue of the trade newspaper *Billboard*, Disneyland executive vice-president Donn Tatum said that in filing the suit Disney firms were not asking for monetary relief of damages. The purpose of the action, Tatum said, was to set the record straight that Disneyland "was designed and built by the Walt Disney organization and that no connection exists between it and the Wood projects".

Tatum contended that Wood's position was that of an operations manager and did not include decisions in creative concepts, design or construction of the park. The suit was settled out of court.

While he claimed Walt considered him like a son, Wood also constantly butted heads with Walt especially about the Mickey Mouse Club Circus and developed his own team that was loyal just to him. He was also known for his off-color jokes something that Walt had never cared for at his studio.

It was Wood who also brought in the legendary Van Arsdale France to create the training for Disneyland and Admiral Joe Fowler who managed the actual construction of the park.

Wood's name was expunged from Disneyland history and some who worked with him at Disneyland like Bob Gurr considered him a con man or simply refused to talk about him after his departure.

Walt wanted managers to be clearly visible to both guests and employees and also to see that the managers were constantly in the park rather than hiding backstage. In the earliest days of Disneyland, managers wore gray suits and orange ties on their white shirts.

"I wore a white shirt and orange tie when I got promoted to manager. That was how people could identify a manager in the park. They wore orange ties. It was something C.V. Wood and his Texans brought in with them because it was their school's colors (University of Texas at Austin), orange and white. In fact they called that burnt orange color 'Texas Orange'," Sully Sullivan told me.

After leaving Disney, Wood formed Marco Engineering, providing market research, design, engineering and construction to the leisure industry. To aggravate the situation, he took along some of the people he had worked with at Disneyland.

He was later responsible for amusement parks like Denver's Magic Mountain (1957), Massachusetts' Pleasure Island (1959) and New York's Freedomland (1960) which had many similarities to Disneyland. He was also responsible for the initial work on Six Flags Over Texas (1961).

Rainbow Ridge

In 1956, with the addition of new scenery to the Frontierland wilderness, the stagecoach ride became the Rainbow Mountain Stagecoach Ride. It themed in with the new Rainbow Caverns as well as the new storyline that The Rainbow Mountain Mining and Exploration Company had begun activity in the area.

While the ways to explore the Frontierland wilderness were authentic, they were low capacity and gave guests a very rough ride. In 1956, Walt invested roughly $400,000 for a new attraction that would provide a more comfortable experience as well as handle more visitors, the Rainbow Ridge Cavern Mine Train.

The little town of Rainbow Ridge with businesses like the Last Chance Saloon and El Dorado Hotel sprung up in the loading area as the fictional Rainbow Mountain Mining and Exploration Company arrived. Guests boarded one of six ore cars (each one holding ten passengers) pulled by a small locomotive on a narrow gauge track to venture on a seven minute frontier excursion.

The four engines were built under the supervision of Roger Broggie and were styled after the industrial steam engines from the turn-of-the-century although there were details like the headlights and wood burner stacks that made them appear even older. They had electric motors and industrial batteries in their tenders. Live narration was provided by either the engineer or the brakeman who was in the last car and heard through individual speakers in each car.

Guests started their trip going through a mine shaft and then passed through rocky cliffs, underneath the Natural Arch Bridge and more including the desert with saguaro cactii that looked somewhat human like the Seven Dwarfs. Guests saw the Devil's Paint Pots with their steaming multi-colored "lava" constantly bubbling before maneuvering between balancing rocks that threatened to fall on the train.

The dramatic conclusion was a trip through the eerie Rainbow Caverns created by Claude Coats where black light effects provided a breathtaking show with the many waterfalls among the stalactites and stalagmites.

Mineral Hall

Mineral Hall was a shop operated by the Black Light Corporation of America (a distributor of Ultra-Violet products in Southern California when black light was still a novelty owned by Thomas Warren) near the exit for the Mine Train in Frontierland and was officially part of the fictional town of Rainbow Ridge (and the famous Rainbow Caverns with its memorable black light finale). In fact, the two story building was meant to resemble the architectural style of the smaller buildings at the attraction.

The location of the shop is now where the Rancho de Zocalo restaurant operates. A second floor window on the front façade of the restaurant is labelled "Mineral Hall".

Walt originally intended Mineral Hall to be a Natural History exhibit similar to one he had seen at the Los Angeles Museum of Science and Industry where a room demonstrated how flourosecent minerals glowed under black lights

However, it evolved into part gift shop and part science exhibit with a series of mineral displays in the back that showed rocks under regular light. Periodically, the U-shaped room would darken and the rocks and minerals would glow eerily under the magic of black light. In addition there were paint and dye samples that did the same. Then the lights would return to normal.

The shop sold black lights so guests could duplicate the experience at home and fluorescent items including over two dozen rock samples that could be purchased for different prices from ten to fifty cents in a blister pack that had a small bubble with the piece on a red and yellow cardboard card that proclaimed: " From True Life Adventures. Walt Disney's Mineral Land. Rocks and Minerals".

In 1956, Walt Disney purchased a small stump from the Pike Petrified Forest in Colorado that he installed in Frontierland. At the same time, he also purchased one ton of small pieces of petrified stone to sell to guests that was sent directly to Disneyland's Mineral Hall.

Indian Village

At Disneyland, Walt Disney wanted Frontierland to be representative of the wild frontier rather than a settled town.

By the time the park opened in July 1955, a temporary Indian Village was located near the border between Adventureland and Frontierland. In 1956, the village was moved to the area now occupied by Critter Country at a cost of $100,000 as part of Disneyland's expansion that year. It was only accessible by a dirt path called Wilderness Trail (while other areas at Disneyland were paved) through a rocky pedestrian tunnel.

A Disney press release declared: "One of the founding principles upon which Disneyland was designed was the preservation of our American heritage.

"This principle may be seen in many of the free shows and exhibits in each of Disneyland's realms—and one of the most popular among many free performances is the preservation of Indian traditions and customs in Frontierland's Indian Village.

"Built on the banks of the Rivers of America, the Plains Indian settlement is authentic in every detail. Animal hide tepees, a birch bark 'long house', spears and other implements and especially the population of real Indians take visitors into a World which has disappeared from the American scene.

"Highlight of a visit to the village is the performance of ceremonial dances by the representatives of 16 tribes.

"With bright feathers and beads decorating their colorful headdresses, moccasins and other articles of clothing, the Indians perform such generations-old ceremonies as the Friendship Dance, Indian symbol of welcome to visiting tribes; the Scout Dance, oldest Indian dance, keynoted by freedom of expression; the Horse Tail, Eagle, Buffalo and Warrior Shield dances.

"All have specific meanings for the Indians—messages that are related to visitors by Chief Shooting Star, a Sioux, while Lee High Sky (Shawnee), Little Arrow (Winnebago), Eddie Little Sky (Sioux) and other representatives of America's true natives perform.

"Nearby, as the sound of Indian chants and drums carry through the settlement from the Ceremonial Dancing Circle, Indian war canoes glide away from shore for a trip around the Rivers of America. Paddled by guests themselves, the canoes are guided on these journeys by Indian braves, skilled in the handling of their craft.

"Among the tribes represented in Frontierland: Apache, Shawnee, Winnebago, Hopi, Navajo, Maricopa, Choctaw, Comanche, Pima, Crow and Pawnee."

In 1956, there was a sign proclaiming: "This is an authentic reproduction of a typical encampment of Plains Indians and their way of life during the years when the white man first entered the vast Indian territory of the west."

In its publications and on park postcards, Disney described it as "full blooded Indians in a peaceful and authentic village" unlike the savage war parties that burned down the settler's cabin and would occasionally attack Fort Wilderness on Tom Sawyer Island.

There were demonstrations of archery in what was known as the Pawnee Arrow Game, displays and demonstrations of arts and crafts like weaving and beadwork as well as short presentations about Native American culture.

The Chippewa Longhouse was authentic and was built by Alexander Matthews Bobidosh, President of the Ojibwe (Chippewa) Tribal Council and a member of the First Nations. The structure had "sewn" Birch & White ash roof, and frame work made of saplings laced with leather.

The village also had a facsimile of a Burial Ground, a stuffed Bison (something most Americans had never seen) and a Navajo Sand Painting exhibit.

The Native Americans only appeared at Disneyland during weekends, summers and holidays. Starting in 1956, guests could grab an oar and climb aboard one of the Indian War Canoes captained by a real Native American at both the front and back and attempt to navigate the Rivers of America around Tom Sawyer Island.

Five Millionth Guest

On October 3, four year old Debra Rutherford of Quincy, Washington became the five millionth guest to visit Disneyland. She was officially welcomed by Jack Sayers, director of customer relations, and given a key and silver pass to the park. Debra accepted a baton and did a creditable job of leading the Disneyland band playing *The Mickey Mouse March*. Then she climbed on top of a big ladder with her father to change the Main Street Railroad Station population sign. From there, Debra and the rest of her family (three year old sister Patricia and dad and mom Mr. and Mrs. W.L. Rutherford) entered and enjoyed a full-day scheduled with rides, treats and eating as guests of Disneyland management.

Other Highlights

- The Disneyland Hotel formally opened on August 25.
- On November 11, Disneyland announced that Liberty Street to parallel Main Street USA is in the planning stages taking the place of the previously announced International Street.

- The Christmas Festival began November 22. From December 15-30, there was a special promotion of "Meet Spin & Marty and Annette in Person!"

- 40% of all Disneyland visitors were from out of state, including visitors from 63 foreign countries.

- The Disneyland Band performed 1,460 concerts.

- It took a crew of more than 200 men--carpenters, craftsmen, artists, and artisans, painters, and electricians to keep Disneyland spotless and in perfect operating order at all times.

- Twenty-four restaurants and refreshments stands in Disneyland were equipped to serve approximately 8,000 persons hourly.

- All animals at Disneyland and their quarters were inspected regularly by officers of the SPCA.

- On one day in the month of August, 1956, Disneyland's visitors took a total of 25,000 boat trips on the Park's seven Water rides.

- Disneyland was designed so that an actual walking disatnce of one and a quarter miles takes a guest through the Park.

- Seventy-two prancing steeds raced around the King Arthur carrousel in Fantasyland. Ten shields on the spears supporting the covering canopy of the carrousel represented ten of the founding Knights of the Round Table. Among those represented: Sir Launcelot, Galahad, Perceval, Tristan, Gawain and Gareth, Bedevere, Lionel and Bors.

- Approximately 270,000 gallons of water per hour are circulated to create the seven multi-colored waterfalls seen in the Rainbow Caverns in Frontierland.

Walt Says

In the Summer of 1956, Walt did a series of interviews with journalist Pete Martin: "It really takes a person more than a day to see the park without exhausting themselves. And as I get these new things in, it's going to take more time. Well, a lot of people come back the third time and just like to sit and listen to the band, see the horses going around. I like to go down and sit by the river and watch the people.

"Chewing gum sticks up things so we don't sell it. And peanut shells. We sell the unshelled. But shelled peanuts, they just crumble them and throw them all over the place. And nothing with round sticks. People trip on them. The ice cream bars got flat sticks and I won't sell any of this spun candy because the kids get it and get it all over everything and people get it on their hands. No liquor, no beer, nothing. Because that brings in a rowdy element. That brings people that we don't want and I feel they don't need it."

1957

- Attendance: 4.3 million
- Employment: 2,960
- Payroll: $10 million
- Highlights:
  - Eight new attractions added
  - Debut of "Christmas in Many Lands" holiday parade
  - Holidayland opens
  - The first New Year's Eve party with 7,500 guests attending. This was an experiment to test an advance-sale ticket program that was so successful it later expanded to Dixieland at Disneyland, Spring Fling and other "hard ticket" events.
  - First Date Nite
  - Disney begins the Community Service Awards program at Disneyland, giving cash awards to local service organizations
  - The Flower Mart begins selling artificial flowers on Main Street, U.S.A. at Disneyland
  - Former Democratic President Harry S. Truman visited the park with his wife and famously refused to have his picture taken by the Dumbo attraction because he felt the elephants were the symbol of Republicans
  - By 1957, Disneyland maintained around 200 head of horses, ponies, mules, and burros overseen by Owen Pope. These included the Belgians, Clydesdales, Percheron-Shire hybrids, and Percheron draft horses that would pull the Main Street Horse Drawn Streetcars.
  - Walt Disney's Magic Kingdom Club (MKC) was created in 1957 as a unique marketing vehicle for the new Park. The Club offered discounted and special-value ticket media to the employees of large companies, industry and military throughout Southern California. It was actually the prototype for the later airline and hotel loyalty membership programs that instilled the sense of a special beneficial relationship.

When Disneyland opened in July 1955, it was incomplete. Tight deadlines and financial restrictions had prevented Walt Disney from doing everything he wanted but he realized that the park was a living entity that he could constantly change.

"The Park means a lot to me in that it's something that will never be finished," said Walt to writer Pete Martin in an interview June 1956 for the *Saturday Evening Post*. "It's alive. It will be a live breathing thing that will need changes. I wanted something that could grow. Not only can I add things but even the trees will keep growing. The thing will get more beautiful each year."

It wasn't just new attractions that were introduced, but enhancements to existing things. For instance, 1957 saw the addition of two new rafts, the *Becky Thatcher* and the *Injun Joe*, to take guests to Tom Sawyer Island.

On the Jungle Cruise, Walt put in a couple of huge but stiff gorillas who moved their arms in a limited fashion like the other electro-mechanicals of the time before Audio-Animatronics, native dancers moved around a dance circle (originally built by Bob Mattey and then quickly re-built by Bob Gurr), a war party with upraised spears threatened from the underbrush and, famously, Trader Sam, the head salesman of the jungle ("He'll trade you two of his heads for one of yours."), made his first appearance.

Walt sought to include amenities for the guests, not just things that required spending more money, so the Baby Care Center opened off of Main Street U.S.A. to assist mothers with their infants. The location included a "Hopper" that looked like a combination of a sink and a toilet. Before disposable diapers, this device was used to wash and rinse soiled cloth diapers.

The Tinker Bell Toy Shop opened in Fantasyland. The second Main Street U.S.A. Omnibus was put in operation to ferry an additional 35 guests. Disneyland welcomed its 10-millionth guest, Leigh Woolfenden, on December 31, 1957.

An adult ticket book with admission and 10 attraction tickets was $3 (a $4.15 value). A child's ticket book was $1 cheaper. The attractions each required the appropriate ticket: "A" ticket ($0.10) "B" ticket ($0.25) "C" ticket ($0.35) and "D" ticket ($0.50).

Disneyland Hotel "in the heart of America's favorite playground" advertised that "a planned trip is a more pleasant trip" and offered single rooms from $10-$15. A suite would run $22-$25. While the Disneyland Hotel had a huge, distinctive marquee sign, Disneyland itself would not get a similar one until 1958.

In these early years, money was tight at Disneyland, so Walt looked for creative but inexpensive ways to "plus" the experience for guests by partnering with local clubs and with businesses that already operated at the park for special events.

Western Regional Pancake Races

The Quaker Oats Company operated the Aunt Jemima's Pancake House in Frontierland since 1955. They also sponsored the Aunt Jemima Community Pancake Days around the country featuring an odd pancake race as part of a fundraising program for local clubs and organizations.

Pancake races were a longtime U.K. tradition in the city of Olney where housewives would race down a street flipping a pancake in a skillet. Starting March 3 -5, 1957, Disneyland sponsored the Western Regional qualifying round in partnership with Quaker Oats until 1964 that determined who would go to the Nationals.

The winner received a check for $100 presented by Aunt Jemima (actress Aylene Lewis until her death in 1964 and sometimes in the 1960s actress Palmere Jackson portraying the character) in addition to a plaque signed by Walt Disney, an enormous Disneyland food basket with items like Aunt Jemima Pancake Flour and Swift canned meats, an Aunt Jemima cigarette lighter, an umbrella, and a fish knife in a sheath.

Real housewives, in housedresses, aprons and high heels, raced down Main Street U.S.A. deftly avoiding the trolley tracks while flipping a pancake from a skillet over three different ribbons that stretched eight feet overhead across the street. Each of the two dozen participants had been winners in their local competitions usually sponsored by a local supermarket or a club like Kiwanis or Lions.

Date Nite

Every Friday and Saturday from June 28 to November 16, Disneyland extended its operating hours from 6pm until midnight to offer teenage Southern California dating couples an opportunity to enjoy a date at Disneyland. It was meant to create a new market for the Park that was generally considered just a daytime experience.

The advertisement stated: "Walt Disney's fabulous attractions are more fun than ever under the stars." The theme song for Date Nite was "Let's Dance at Disneyland" and was performed by The Elliott Brothers Orchestra.

It was originally focused at Carnation Plaza Gardens because of the availability of a large dance space and being adjacent to a food location that served burgers, fries, sodas and more. The "house" band was the fourteen piece Elliot Brothers Big Band orchestra. Special Disneyland

Date Nite Ticket Book that had two admissions and ten attractions for $6.50. It permitted entrance after five pm.

The *Los Angeles Times* ("Fountain of Youth Overflows With Disneyland Date Nighters" by Barbara Jo Willcockson, August 18, 1957):

"Fantastically, nearly 8000 young people (70% of the attendance) are tallied every Friday and Saturday night as they enthusiastically pour in. They are noisy, they are delightful, they are everywhere. The management's understandable qualms have melted into applause for 'that terrific bunch of kids'.

"College age or high school, their whole hearted, trouble-free response has proved that this was just what they were looking for—plenty of room, infinite variety, minimum cost and a complete absence of liquor anywhere on the premises."

Walt Disney himself insisted that as long as the park is open, any guests must experience the full Disneyland show, and thus all attractions should remain open. It was immediately popular so that Disneyland in July 1957 extended the hours to one am and it became an annual event for many years. By September 1958 Disneyland claimed that more than a half-million people had already become "Date Niters".

With the growing popularity of the park, Walt was desperate to increase capacity so several well-loved attractions premiered although some of them were already considered temporary and only lasted a few years or at most a decade.

Viewliner

Walt had initially wanted a monorail in Tomorrowland, but neither the money nor technology existed to provide him that dream. Eventually, it would materialize in 1959 and become a historic icon.

Walt had a keen awareness of anything new that was being developed and experimented. General Motors was promoting a new type of streamlined, lightweight train dubbed the Aerotrain that could average speeds of 100 miles an hour. It was hoped it would encourage travelers who were being lost to airlines and their own personal automobiles to return to train travel.

In 1956, one ran from New York City to Pittsburgh, while a second ran between Cleveland and Chicago and a third from Las Vegas to Los Angeles.

It seemed as if it would be the train of tomorrow, or at least of the immediate future. The Santa Fe & Disneyland Railroad represented the old steam trains of the past but Disneyland's Viewliner (also sponsored by Santa Fe) was the predicted future of train travel.

The half-scaled version of the actual Aerotrain was done for Disneyland by Imagineer Bob Gurr who had ridden the Las Vegas to Los Angeles route. It was described as "a prototype interurban express train of the future."

The Viewliner consisted of an "engine," four coaches, and an observation coach at the rear. The Viewliners were designed, engineered, and assembled at the Disney Studios in Burbank.

Each of the coaches measured 16 feet 10 inches in length, with a capacity of 32 passengers each, and weighed 1,980 pounds. The bodies were constructed out of aluminum on steel frames and had conventional railroad wheels that operated on a 30-inch gauge track. The Disneyland steam locomotives ran on a 36-inch gauge track.

There were two Viewliners: a red one that operated out of Tomorrowland (with the station about where the Monorail station would later be) and a blue one that operated out of Fantasyland (with the station near where the Matterhorn would later be built). They both maneuvered around a track loop that at one point paralleled the steam trains. The Viewliners passed over the Motor Boat Cruise and glided by both the Tomorrowland Autopia and the Junior Autopia.

The names of the Fantasyland cars were Alice, Cinderella, Pinocchio, Bambi, and Tinker Bell. The names of the Tomorrowland cars were Jupiter, Venus, Mars, Mercury, and Saturn. One Imagineer joked that Walt should make a spare car named Pluto so it could be used on either train. The Viewliner cars were permanently coupled together so adding an additional one was impossible.

The engine was unique because it was a 1954 Oldsmobile 88 coupe. There was a 14-inch section in the center of the dashboard for a radio that had to be removed so that the chassis was not too wide for the track. That's why examining photos of the front of the train show a vertical seam down the middle of the windshield.

It had a steering wheel (that Gurr moved over to the other side), automatic transmission, reverse gear, and brakes. It operated on gasoline and ran on a standard Oldsmobile Rocket V8 engine. The engine was 18 feet 10 inches in length and weighed approximately 5,000 pounds.

On its opening day in June, electrical wiring shorted out and smoke billowed out from the front. Gurr had to pop open the front hood (since it was a car) to make adjustments so he and Walt could pilot the inaugural run.

The Disneyland attraction lasted only 15 months until September 30, 1958, and then disappeared to make room for construction of 1959's first three "E" Ticket attractions. During its short career, the vehicles carried 1,452,870 guests and required a twenty-five cent "B" ticket.

Motor Boat Cruise

When Disneyland opened, it had a Tomorrowland Lagoon where the Tomorrowland Boats (later renamed the Phantom Boats) operated. The poorly designed fiberglass bodies resulted in the outboard motors overheating and stalling and eventually required a cast member as the captain. There were officially retired in the summer of 1956.

Walt saw that guests liked the idea of a boat ride and eventually came up with a fleet of motorboats from Arrow Development with the steering wheel in the center so everyone on the bench seat could have access to it. The wheel was basically non-functioning but in the early years could be moved slightly, sometimes resulting in the boat getting stuck because it had slid off its rail.

The boats were made out of mahogany plywood and painted white with one additional solid color of red, blue, green or yellow on the hull.

The attraction was on a pipe rail track, so there was no danger steering into the rocks or bridge pylons along the way. A gas pedal did not increase the speed but did produce a louder sound.

There was landscaping and a chance to glimpse some other operating attractions but no storyline and nothing unique to see. However, it was popular for children because "young skippers can pilot their own private yachts on a cruise through narrow straits and white water rapids with rock-filled currents". This attraction required a twenty-five cent "B" ticket and lasted for approximately 35 years.

Frontierland's Petrified Tree

By the edge of the Rivers of America, not far from the entrance to the Mark Twain Riverboat, is a plaque in Frontierland that states:

"Petrified Tree from Pike Petrified Forest, Colorado. This section weighs five tons and measures 7 ½ feet in diameter. The original tree, estimated to have been 200 feet tall was part of a sub-tropical forest 55 to 70 million years ago in what is now Colorado. Scientists believe it to be of the Redwood or Sequoia species.

"During some prehistoric era, a cataclysmic upheaval caused silica laden water to overspread the living forest. Wood cells were changed during the course of time to sandstone. Opals were formed within the tree trunk itself. Present to Disneyland by Mrs. Walt Disney September 1957."

The story that has been told for decades is that in 1956, for his 31st wedding anniversary, and while vacationing in Colorado, Walt purchased this fossilized tree stump as an anniversary gift for his wife, Lillian. When it was shipped to their home, Lillian found she did not care for the oddity and so gave it to Disneyland the following year because it "was too large for the mantle at home" the press was told.

On the evening of July 11, 1956, Walt and Lillian visited Pike Petrified Forest, now part of Florissant Fossil Beds National Monument in Colorado. Lilly was much less interested in the experience and stayed in the car but Walt decided he wanted to buy "a small specimen." The price was $1,650 negotiated with Jack Baker who bought and sold fossils through his company Pike Petrified Forest Fossil.

The tree was never sent to the Disney home or was Walt's actual wedding anniversary gift to Lillian. It was merely another of the many antique curiosities that Walt delighted in displaying in the park and the basis for a "good story" that made people smile.

The 10-foot-tall stump and one ton of small pieces of petrified stone were sent directly to Disneyland's Mineral Hall in late July-early August. The moving of the stump was left to B & R Construction Company of Colorado Springs.

Sleeping Beauty Castle Walk-Thru

To help explain the story of Disney's interpretation of the fairy tale *Sleeping Beauty* to the guests, to promote the upcoming Disney animated feature film, and to allow guests an opportunity to go inside the castle, a narrow walk-through series of dioramas of miniature scenes was designed by Imagineer Ken Anderson for the interior of the castle.

This "A"-ticket walking tour costing a dime took guests up narrow winding stairs in the dark to view miniature dioramas concentrating on key moments in the story. Illuminated manuscripts in leather bound volumes helped guests follow the storyline as they walked from one end of the castle to the other over the archway. There was music and sound effects including an "echo" effect at one point.

The dioramas were dimensional plywood cutouts that had some elements of movement. For instance, Maleficient had Diablo the Raven on her shoulders and his wings slowly flapped thanks to a small motor mechanism. It was very similar to the sets and figures in the original Fantasyland dark rides.

There were almost a dozen scenes including "Burning of every spinning wheel in the kingdom," a series of flats with a lighted burning effect down in the courtyard similar to an effect later used in Pirates of the Caribbean; "Three fairies watching over the little princess night and day," where the fairies would appear to float over the cradle using the "Pepper's Ghost" technique later used in the Haunted Mansion ballroom scene); "Meet Maleficient's demons," where the guest could peak through keyholes to see the goons (a last-minute addition since the original plans indicate that the guests at this point were to wander outside onto the rear balcony for a view of Fantasyland but that never happened); and

"Love's First Kiss" (when the prince leaned over and kissed the cut out of Aurora she fluttered her eyelids and opened her eyes).

The official dedication of the new walk-through took place on Sunday, April 29, 1957 at 3 p.m. with the Disneyland Band playing "When You Wish Upon a Star" in the courtyard. Walt escorted actress Shirley Temple Black through a pathway created by the band led by Vessey Walker to the entrance of the walk through.

Mrs. Black, dressed as a princess wearing a gold crown and a floor length red velvet cloak, accompanied her three children: oldest daughter Linda, son Charles Jr., and youngest daughter Lori. They stayed at the Disneyland Hotel and apparently enjoyed some time together at the park earlier that day before the dedication ceremony.

After Walt spoke to the crowd briefly, he introduced Black and she told the story of *Sleeping Beauty*. Then, with Walt, she cut the chest-high ribbon to open the attraction and went inside. Later, she waved to photographers and guests from the upper balcony.

This was the first time in Disney history that an attraction based on a film opened prior to the film's debut. The castle opened four years before the release of the film and the walk through two years before the film debuted..

Frontierland Shooting Gallery

Disneyland featured several different shooting galleries. The Main Street Penny Arcade had one from 1955 to 1962 and Adventureland had another from 1962 to 1982. The most popular, and probably the most appropriate, was the one in Frontierland that opened in July 1957 and still operates today. All of these shooting galleries required quarters, not tickets, for decades.

Even Walt had to pay to use them. Walt did not hunt for sport, but enjoyed the skill needed to hit a target in a shooting gallery.

Frontierland featured 16 rifles (reminiscent of the ones used by Davy Crockett in the Disney television series and comparable in power to a .22 caliber rifle) and guests got 14 shots. These extra-soft lead bullets were imported from Australia.

The heavy guns were positioned in a cradle to prevent guests from aiming outside the gallery. After each firing session, a cast member would have to reload each rifle with pellets. The targets were the tra-ditional chain-driven images that moved back and forth on a loop in front of a backdrop.

MacGlasshan Guns supplied the Disney shooting galleries with their rifles beginning in 1955. Every night the targets had to be repainted to cover the dings made by the lead pellets. It was discovered that more than 2,000 gallons of paint were being used every year and that the excessive maintenance time could be best allocated elsewhere in the park.

The guns were replaced with 18 new infrared light beam rifles in 1985 and the gallery was updated, as well including humorous sound effects, and it was renamed Frontierland Shootin' Arcade.

Monsanto House of the Future

Monsanto had sponsored the Hall of Chemistry in Disneyland's Tomorrowland since 1955. Monsanto wanted to expand its presence in Disneyland, but also in the booming home construction industry.

They felt that they might be able to develop a method of using its plastics in construction, not simply to replace existing wood at a less expensive price, but explore the possibilities for new structural, durability and aesthetic options.

In 1953, Monsanto's Plastic Research Laboratory partnered with the Massachusetts Institute of Technology (MIT) to develop on a larger scale something that was already being done with furniture, like molded plastic chairs.

It was decided that only a full-scale display house would best demonstrate these new applications both to builders and the public. As a result, it was offered as a free attraction at Disneyland to guests to walk through and discover the wonders of future living.

Walt, of course, was excited because his original concept of Tomorrowland was to have guests experience the world of the immediate future just around the corner. It would also offer another attraction to the growing list of attractions, especially for Tomorrowland, which was sorely in need of something new rather than the last-minute exhibits about plumbing, painting, and dairy products that filled the area.

The house was located to the left side of the entrance to Tomorrowland and was a white cruciform with four gracefully curved fiberglass wings cantilevered from a 256-square-foot central core. It was like a cross or a "plus" sign and was chosen because it not only provided full daylight for each individual room, but sound reduction, privacy, and the ease in adding extra modules.

Each wing was 8-feet tall, 16-feet wide, and 16-feet long. Overall, the house was 1,280-square feet and had three bedrooms, two baths, a living room, a dining room, a family room, and a kitchen. The house opened June 12, 1957 after a media preview a day earlier.

The Kelvinator Division of American Motors Corporation, which had been an original Disney lessee, designed the kitchen. The "Atoms for Living Kitchen" had appliances that either dropped down from overhead, like the "cold zone" units that took the place of a refrigerator, or popped up from the counter, like the new microwave oven. An ultrasonic dishwasher was included to clean plastic dishes, bowls, cups, and more. It also served as a storage cabinet for them, as well.

Sylvania Electric Products Company provided adjustable panel lighting behind polarized plastic ceiling tiles that could mimic "the glow of natural sunlight," as well as bright "shadow-less light." Bell Telephone contributed the push-button speakerphone (that would make its general public appearance years later at the 1964 New York World's Fair) with "pre-set" dialing to call selected numbers, like a doctor or the school. In the bathroom there was a phone with a video screen so you could see who was at the front door, but they couldn't see you.

The bathroom featured a movable sink that, at the push of a button, could adjust higher or lower for the person using it. Devices included an electric razor and an electric toothbrush with an attached cord. The living room had a large, wall-mounted (non-working) television screen and, of course, a built-in stereo sound system.

While today, many of these innovations seem quaint and unexceptional, it must be remembered that at the time they were considered revolutionary. Coordinating the design and building of the House was Imagineer John Hench, who supplied his personal touch both inside and outside the attraction.

Working with landscaper Bill Evans, Hench helped design the exterior multilevel waterfall and horticultural terraces. The area surrounding the building was meant to resemble a calm, beautiful Japanese garden that appeared to float above the water.

Within the first three years, the house welcomed more than six million guests. During that time, the entire structure settled less than 1/20th of an inch. More than 20 million people (more than the entire population of the state of California at the time) visited by the time the house was finally removed in 1967.

It was estimated that the cost of such a house would be in the $15,000-$18,000 range (roughly 10 times that cost today) although that price would increase with other options, including the ability to have a rotating base.

The house proved more durable than expected when the original plan for a one-day demolition in late 1967 turned into a long two-week project. The building had to be hack-sawed piece by piece according to Hench and parts crushed with wrapped chains into removable pieces when the wrecking ball kept bouncing off the sides of the house.

Midget Autopia

The Autopia attraction in Tomorrowland was instantly popular, resulting in Walt opening the similar Junior Autopia in Fantasyland in 1956 to try to handle the demand.

In Fantasyland, near the Storybook Land Canal Boats in 1957, Walt introduced the Midget Autopia for the smallest of Disneyland's guests who might not be able to steer or operate the gas pedal on the other Autopia attractions.

Unlike other Disneyland attractions, no adults were allowed on the Midget Autopia. It was more like a cartoon experience than a miniaturized driving opportunity for two people. It was an off-the-shelf amusement park ride that was purchased and enhanced by Arrow Development. The cars included headlights from a '56 Pontiac and hood ornaments from a '57 Chevrolet.

Unlike the larger cars that ran on gas, these smaller, rounder cars ran on electricity on a bus bar track much like the popular dark rides so the drivers could not accelerate or brake like the other versions. The route was not the freeway but a gentle, winding, rural road. The journey went over a small hill, through a short tunnel and a yellow garage barn where the doors swung open at almost the last minute.

"They were just simple four-wheel dark ride cars," recalled Imagineer Bob Gurr in 1997. "Arrow had been building and selling them to other parks for years, and these were not Autopia cars in the sense that you could drive or control them. The Midget Autopia was a 'kiddie' ride with the same technology used on almost all dark rides."

There were two steering wheels so each passenger had access to one, but the wheels were unconnected to anything. The attraction was generally just open during the peak park hours during summer, holidays and weekends.

After the attraction was dismantled in 1966, it was donated to Walt's hometown of Marceline, Missouri, where it operated in the Walt Disney Municipal Park for eleven years until maintenance and insurance became major challenges and it was closed.

Holidayland

Holidayland was a nine-acre picnic-type area designed as a space that could be rented by corporations or outside groups for an outdoor event. It could accommodate up to 7,000 people.

It had playgrounds with swings, slides, and more. It also featured baseball fields and picnic areas, along with a raised stage for entertainment under "the world's largest candy-striped circus tent" that had been used for the ill-fated Mickey Mouse Club Circus in 1955.

Holidayland also had a separate gated entrance into Disneyland through Frontierland. It resembled a city park and was located roughly where New Orleans Square is today. Basically, the show building for Pirates is where the baseball fields were and the Haunted Mansion show building is where the circus tent stage area was.

Primarily it was Milt Albright who was put in charge as overall manager and he tried his best to make it a success but many factors undercut his efforts.

The first event held in Holidayland was the Los Angeles Elk's Lodge No. 99 Picnic on Sunday, June 16, 1957, for 5,000 members and their families. The event included a performance by the Disneyland Band and a 30-minute performance by the Mouseketeers. (Smaller sized groups had to settle for their own entertainment, like sack races and bingo games.)

Since it was technically not in Disneyland, it had concession stands that included the sale of beer. Guests could purchase a picnic basket lunch prepared by the Red Wagon Inn that included all the beer you could drink.

"Walt thought beer was a basic part of a picnic," said Jack Taylor, the first operations supervisor at Holidayland. "But he never wanted it inside Disneyland."

Admission to Holidayland did not include admission into Disneyland, although some people tried to sneak in across the railroad tracks. Admission tickets and a reduced price ticket book were offered.

In the beginning there were only very small restrooms and no nighttime lighting. Walt soon introduced portable restrooms, and eventually built permanent restrooms just before the area closed forever in fall 1961. The previous year strong winds had literally torn the circus tent to shreds.

By the way, it was called Holidayland because the promotional information for the area declared it to be "A recreational park where every day's a holiday."

Don DeFore's Silver Banjo Restaurant

"The finest barbecue this side of the Mississippi" was served at Don DeFore's Silver Banjo Barbecue restaurant on New Orleans Street in Frontierland. It took over the old location of Casa de Fritos that was next to Aunt Jemima's Pancake House.

The restaurant was named and operated by actor Don Defore who was a friend of Walt Disney. Walt asked DeFore if he would like to run a restaurant in Frontierland. DeFore and his younger brother Verne eagerly accepted the offer and took a 45-hour business management night class at UCLA Extension.

The restaurant was cafeteria-style with a cashier at the end of the line and served sandwiches, ribs, chicken, baked beans, cole slaw, and fries. It had its own special barbecue sauce based on the one served in the chain of Love's barbecue restaurants.

In his spare time, DeFore helped out as a chef while his brother managed the location. The name of the restaurant came from a prized childhood possession. The two brothers' children worked at the restaurant in various capacities.

The kitchen area was too small by Orange County Health Department standards and the storage freezers were outside in a shed, so the restaurant closed in 1962 (not the usually stated 1961) because it could not meet the requirements. Aunt Jemima absorbed the kitchen and dining area and expanded.

Disneylander

In the earliest years of Disneyland, employees were not yet known as "cast members". They were referred to as "Disneylanders" and in the internal Disneyland periodical newsletter for May 1957 entitled the *Disneylander* the term was explained:

"What is a Disneylander? A Disneylander is both male & female, comes in assorted sizes, shapes and colors. Never seems to have a last name, answers to Jo, Louie, Hutch, Chuck, Judy, Joan, Alice, Mary, Walt and Hey you!"

1958

- Attendance: 4.4 million
- Employment: 3,450
- Payroll: $10.5 million
- Highlights:
  - Third engine for the Disneyland Railroad debuts
  - Ken-L Land Pet Motel opens in January
  - Disneyland Marquee sign installed
  - First Candlelight Processional held in December
  - Debut of first large park map drawn by Sam McKim
  - Zorro Days debuts
  - First issue of *Vacationland* magazine published
  - Disneyland closed Monday and Tuesday to *"provide the necessary time for rehabilitation and maintenance"*.
  - The motorized Fire Engine designed by Bob Gurr debuts traveling five miles an hour although it had a maximum speed of thirty-five mph. The truck was inspired by turn-of-the-early 20th century Fire Engines, such as the 1907 Rambler and vintage LaFrance fire trucks.
  - Milt Albright with the support of Jack Lindquist expands the Magic Kingdom Club. At its peak, the MKC had over five and a half million members from more than 8,000 companies worldwide and was responsible for bringing in over a hundred million dollars annually in revenue to Disney.

As the previous year closed on December 31, 1957, and Disneyland hosted its first New Year's Eve party, the 10 millionth guest, Leigh Woolfenden, walked through the gates. Yearly attendance at the Park increased.

The year 1958 brought many significant additions to the park as well including new attractions like the Columbia Sailing Ship, the Alice in Wonderland dark ride, and the Grand Canyon Diorama.

Imagineer Bob Gurr told me, "Looking back in recent years, I'm still amazed at how much work was done so fast by so many back in 1958-1959. I think this was Walt's golden age in building Disneyland. When you look at all the complicated civil engineering, the massive amounts of concrete work, to say nothing of engineering from scratch, this was unprecedented in the theme park industry."

Sailing Ship Columbia

Walt stood alongside Dick Nunis looking at the busy Rivers of America with the Mark Twain, the keel boats, the rafts going back and forth to Tom Sawyer's Island, and Indian war canoes paddling furiously near the shore. He turned to Nunis who thought Walt was going to comment on how busy the river was and said, "What we really need is another big boat!"

Walt Disney considered adding a replica of Robert Fulton's first commercial steamboat The Clermont to the Rivers of America. Admiral Joe Fowler, head of Disneyland construction, after exhaustive research at multiple maritime museums suggested instead the "Gem of the Ocean", Columbia Redivivia ("freedom reborn"), the first American ship to circumnavigate the globe in 1787-1790. It was a merchant ship and a private vessel so that is why it is not preceded by "U.S.S."

At the time of its construction, it was the first three-masted windjammer built in the United States in more than 100 years. It was designed to follow the same hidden track used by the Mark Twain. The flat-bottomed steel hull was constructed at Todd Shipyards in San Pedro, California as well as the masts, rigging, spars and sails. Steel plates were added to the hold below the water line to keep the ship from tipping over because of the tall masts.

Architect Ray Wallace, who had a love of classic ships, was commissioned by Fowler to design and build the ship. Wallace was Errol Flynn's first mate on his sailboat that they took to Catalina. Wallace is also the person responsible for the Min and Bill ship at Disney Hollywood Studios.

Only one known picture was known to exist of the ship, "Columbia in a Squall," but Wallace used research from the Library of Congress, as well as the blueprints for the H.M.S. Bounty built two years earlier by the same shipbuilders. Authentic teak, oak, and maple wood was used in the construction of the outer hull, decks, masts and other areas. Blaine Gibson sculpted the figurehead.

The ship was launched at a ceremony on June 14, 1958 at 5 p.m. Following nautical tradition, Walt had placed a new silver dollar under each of the masts for good luck, but they disappeared when the masts were replaced in the 1990s. The main mast is 84 feet tall.

Disneyland claimed that the cost to build the ship was $100,000, although some estimates put the final cost at much more.

U.S. Coast Guard Admiral Alfred Carroll Richmond presented a Bible to the Columbia's acting skipper, in accordance with maritime tradition. And the Admiral's wife, Gretchen Richmond, christened the Columbia with a bottle of champagne as Walt looked on proudly.

Even though Richmond retired in 1962, he returned in full uniform to inaugurate the below deck museum in 1964.

A new dock and landing were built for the ship to be in drydock, dubbed Fowler's Harbor after Admiral Joe Fowler retired from the U.S. Navy and who was in charge of construction of Disneyland. Walt jokingly referred to it as "Joe's Ditch."

Fred Gurley Train - Santa Fe & Disneyland Railroad

Between 1955 and 1956, the trains circling Disneyland had carried more than 775,000 passengers and that number doubled between 1956 and 1957 and then nearly doubled again by the beginning of 1958 so the system was struggling to handle more than two million guests a year.

The third engine on the Santa Fe & Disneyland Railroad came into service on March 28, 1958. It was named after Fred Gurley who was the president of the Atchison, Topeka and Santa Fe Railway, one of the largest railroads in the United States. He was a good friend of Walt Disney's and was the man who brokered the deal for the Santa Fe to become involved as a lessee at Disneyland.

On Disneyland's opening day July 17, 1955, Gurley was in the cab of the E.P. Ripley with Walt Disney riding into Main Street Station. The first two engines (E.P. Ripley and C.K. Holliday) had been built from scratch and were based on Walt's handmade Lilly Belle engine for his backyard Carolwood Pacific miniature railroad. Just building the frames alone cost almost $50,000 each.

To save time and money, it was decided that any new additions would be previously existing engines with the frames retained, but the rest rebuilt. The Fred Gurley was originally built by the Baldwin Locomotive Works of Philadelphia in August 1894 and spent much of its time working carrying sugar in Louisiana. It was officially retired in 1956 and purchased by Disney for $1,200 plus $300 for shipping to Los Angeles.

The years of hauling sugar in humid weather had taken its toil on the little engine and much of it was rusted and with wood rot. However, some important things were salvageable, including the frame, wheels, cylinders, domes and more including the bell that still rang clear despite decades of grime and soot.

It was entirely taken apart for careful examination and then re-built at the Disney Studios in Burbank including a new boiler, tender tank and an enclosed hardwood cab based on an authentic design among other things. Even after all of this work, the total cost was $37,061, which was significantly less than the first two engines.

One of the things that made this train different is that the cars it pulled were excursion cars with all seating facing to the right toward the inside of the park, making it more effective to see things and easier to board and exit each car. This was done primarily to better see the new Grand Canyon Diorama.

Work was started on the fourth engine, the Ernest S. March, which would be introduced to the park in June 1959.

A new 202-foot-long train station was opened in Tomorrowland in April. It was not as elaborate as the other train stations, because it was supposed to represent "a futurist's design of a transport loading station," so it was basically just a concrete block with an aluminum cover supported by tubular steel.

The large round holes in the beams were a popular "futuristic" architectural design element in the 1950s. It was a similar design to the earlier Viewliner station. The station was also meant to obscure the view of vintage railroad trains stopping in the future. There was a ticket booth in front of the station, as well.

Grand Canyon Diorama

In 1958, Walt Disney produced a film titled *Grand Canyon* that won the Oscar for the Best Live-Action Short Subject. The film features scenes of the Grand Canyon—from sunrise to sunset, including thunderstorms, and many of the different species of wildlife that inhabit the canyon set to Ferde Grofe's *Grand Canyon Suite*.

Walt became intrigued by dioramas while visiting museums and he contacted Bob Sewell, who had worked for a decade at the Los Angeles Museum of Natural History to help his team create one for Disneyland. Imagineer Claude Coats was put in charge and sent on a field trip to the Grand Canyon.

Total staff time to create the attraction was more than 80,000 hours at a cost estimated at $367,814, plus an additional $2,374 for the new sound equipment in the passenger cars.

The Grand Canyon Diorama was added to the Disneyland theme park on March 31, 1958, at 11:30 a.m. A 96-year-old Hopi Indian chief, Chief Nevangnewa, blessed the trains on the diorama's opening day as well as other members of the Hopi tribe including a very young boy Little White Cloud who seemed to delight Walt.

The new third train was officially dedicated as the Fred Gurley on that day as well. Walt Disney and Fred Gurley, chairman of the Santa Fe Railroad, wore railroad caps and proudly smiled standing by a sign proclaiming the entrance to the attraction and then steamed it through the new wooden tunnel that had been built.

Musical entertainment was provided both by The Disneyland Band, as well as the Santa Fe All-Indian Band from Winslow, Arizona. Over forty newspaper and television writers and cameramen were present for the dedication and hundreds of park guests as well.

Painted on a single piece of seamless, hand-woven canvas and representing the view from the canyon's south rim, the rear of the diorama measured 306-feet long, 34-feet high, 45-feet wide and was covered with 300 gallons of paint. It featured the work of prolific scenic artist Delmer Yoakum and was described at the time as the "longest diorama in the world."

Within the diorama it's possible to find a mountain lion, porcupines, skunks, a golden eagle, rattlesnakes, rabbits, deer, crows, wild turkeys and plenty of sheep, surrounded by aspens and pine. All of the animals were real taxidermied animals that were treated extensively with flame retardants.

Emile Kuri, who had designed Walt's apartment and exterior elements on Main Street, directed the taxidermy staff to get a sense of realism and motion. One day, Walt looked in a freezer and discovered the skinned carcass of a coyote and was so appalled that he decreed this was the last time that real animal skins would be used for a Disneyland attraction.

Imagineer Marvin Davis suggested that it should be a diorama featuring all the National Parks like Yellowstone and Yosemite. However, Walt was adamant that it would be just the Grand Canyon, but had to be convinced by Imagineer Claude Coats there were wild turkeys that lived there.

When other Imagineers said it made no sense to have a train leave Tomorrowland and then go into the Grand Canyon, Walt argued that the train ride needed a grand finale before returning to the Main Street station.

Zorro Days

Walt wanted to cross-promote his own television shows so in addition to having the Mouseketeers appear at the park and sign autographs, he scheduled Zorro Days weekends where the stars of the ABC television show showed up at the park. There were five major Zorro appearances at Disneyland: April 26-27,1958 ; May 30-June 1, 1958; November 27-30, 1958; November 26-29, 1959; and, finally November, 11-13, 1960.

There were four shows each day. The first three included a parade down Main Street ending in Frontierland where actor Guy Williams costumed as Zorro got off his horse and ran into the Golden Horseshoe Revue and Buddy Van Horn, his stunt double, appeared on the roof in costume battling the Spanish soldiers and swinging down to the balcony.

The fight continued over to the upper decks of the Mark Twain steamboat where Zorro forced at sword point the evil Captain Monastario into the Rivers of America along with some of the other soldiers.

The final show took place at Magnolia Park where Williams as Zorro signed autographs and did fake sword fights with children who had come to the park dressed in black capes and masks.

Other Highlights:

On January 18, the **Ken-L Land Pet Motel** pet boarding facility (sponsored by Ken-L Ration) opened outside the Disneyland main gate. It could house up to 160 pets for twenty-five cents each a day, which included food and water. It lasted until 1968 when sponsorship was taken over by Kal Kan and then even later by other sponsors.

Participating in the opening ceremonies were Old Yeller's son, Duke, and Kevin Corcoran, the youthful star of the 1957 film *Old Yeller*. It was Walt's idea to have the location because he was afraid that people visiting Disneyland would leave their pets in their cars. Because he loved animals, he wanted a safe and secure place for those pets, rather than roasting in the hot Anaheim sun with a small cracked opening in a window.

The **Mad Hatter of Main Street** shop and **The Hills Brothers Coffee House** opened in Town Square in June as evidence that new businesses were always appearing in the park.

The iconic **Disneyland Marquee** sign on Harbor Boulevard made its first appearance in 1958 inspired by a similar design for a sign outside the Disneyland Hotel since 1956. On each of its two sides, a huge "D" on a yellow panel was followed by the other letters on separate white panels. At night, the backlit panels would glow. Tall poles supported colorful, rigid banners.

Underneath was a rectangular panel where information in plastic letters was posted like operating hours, special events, etc. The lettering was done by hand with a long pole like for the marquee of a movie theater. The original sign stood with a few changes (including the removal of the banners) over thirty years and was replaced in 1988.

Disneyland sponsored **Disney Night at the Hollywood Bowl** on August 1. Highlight of the entertainment was a 1,000-foot glide over the audience by aerialist Tiny Kline dressed as Tinker Bell and that gave Walt an idea. Kline, a grandmother, would be flying over Sleeping Beauty Castle three years later in 1961.

August 16 brought Bob Gurr's **Motorized Firetruck** to Main Street, and it became one of Walt's favorite vehicles. The last public photo of Walt at the park was taken with him behind the wheel of the truck and Mickey Mouse by his side.

Gurr purchased a 1938 Chevrolet fire engine from the Crown Coach Fire Engine Company for $150 just to get all the fire equipment that came with it. Imagineer Ward Kimball suggested some improvements including a more impressive looking front end with big Rushmore headlamps.

Gurr drove it down the Santa Ana Freeway from the Disney Studio in Burbank to Disneyland to help break in the engine. When he got near the park, he stopped at a corner and a little boy shouted out that by the time he got to the fire, the place would have burned down.

It was the last motorized vehicle introduced to Main Street. It operated concurrently with the horse drawn fire wagon for a few years.

The **Junior Autopia** and **Viewliner** closed in September to make way for the 1959 improvements since Walt's 1958 European trip had shown him a new type of monorail and the majesty of Matterhorn Mountain when he visited the film set for his 1959 live-action film *Third Man on the Mountain*. It is amazing that Walt thought of these attractions in late 1958 and they became a reality by June of the following year.

Another event that year that would also influence Disneyland was the outdoor amusement venue **Pacific Ocean Park** opening July 26, 1958, in Santa Monica to take advantage of the success of Disneyland. It was a joint venture of CBS and Santa Anita Park racetrack and would become the backdrop for the Lawrence Welk television show.

The park included bubble-shaped gondolas that went out over the ocean like the Skyway, Mystery Island Banana Train Ride, Flight to Mars, King Neptune's Courtyard, Sea Serpent Roller Coaster, and more.

Unfortunately, it started to fall into disrepair as early as 1965 with nearby construction of the surrounding area discouraging people from going to the pleasure pier and it closed permanently in 1967. It instituted the "Pay One Price" (POP – Pacific Ocean Park) policy in an attempt to undercut Disneyland and its ticket books.

It cost $4.25 for adult admission and 15 attractions—but that was actually a $5.85 value, so the ticket book was a real bargain. A ticket book with admission and 10 rides was $3.25.

Disneyland was open Wednesday through Sunday from 10 a.m. to 7 p.m. generally (summer and holidays had extended hours usually 9 a.m. to midnight). It was closed Monday and Tuesday because it "provides the necessary time for rehabilitation and maintenance," but was open every day during the Christmas holidays, starting December 17.

In 1958, three different variations of the souvenir park map, drawn by Sam McKim, were issued. Some variations are slight, like the inclusion of Cascade Peak, or the color of the water for the Jungle Cruise, while others are more significant, like the first version that still featured the Viewliner, which would disappear by the end of the year.

Also the first issue of *Vacationland* published by Disneyland appeared in the fall. Previously the colorful slick magazine had been called *Disneyland Holiday* and was offered free at local hotels. It has been speculated that the name change was to be more inclusive of other Southern California tourist attractions, like Knott's Berry Farm.

On May 27 thanks to animator Ward Kimball's connections with the Horseless Carriage Club of America, Walt arranged an annual event where the members attired in turn-of-the century costumes showcased their vintage vehicles in a parade down Main Street and then parked them in the Town Square for the guests to examine.

On March 30 was the first Kids Amateur Dog Show sponsored by Ken-L Ration dog food. It was so popular it became an annual event for several years. Kids entered the Qualifying Kids' Amateur Dog Shows throughout Orange County, California, with the hopes of being selected as a semi-finalist and getting the chance to go for a walk with his or her pup down Main Street, U.S.A.

Even the dogs and masters who did not get selected for the finals left with prizes such as Ken-L Club badges, Ken-L Club T-shirts, and an assortment of other Ken-L products.

Thanks to Disneyland Hotel owner Jack Wrather who owned the rights to the character, Sergeant Preston of the Yukon (actor Richard Simmons was portraying the character on television), the fictional Canadian Mountie and his dog Yukon King were in attendance to give out the awards.

After several trials and tests at Disneyland, the first place winner, which was decided out of the top performers from the ten individual class categories and ranging from "Largest Dog" to "Prettiest Dog," rode away with a new bicycle for their master and a special dog blanket. "Most Popular Dog" was decided by audience applause.

The dogs were put to the test at Disneyland in the Semi-Finals at 2 p.m. on Saturday, March 29, 1958, and the Finals, also at 2 p.m., the day after. Those dogs asked back for the Finals got to march in the 2:30 p.m. "Parade of Champions" on Main Street, U.S.A. The parade route started at the double gates next to the Opera House, went up Main Street, around the Plaza, down Main Street, around Town Square, and then they exited back through the double gates next to the Opera House. The Disneyland band provided music during the show of the dogs.

Alice in Wonderland

When Fantasyland opened in 1955, it had three dark rides. One was scary (Snow White), one was funny (Mr. Toad) and one was beautiful (Peter Pan). Walt decided there needed to be one that depicted craziness common in cartoons.

Walt assigned Claude Coats to the project, who had done color styling for the 1951 animated feature film *Alice in Wonderland* and had shown a skill at utilizing black light on early Disneyland attractions.

Coats was in charge of everything from design and layout to creating the contemptuous caterpillar vehicle with a sneer on its face. He had originally suggested using playing cards as a vehicle, but it was Walt himself who said, "Use the caterpillar."

As a result, neither Alice nor the caterpillar appeared in the original version of the scenes. Blaine Gibson sculpted the vehicle from Coats' illustration. The design was patented on January 12, 1960 (the application was submitted May 8, 1959) in Coats' name and he signed over the patent to Disneyland Inc. for $10.

The vehicle was longer than the other dark ride vehicles, so it could seat more people, and it went slower because it was heavier, and the lowest gear had to be used in order for it to get up the incline to the second floor.

It was the only two-story dark ride in Fantasyland and that second story was over the Mr. Toad's Wild Ride attraction. Bob Gurr assisted with mounting the fiberglass caterpillar onto a ride vehicle purchased from Arrow Development. He also helped install some of the moving gags with Roger Broggie Jr.

Coats was assisted in the artwork on the plywood two-dimensional cutouts by Colin Campbell, Blaine Gibson, and Ken Anderson.

Most of the gags were some character moving up and down (like the Dormouse's head popping up the lid on the sugar bowl at the Mad Tea Party or the Accordion Owl stretching its neck in the Tulgey Woods), that was accomplished fairly simply by air cylinders and, when the value was shut off, something would come back down.

The scenery and figures, like the smiling Cheshire Cat, were "flat" on plywood or masonite and painted so that ultraviolet black light would make the colors more intense, unreal and seem to glow.

Kathryn Beaumont, the young actress who had provided the voice for Alice in the film, recorded the lines for the attraction. She was about 21 years old at the time.

Mouseketeer Karen Pendleton, dressed as Alice, appeared at the ribbon-cutting ceremony roughly two months after the ride officially started operating on June 14, 1958. She and Walt were taken to the entrance of the attraction in a horse-drawn carriage.

The ride was a "C" Ticket or thirty-five cents. The eight-foot-tall ticket booth was a giant mushroom with an open Alice in Wonderland storybook on top. Sometimes the female ticket seller inside wore an Alice in Wonderland costume.

Candlelight Processional

According to legend and an unpublished manuscript about the history of Disney entertainment by Ron Logan, one day in 1958, Walt Disney supposedly remarked to his friend Dr. Charles Hirt of the University of Southern California, "We need Christmas carolers at Disneyland. Can't we have a choir assembled at the hub of Main Street by the Railroad Station in Town Square? Have them sing to the guests there, and I'll listen from my office over the Fire Station."

There were already Christmas carolers at Disneyland that very first holiday season in December 1955, mere months after the park officially opened. During December 1955, there was a group of 12 Dickens Carolers (from the University of Southern California), under Hirt's direction, who performed throughout the park and guest choirs were invited to perform daily in the Main Street bandstand, which had been recently moved to the Magnolia Park area of Adventureland by the Jungle Cruise.

In addition, in 1955, for the opening afternoon of this holiday tradition, the Dickens Carolers and a 300-member massed chorus made up of visiting choirs stood together on the Main Street Train Station steps and sang Christmas carols accompanied by visiting school bands. They stood on the steps so they could be seen clearly and easily by the guests.

By Christmas 1956, this holiday entertainment event was officially christened the "Christmas Bowl," perhaps borrowing from the concept of the "Hollywood Bowl" that provided holiday concerts. A sign proclaiming that title was placed over the entrance to the bandstand area in Magnolia Park. Under Hirt's direction, the carolers and singers from eight visiting choirs also performed as a group on the train station steps, this time accompanied by the Disneyland Band.

The choirs and carolers were so well received by Disneyland guests that, in 1958, Hirt suggested to Disney Entertainment that performances by a larger massed choir group would be a welcome addition to future holiday events.

As Hirt remembered in later years, "When we first did the ceremony in 1958, the carolers all gathered around the flagpole in Town Square. It was a beautiful ceremony, but we made one mistake: it was difficult for people to see since the singers were all in a circle with me in the center conducting. So the next year, bleachers were constructed adjacent to the Train Station so that the carolers were facing the spectators on Main Street."

Celebrity narrators were introduced in 1961, with actor Dennis Morgan having the distinction of being the first one. He performed that role 1961-1964 and again in 1966. Dick Van Dyke, to help promote *Mary Poppins*, was the narrator in 1965.

Edison Square

Not everything that Walt planned for 1958 was realized. One of his ambitious proposals was for a side extension to Main Street to be called Edison Square and would feature his first attempt at the Carousel of Progress.

At the end of Main Street, on the right side of The Hub, would have been another more urban, residential street named Edison Square. It would have been built on what was then known as "Plaza Street" near the Plaza Inn (at that time called the Red Wagon Inn). It was announced that Edison Square would open Easter 1959.

There would be a brick paved street, the most modern of electric and gas-powered "horseless carriages" and, of course, "brand new" electric street lights instead of Main Street's gas lamps.

The facades of the buildings would recall the red brick houses of Philadelphia, New York's brownstones, the wooden edifices of St. Louis and San Francisco, the graystones of Chicago, and the colonial brick of Boston—truly making it part of a larger Main Street U.S.A., rather than just a small Midwestern town.

Prominently displayed at the center of this cul-de-sac area in a little fenced-in circular, green park would have been a life-sized statue of inventor Thomas Edison, with his right arm raised high in the air and his finger pointing upward.

After the opening of Disneyland Park, General Electric's Lamp Division had visited Walt at WED to discuss the possibilities of sponsoring an attraction at Disneyland. While they were clear about what they wanted to advertise, they left it to Walt's storytelling to come up with an appropriate showcase.

The result was a new area for the park spotlighting a unique four-act play with a prologue and epilogue titled "Harnessing the Lightning."

Walt saw the play *Our Town* at least three times at the urging of Imagineer John Hench when it was performed in Los Angeles and used it as the inspiration for the show.

"Harnessing the Lightning" would be performed in a hidden horseshoe theater with multiple stages inside the buildings at the far end of the cul-de-sac of Edison Square. In four acts, it would follow a typical American family through the decades with each step showing how G.E. had made the future brighter and better.

Mr. Wilbur K. Watt, the "K" standing for "Kilo", would be the on stage narrator for the show. According to the brochure prepared for G.E.: "Our narrator, Wilbur K. Watt, is an incredible electro-mechanical man. As he rocks back and forth in his armchair, he describes the scene we see on stage. It is almost as though Mr. Watt were alive, for his movements are synchronized and life-like as he describes the play."

At the appropriate time, a group of roughly 125 people would be funneled into the first theater. The audience would stand on a four-tiered platform, with each tier separated by continuous railing, very similar to the pre-show of Stitch's Great Escape attraction at Walt Disney World.

When the scene was finished on the first stage, the lights would dim and automatic doors would open to allow guests to move into the next area to see the next scene while another group was funneled in behind them to see the first act.

With some script revisions, the show would later evolve into The Carousel Theater of Progress and finally just The Carousel of Progress for the 1964-65 New York World's Fair.

1959

- Attendance: 5 million
- Employment: 3,650
- Payroll: $12 million
- Admission: Adult ($1.25), Junior ($1.00), Child (fifty cents)
- Highlights:
    - Submarine Voyage, Disneyland-Alweg Monorail, Matterhorn Mountain and Bobsleds, Motor Boat Cruise debut as the first "E Ticket" attractions
    - Tradition of Rose Bowl teams visiting Disneyland begins with the University of Washington and the University of Wisconsin
    - Premier Khruschev of Russia denied Disneyland visit
    - Dapper Dans debut on Main Street U.S.A.

For Disneyland, the year 1959 was a transformative year that Walt himself described as "the second opening of Disneyland". Disneyland shifted from a regional attraction with its primary attendance coming from the Southern California area to truly a larger national destination with a higher percentage of its guests coming from other states and countries.

There were 11 attractions listed on "E" tickets in the Disneyland ticket books of 1959. An "E" Ticket was valued at fifty cents although it would rise in value over the decades.

However, a closer look shows that the *Santa Fe & Disneyland Railroad* was actually listed four times because guests could board the trains in four lands (Main Street, Frontierland, Fantasyland, Tomorrowland).

Besides the three brand new ones, there were others that had been promoted from "D" tickets, which had previously been the highest: TWA Rocket to the Moon, Jungle Cruise, Mark Twain Steamboat, Tom Sawyer Island Rafts, Sailing Ship Columbia, Rainbow Ridge Pack Mules and Rainbow Ridge Stagecoaches.

The expression "E Ticket" came to mean any activity or event that was especially worthwhile or top tier. Astronaut Sally Ride, describing her first Space Shuttle voyage, said, "This is definitely an 'E' ticket!"

Western Weekend

Walt often brought in television stars to increase attendance and entertain guests. Western Weekend was held February 21-23. It featured stunt shows and gun fights and in attendance was Warner Brothers television westerns stars like Ty Hardin as Bronco Lane and Will Hutchins as Sugarfoot. The cast of television's Rin-Tin-Tin with Rinty himself was there as well as Robert Loggia from Disney's Elfego Baca. Thanksgiving weekend November 26-29, 1959 were once again the Zorro Days event that had begun in 1958.

The Dapper Dans

The Dapper Dans are a singing group who bring a greater sense of authenticity to Main Street U.S.A.

In 1957, Disneyland entertainment director Tommy Walker arranged for a barbershop quartet to perform on Main Street to add a little more atmosphere to the 1890-1910 time frame of the location. Chuck Corson, a former stage manager for the Fred Waring Chorale who was talent booker for the park, gathered four singers from that group to form Disneyland's first Main Street Quartet. Corson also handled talent booking at Walt Disney World.

Corson, who primarily handled the bigger entertainment "names" in talent booking, worked with Sonny Anderson, who handled the musical "atmosphere" entertainment for the park (and later Walt Disney World). In 1959, Anderson wanted more than just a singing group on Main Street U.S.A. He wanted one that could do some vaude-villian-style comedy interaction with the guests and maybe a little tap dancing.

The bass singer T.J. Marker, who was the leader of the quartet, came up with the new name, The Dapper Dans, for the re-imagined group in 1959. ("Dapper Dan" was a turn-of-the-last-century phrase referring to a well-dressed and groomed gentleman who was "dapper" or stylish.)

"We had a quartet but all they did was stand up there and sing," Anderson told Charles "Bub" Thomas who joined the Dapper Dan group in Disneyland in 1969. "I wanted some entertainers. We have plenty of entertainment for the kids. But we need a quartet that could entertain their parents... the older people."

The superb four-part harmony sung a cappella by this quartet became an institution on Main Street U.S.A., with a song list of more than 100 songs in the repertoire. The jokes always brought laughter from the audience, especially when they announced the songs they would sing: "She Was Kind to the Regiment but Rotten to the Corps" or "Let Me Call You Sweetheart... because I've forgotten your name."

Walt considered the Dapper Dans the ambassadors of Main Street because they actually talked with the guests and sometimes involved them directly in the performance.

3-D Jamboree

3-D Jamboree at Disneyland was a roughly 26 minute show that premiered in the Mickey Mouse Club Theater (near the carousel) in Fantasyland at Disneyland Park around June 16, 1956 and ran until sometime in 1959. The presentation combined the 3-D versions of the 1953 Disney Studios produced theatrical short cartoons: *Adventures in Music: Melody* and *Working for Peanuts*.

Disney executive Harry Tytle remembered. "Walt proposed a show, utilizing 3-D cartoon shorts which we made years before. He had director Bill Beaudine, direct a special 3-D live-action opening, utilizing the Mouseketeers. The attendance at the Mickey Mouse Theater grew and grew."

So many glasses were used (almost 4,000 a day) that Tytle talked to people working there about the possibility of cleaning the glasses for re-use.

The souvenir book from the time only claimed "30-minute cartoons running continuously from 11 a.m. to closing" and it would have taken a "B" ticket to attend.

Autopia

The Tomorrowland Autopia was instantly popular when it opened with the park in 1955, but it led to guest challenges with long lines and disappointed smaller children not tall enough to operate the vehicles.

The Junior Autopia in the Fantasyland area opened roughly a year later in 1956 to alleviate those problems by offering more cars, but with foot pedals and booster seats designed to accommodate smaller children. Unlike its predecessor it featured a guide track for the cars.

In 1959, the Tomorrowland and Fantasyland Autopias were combined and featured similar double-sided boarding areas for the two tracks at each attraction, beautifully landscaped straight-aways, bridges, and cloverleafs. At one point, all four ride tracks converged creating briefly a four-lane superhighway on top of the pine covered McKim Hill (named after Imagineer Sam McKim) which was actually the top of the Submarine Voyage show building.

In 1959, the new Mark V design for the cars was introduced for both attractions that were sponsored by Richfield Oil which offered a Disneyland driver's license to guests.

Motor Boat Cruise

The Motor Boat Cruise located between Tomorrowland and Fantasyland opened in 1957. The little boats themselves were well crafted of mahogany plywood and allowed young skippers to seemingly navigate through some treacherous obstacles like outcroppings of rocks. The boats were painted white with one additional solid color of red, blue, green or yellow on the hull.

The murky water was only a few feet deep, but gave the impression of being much deeper and the crafts glided along on a track much like the Mark Twain steamboat. The trough was the guide all the way around the loop. Two guide wheels (one in front and one in back) mounted on a vertical axle would guide the boats, but allow them to float.

For 1959, not only did the boat ride pass underneath the new Autopia and Monorail tracks but added a rushing "white water rapids" section.

The Disneyland Railroad

With the new 1959 attractions, Walt realized he would need added passenger capacity for the Disneyland Railroad, one of the most popular attractions at the park. He authorized Imagineer Roger Broggie to locate another vintage Baldwin engine to restore rather than building a new train from scratch to save some money.

The passenger cars, however, in order to be durable and safe enough for the guests needed to be custom built. Broggie found a train in New Jersey that had been built at the Baldwin Locomotive Works of Philadelphia in April 1925, the same company that had built the Fred Gurley. It had spent decades hauling sand for the Raritan River Sand Company of New Jersey and an additional eight years operating at a small amusement park near Freehold, N.J.

Broggie paid $2,000 for the engine, but after all the restoration was done over a year's time, the final cost was nearly $58,000. The train got lost in shipping from New Jersey to California and an angry Walt called the president of the Atchison, Topeka and Santa Fe Railway, Ernest S. March, who located the car with the engine somewhere in Pennsylvania and got it re-routed to Los Angeles.

Walt decided to name the engine after Marsh. Animator Ward Kimball suggested the engine be made over to resemble the Montezuma, the first locomotive built for the Denver & Rio Grande Railway and Walt eagerly agreed. It was painted a bright red with gold trim and was nicknamed by cast members the "Holiday Red". It was officially added to the railroad on July 25, 1959.

Dark Rides Enchancements

Imagineers Yale Gracey and Rolly Crump were teamed up to update the effects on the Fantasyland dark rides. They added glow-in-the-dark eyes in the Snow White forest scene. Mr. Toad's barrels became three-dimensional instead of cut-outs. Peter Pan got an improved volcano effect. Alice in Wonderland got the gag of the Mad Hatter pouring an endless stream of tea.

Car Club Day and Autocade

Perhaps one of the most unusual events took place at Disneyland on September 5, 1959. It was the first (and last) annual Car Club Day and Autocade.

It was a one-day event with the participants driving their cars down Main Street USA and continued on to the Holidayland area where they were displayed outside the old Mickey Mouse Club Circus tent for judging.

There were a lot of stock Model Ts and a couple of Corvettes, as well. As soon as the "hot rodders" showed up, Disney management got nervous as they were not the typical Disneyland guest.

Ray Anderegg was there. Bob Johnson's car was in the show and Ed Roth later bought it and modified it into Tweedy Pie. The pre-bubble top X-Sonic Tony Bachiero's 57 Ford Custom Corvette was there. All the participants were given a special dash plaque featuring Sleeping Beauty Castle on the right and a hot rod facing the viewer on the left. In the upper left was the date.

Ed "Big Daddy" Roth was an iconic car customizer who opened his own shop in 1959 where he built his scratch-made custom hot rod The Outlaw using fiberglass. He was often paid to bring it to display at car shows and he attended this event.

His most popular creation, Rat Fink, was created after this show. Rat Fink was a green, comically grotesque and depraved looking rat in red overalls. The story Roth told was that he sketched the creature as the antithesis to Mickey Mouse after becoming sick of seeing so many children wearing the trademark ears. The word "rat fink" was already part of the popular vernacular.

The show itself was covered in the March 1960 issue of *Rodding & Re-Styling* magazine.

For decades there were rumors of the participants drinking heavily and some of the kids who worked at Disneyland getting into a rumble in the parking lot that resulted in future events being cancelled, but these are just urban legends. Since a police officer had backed the event, there was a heavy police presence so it was doubtful any trouble occurred.

Lee Karjala wrote on August 30, 2011: "My brother-in-law at the time was the president of the Road Lords car club of East Los Angeles and was well connected to the custom car builders in the Los Angeles area as well as knowing many members of the Los Angeles police department.

"He was really good friends with a police officer back then who suggested that he hold a car show at Disneyland and the officer had some connections with the management there. At the time the park was only about four years old and they were hungry for special events to bring more customers to Disneyland. My father and brother-in-law bought all the trophies and plaques with their own money.

"I remember that George Barris and Big Daddy Ed Roth were two of the more prominent business owners that showed their wares, with Ed and his staff producing T-shirts with his custom airbrush designs. I remember such cars as the Kopper Kart, Norm Grabowski's 'Kookie T' which was featured as Edd Byrne's character's car (he was "Kookie" on the TV series 77 *Sunset Strip*), and Ed Roth's Outlaw.

"I suspect that the one-day show was not a financial success for my father and brother-in-law because they never duplicated it or talked about it after the one day event."

Special Events

The tradition of annual Rose Bowl teams visiting Disneyland began when the University of Washington and University of Wisconsin players toured the park prior to their January 1, 1960 game.

In addition, previous special events were held including Zorro Days on Thanksgiving weekend November 26-29, the Western Regional Pancake Races on February 7-8. Horseless Carriage Day on September 27 and Kids Amateur Dog Show in April.

John F. Kennedy visited the Park on November first. The Stanford Research Institute presented an economic impact report to the Orange County Board of Supervisors for the year 1959. It stated that more than 16.6 million guests had visited the park, or roughly one in every ten Americans. The 15 millionth visitor went through the turnstiles in April 18th.

Nikita Khrushchev

Nikita Khrushchev, premier of the Soviet Union and a fiery opponent of American capitalism, arrived in the United States on September 16, 1959 for an extended eleven day visit to the United States. During his trip, he visited several American cities, including a stop in Los Angeles on September 19, where he started his day on a soundstage at Twentieth Century Fox Studios seeing a scene from the movie *Can Can* being filmed.

Supposedly, at lunch, comedian Bob Hope and actors Frank Sinatra and David Niven urged Mrs. Khrushchev that she should visit Disneyland and that they would take her there themselves because it was so safe. The Khrushchevs had previously requested such a visit, but the Secret Service had strongly urged against it for security reasons.

Khrushchev angrily vented,"Just now I was told that I could not go to Disneyland. I asked 'Why not? What is it? Do you have rocket-launching pads there?' I do not know. 'We', which means the American authorities, 'cannot guarantee your security if you go there.' What is it? Is there an epidemic of cholera there or something? Or have gangsters taken over the place that can destroy me? This is the situation I am in. I can not find words to explain this to my people."

The newspaper reports focused on Khrushchev's outburst at not being allowed to visit Disneyland instead of the prepared speech he gave later that evening. Soon, editorial cartoons and comedians were commenting on the tantrum and providing additional publicity for Walt's park as well as sparking curiosity to go and see what the Soviet leader had missed.

Walt talked about the incident in the September 25, 1963 interview with Fletcher Markle for the Canadian Broadcasting Corporation's television show *Telescope*:

"We didn't refuse him permission. No, we were all set. You see, we work according to what the State Department wants to do and Khrushchev was a guest of the government. Both the State Department security and the Soviet security had come and cased Disneyland and they were all set. And I was all ready.

"We had different shots, places where we'd take pictures with Khrushchev and I had one that was my favorite. We'd be lined up in front of my eight submarines. I'd be pointing to Mr. Khrushchev and saying, 'Well, now, Mr. Khrushchev, here's my Disneyland submarine fleet. It's the eighth-largest submarine fleet in the world'."

Sunday June 14, 1959:
Press Preview and Dedication Ceremonies

Guests visiting Disneyland that day were given a flyer that featured the following information: "Yes, today is a special day at Disneyland… the occasion of our Press Preview and Dedication Ceremonies for Disneyland '59 and all its new adventures.

"TODAY, all of these new adventures, including the Matterhorn Mountain and its bobsled runs; the Submarine Fleet on the Underseas

Voyage; the Disneyland-Alweg Monorail Trains; the new Fantasyland Autopia, and the Motor Boat Cruise have been reserved for the press, celebrities and dignitaries who are taking part in the actual dedication ceremonies being staged for Press and Television cameras.

"Of course all of Disneyland's other wonderful attractions will be open today for your entertainment and enjoyment. TOMORROW, Monday, June 15th, all of the new Disneyland '59 attractions will officially open to the public.

"A special Disneyland '59 Dedication parade will take place today beginning promptly at 1:30 p.m. on Main Street, and you are cordially invited to view this pageant which will start in Town Square, and follow a parade route down Main Street and around the Hub area.

"Today's Parade and Dedication Ceremonies will all be on television tomorrow night over the ABC network in a special 90 minute program *Kodak Presents—Disneyland '59*. In the Los Angeles area, this program will be shown over KABC, Channel 7 from 7:30-9 p.m."

Walt, of course, realized that not all of his potential audience would be able to see this once-in-a-lifetime, never rerun, show. So he edited color footage of the event into a 27-minute featurette titled *Gala Day at Disneyland*, released to theaters on January 21, 1960.

Even people who had watched it on a small black-and-white television set loved seeing the tightly edited version on a huge screen in Technicolor. Ever the showman, Walt even included the flub when Richard Nixon's daughters were unable to cut the ribbon for the monorail dedication and Walt had to help tear it. In the television broadcast, that segment was edited out.

Walt included footage from this featurette as the first part of his weekly television show episode *Disneyland '61/Olympic Elk* (May 28, 1961), as well.

Schedule of Events

Walt had invited approximately 2,000 members of the press to attend. ABC personnel arrived at 7:30 a.m. in the morning to set up and rehearse.

9:15 a.m.

Vice-President Richard Nixon and his family met Walt at the monorail station for press photos for newspapers east of the Rocky Mountains who needed them for their Monday morning editions. This is when the famous Bob Gurr "kidnapping Nixon" on the monorail incident took place. Then, Nixon left and attended church services in Whittier with his mother.

The Nixons had stayed at the Disneyland Hotel Saturday night in owner Jack Wrather's personal suite.

Noon

Parade starts forming. Lunch at Red Wagon Inn for celebrities.

12:15 p.m.

Nixon and his family have an informal luncheon at Walt's apartment above the Firehouse.

1:15 p.m.

Certain celebrities board "horseless carriages" to take them from City Hall to the official reviewing stand in the Hub. Walt rode with his grandchildren Christopher and Joanna in a 1906 Buick driven by E.J. Antonik. Mrs. Disney who was notoriously shy did not ride with Walt but was at the ceremonies along with her son-in-law Ron Miller and his wife Diane Disney Miller. Nixon rode in a 1909 Cadillac driven by Barney Rademacher.

1:30 p.m.

Disneyland '59 Dedication Parade and Pageant begins. Special reserved grandstand for press guests located adjacent to Plaza at end of Main Street.

Reviewing Stand Official Guests

- The Honorable Richard M. Nixon, Vice-President of the United States, Mrs. Nixon and their two daughters Julie and Tricia
- Mr. and Mrs. Walt Disney
- Mr. and Mrs. Art Linkletter
- Mr. and Mrs. Roy O. Disney
- Rear Admiral Charles C. Kirkpatrick, United States Navy
- Chief Machinist Mate Stuart M. Nelson, United States Navy, Mrs. Nelson and Family
- Mr. Edward Fernet, Consul General of Switzerland and Family
- Mr. Meredith Willson

Vanguard

- Mickey Mouse, Chip'n'Dale
- Disneyland Band, "The marchingest band in America," - Vesey Walker, director
- Armed Forces Color Guard
- Grand Marshall, Walt Disney
- Roy O. Disney with wife Edna
- Vice-President Richard Nixon and family

- Celebrities including Roberta Shore, Annette and the Shaggy Dog, Guy Williams dressed as Zorro riding a black horse, Henry Calvin (Sgt. Garcia on Zorro) in a carriage, and more, including the cast of *Lassie* television show (Jon Provost, June Lockhart, Lassie).

International Group

"Disneyland is dedicated to all people of all nations around the world. This section reflects that principle"—narrator "Gala Day at Disneyland" (1960)

- Massed Flags Float (a twirling globe)

Japan

- Japanese Kansuma Kai - Fugima Kansuma, director
- Japanese Float

Austria

- Austrian Mountain Dancers - Charles Bausback, director

Mexico

- Disneyland's Gonzales Trio
- Mexican Equestrians - Peter Martinez and Thelma Kurtt
- Corina Valdez Dancers - Corina Solis, director
- Los Angeles County Sheriff's Mounted Charro Posse - Capt. Ben Oberstein, leader

China

- Los Angeles Chinese Drum and Bugle Corps - Philip Kwan, director
- Rickshaws- June Gong "Miss San Francisco Chinatown" and Jean Chew "Miss Los Angeles Chinatown"
- Chinese Dragons, one of which was 150 years old at the time.

Greece

- Greek Gandy Dancers - Dean Linscott, director
- Greek Musicians from Athens

Spain

- Spanish Equestrian - Norma Gootjes
- Lilly Aguilar Dancers and Musicians - Lilly Aguilar, director
- Spanish Ceremonial Masks

- Many Hispanic festivals include costumed figures known as gigantes y cabezudos, or roughly, "Giants and Big-Heads"
- Spanish Equestrians - Rollo Grover, Clyde and Dee Goehring, Bob Phillips and Hazel Kirkpatrick, Marjorie Wurman, Barbara Dillion and Kathleen Swift

Italy

- Italian Dancers and Sicilian Cart - Nate Moore, director

Scotland

- San Diego Highland Dancers - Mrs. Clark Sutorius, director
- San Diego Bagpipe Bands: Campbell Highlanders - John Haywood, Pipe Major and Cameron Highlanders - John Rosenberger, Pipe Major

Disneyland Division

Main Street , U.S.A.

- Firehouse Five Plus Two - Chief Ward Kimball
- Horsedrawn Firewagon
- Horseless Carriages - Courtesy of Horseless Carriage Club of Southern California
- Main Street Horsecar and Dancing Group performing the "Horsecar Ballet" as they jumped off the Horsecar when it stopped and danced along either side of it.
- Omnibus - The Elliott Brothers and "Disneyland Dateniters" Band (The Elliott Brothers played events like Disneyland's Grad Nites for years. In 1958, they released their album "Date Nite at Disneyland with the Date Niters." Their sister Mary was a singer who gave up her career to become the third wife of actor Bob Cummings. Both of them were in attendance at this preview.)

Adventureland

- African Safari
- Elephant Hunter (Wally Boag) riding a real elephant and shooting off a trick rifle that fired coiled up covered springs.
- Watusi Warriors
- Gorilla and Chimpanzees
- Adventureland Float (a Jungle Cruise launch)
- Polynesian Women

Frontierland

- Huntington Park Youth Band - Phil Moore, director
- Stagecoach
- Western Silver Mounted Equestrians - George Putnam, George Ryan, Al Garcia, Ernest Specht, George J. Sherman, L. D. Wardle, Lyle and Grace Williams, Harold and Thelma Esseberg, Frank McCoy, Harold Dukan, Wally Blomquist, and Dr. Dale Wurman
- Columbia Float
- Disneyland Indians
- Golden Horseshoe Float (done up like an old West saloon with two can-can dancers sitting on the bar while stuntmen performed a staged fight)

Tomorrowland

- South Gate City Youth Band -Dale Eymann, director
- Super Autopia Mark V Cars (The cars held a driver and a celebrity including: Darren McGavin, Chill Wills, Lawrence Welk, Lennon Sisters, Jeffrey Hunter, Marvin Miller, Richard Crenna, Dennis Hopper, Clint Eastwood, Rex Allen and others)
- Disneyland Alweg Monorail Float - (Futuristic domed buildings with a miniature operating monorail running through the display that host Art Linkletter called "an actual working model".)
- Swiss Singing Society "Harmonie" - Fred Erich Bannasch, director
- Matterhorn Float - (The scale model Matterhorn featured on that float was one of three large-scale Matterhorn models built by Imagineer Harriet Burns to guide engineering, architectural, and construction teams as they worked on the attraction.)
- San Diego Naval Training Center Band - W/O F.L. Emond, director
- Submarine Voyage Float (King Neptune and four mermaids who threw treasures from Davy Jones' Locker to the guests)

Fantasyland

- Independent Order of Foresters
- Robin Hood Band - David Baskerville, director
- Tumblers
- Walt Disney Cartoon Characters (Like Opening Day at

Disneyland, these costumes were borrowed from John Harris' Ice Capades show and included Mickey Mouse, Three Little Pigs, Pinocchio, some Disney princesses and more.)

- Roy Williams, the "Big Mooseketeer"
- Horseketeers Drill Team (in the Mickey Mouse Club horse costume where it looked like they were riding a cartoon horse when they were standing up.)
- Fantasia Group (including the mushrooms from the film)
- Arabian Equestrians - Don Hudson Barnstetter and Marvin Moore
- "76 Trombones" (Meredith Willson, the composer of the Broadway hit *The Music Man*, which was still running on Broadway at the time, was in the reviewing stand. Apparently, this band of 76 trombone players all dressed in tuxedos with white bow ties was a surprise to him. "I've been saying it all afternoon, but Walt Disney, when he does anything, he does it right, doesn't he? Listen to that!" remarked Willson to co-host Linkletter. Leading the band like a drum major was a strutting Tommy Walker, Disneyland's director of entertainment, also in a tuxedo. He handed his cane and hat to Willson who proceeded to conduct the orchestra.)
- Silhouettes of Western High School Anaheim - Ruth Miyano, director
- Colorful balloon release near Town Square including two-toned Mickey Mouse headed balloons.

2:30 p.m.

Matterhorn Musical Pageant. Reserved grandstands for Press Guests located at base of Matterhorn Mountain adjacent to the Main Street Plaza.

- Mountain Climbers (from the Sierra Club who climbed the structure, planted both the Swiss and American flags at the pinnacle, and then rappelled down the slope)
- Swiss Singing Society "Harmonie" - Fred Erich Bannasch, director
- Swiss Alpine Horn Player
- Swiss Dancers (in red and white outfits)
- Yodelers
- Performance on raised stage by Silver Medal Olympic skating champion Ronnie Robertson who was then touring with the Ice Capades where he was nicknamed "The Human Blur" - choreography by Tommy Mahoney

3 p.m.

Following the Matterhorn Pageant, the new Matterhorn Mountain Bobsleds, Fantasyland Autopia and Motor Boat Cruise were open for the Press Guests and their families to enjoy.

4 p.m.

Dedication Ceremonies: Submarine Voyage and Disneyland-Alweg Monorail Trains. Press Guests were invited to follow the directional signs and view these activities from area surrounding the Coral Lagoon.

Submarine Voyage Dedication

Participants

- Chief Machinist Mate, Stuart M. Nelson of the U.S.S. Nautilus and his first wife Mildred Nelson
- Rear Admiral Charles C. Kirkpatrick
- Walt Disney
- Art Linkletter

There was a Mermaid Ballet in Coral Lagoon by eight mermaids.

Mrs. Nelson christened the Disneyland Submarine D-301 shouting "I christen thee Nautilus." Walt had handed her a ribbon-decorated bottle of champagne that was sitting on the top of the submarine and she smashed it with such vigor that she almost lost her balance and Walt had to steady her. Walt accompanied her, her children, Nelson and Kirkpatrick aboard for the first maiden voyage of the Nautilus.

Nelson died on February 12, 2007 in Gainesville, Florida at the age of 79.

Nelson was one of the pioneers of the U.S. Navy nuclear submarine service. He served aboard the first U.S. nuclear submarine, the Nautilus, (SSN 571) which is why he and his family were selected for this christening.

By 1957 he was chief machinist mate aboard the Nautilus, where he was in charge of the propulsion plant during the first submerged trans-polar trip in 1958. In 1960 he was commissioned an officer and remained aboard the Nautilus until 1961.

Admiral Kirkpatrick, who had been persuaded to participate in this christening at the urging of Nixon, said that Nelson was "a man who does what other men can only imagine" and that Nelson was "officially commended for outstanding leadership, technical competence and devotion to duty in the first transpolar cruise in history under the sea in submarine".

Kirkpatrick turned to Walt and said, "Walt, this is a real Navy family [referring to Nelson, his wife and their three young sons who were standing nearby]. I don't believe you can put the christening of a ship in better hands or better company."

Disneyland–Alweg Monorail System Dedication

Press guests were invited to view these activities from the area surrounding the Coral Lagoon.

Walt: "To open the first operating monorail system in America, it is our good fortune to have our friend and fellow Californian, the Vice-President of the United States, Mr. Richard Nixon and his charming family, Mrs. Pat Nixon, "Julia" (actually her name was Julie) and Patricia, his daughters. (Julie was roughly 10 years old and Tricia about 13.)"

Richard Nixon: "Thank you very much, Walt. I want to say this has really been one of the most exciting and interesting days that I've ever had in my life and I'm sure that's true of all the others who are here at Disneyland to participate in these various ceremonies opening these wonderful new exhibits which we have here.

"I think you will be interested to know, Walt, and I know our television and radio listeners will be interested to know when my wife and I were planning this trip and talking it over with our two daughters and we asked them what they wanted to do most when they came to California, they said, 'We want to see our grandmother and go to Disneyland'.

"Now, I can tell you, however, that is not just the case with regard to young people all over the country but it's true of the dignitaries who come to Washington from other lands. I remember President Sukarno [of Indonesia] also wanted to come to Disneyland and he has been here as you know.

"The king of Belgium, the king of Morocco...from all over the world people whether they are adults or children want to come to Disneyland...to see America, the past, the present and the future and so consequently, I just want to take this opportunity to say what a fine job we think Disneyland has been doing in letting all of us for a brief few hours have an interlude in our rather busy life and participate in a feeling about the traditions, the dreams, the hopes of this great country of ours.

"Now, of course, comes the time for the dedication although you and I, the adults up here, are probably just as interested in riding this as the children. Since this first monorail system is a system for the future and since Disneyland is a place which children love above everything else, I think it would be nice if our two daughters Patricia and Julie cut the ribbon."

4:30 p.m.

Press Guests and their family were allowed to ride the Submarine Voyage and the Monorail.

5:30-7:30 p.m.

Informal Buffet Dinner and Entertainment in Holidayland. Special Santa Fe and Disneyland Trains departed from Fantasyland Station at five-minute intervals beginning at 5:30 p.m. and dropped off at the Frontierland Station. Nixon and his family then went to Knott's Beery Farm for a family reunion and received special attention from Walter Knott.

8 p.m.-Midnight

Dancing at the Plaza Gardens

9 p.m.

Fantasy in the Sky fireworks. Reportedly, there was also a fireworks display around 6:15 p.m., but I have been unable to confirm it.

At the end of the televised show, Linkletter was in one of the Skyway buckets in Tomorrowland:

Linkletter: "My happy job as co-host is just about wrapped up. I'm going to have some fun on these rides we've been talking about. Where's Walt? [*pointing down*] There he is down there with some children naturally. So for one last bit of official business, I give you the happiest kid in the park...Walt Disney!"

Walt: "Disneyland was made possible by all of you...the millions who have already been here, the people here today...and those we hope to see some day. I think it is appropriate for the occasion to ask these children of the visitors here today to help me officially open Disneyland '59 for its only purpose...the pursuit of happiness for all."

Ropes were then opened allowing a mass of children to enter the Tomorrowland area with the new attractions.

The First Three "E Ticket" Attractions 1959

The Matterhorn

The Matterhorn Bobsleds attraction can claim numerous milestones:

- First thrill ride in Disneyland

- First tubular steel track roller coaster in the world. Previously roller coasters were built on wooden frames.

- First roller coaster with multiple cars on the same track made possible through individual braking zones and an electronic dispatch system

- First roller coaster built by Arrow Development (later Arrow Dynamics), which went on to become a leading, worldwide supplier of roller coasters.

- World's first themed indoor-outdoor roller coaster

- The Matterhorn is unique to Disneyland and does not exist in any other Disney theme park.

- It is the highest point in Disneyland since 1959 and was the highest point in Orange County for many years and could be seen from the Interstate 5 Freeway

In the process of digging the moat around Sleeping Beauty Castle, there was a twenty foot pile of dirt left behind put between the entrance to Fantasyland and Tomorowland. Because it would cost too much to remove it and nothing to replace it, Walt simply leveled off the top of it, added some trees and landscaping and a few picnic benches and it was labeled Lookout Hill but Walt always called it Holiday Hill.

He chose the name not just because of its alliterative nature but because he had been thinking of having that area be devoted to celebrating holidays, something he would later create elsewhere in 1957 with Holidayland.

When the Disneyland Skyway opened on June 23, 1956, the hill became the home for a large steel tower used to support the buckets that traveled from Fantasyland to Tomorrowland and back.

That summer, Walt sat on the hill with Admiral Joe Fowler who was in charge of Disneyland construction and talked about the possibility of transforming the hill into a toboggan ride with real snow.

In 1938, Walt wrote a letter to the *Marceline News* in which he reflected on the joys of growing up in Marceline, Missouri and recalled, "What fun I used to have on winter days going down the hillsides lickety-split on a sled."

The good Admiral was aghast at the logistics and expense of trying to get a working snowmaking machine to generate enough snow to accommodate Walt's vision. He argued that in the summer heat it would all quickly turn to slush, and that there would be drainage problems. He steered Walt away from the idea by talking about all the other things needed in Disneyland at the time.

Walt's response was to start calling the area "Snow Hill" and the name evolved by the end of 1957 into "Snow Mountain" as Walt kept thinking bigger. One day a female employee found Walt sitting on a bench between Fantasyland and Tomorrowland and staring up in the sky.

"What are you looking at, Walt?" she asked. "My mountain," he quietly replied.

Amorous couples quickly discovered that this secluded, out-of-the-way location could be a somewhat private location which resulted in a Security Report dated July 18, 1957 that it was a favorite spot for guests who were "using the viewing area for love-making" and that Security needed to patrol the area more vigorously and make "frequent inspections".

In October 1957, Disneyland executive Jack Sayers read an article in *Funspot* magazine about a "wild mouse" coaster that could make quick turns and sharp drops, and he passed the article along to Walt, who passed it along to Dick Irvine.

By May 15, 1958, Bill Cottrell was talking at a meeting about converting Holiday Hill with "a pair of wild mouse bobsleds" with a little bit of artificial snow. It was hoped that by having two separate tracks it could accommodate capacity issues.

In production at the same time was the Disney live action film, *Third Man on the Mountain* (1959) based on a true story of a famous mountain climber who had died trying to climb the Matterhorn and his determined young son attempting to complete the task.

Walt went to visit the location for the filming for about a week, traveling by train to the Alpine village of Zermatt, at the foot of the Matterhorn. He became more and more enamored of the impressive peak. Disney publicist Leonard Shannon who was there as well remembered, "He would stand and literally look at that thing for an hour or so."

Walt bought a souvenir postcard with a photo of the mountain and sent it back to Burbank to one of his art directors, Victor Greene, with the terse message: "Build this!"

Amazingly, Greene who would become the attraction's art director was able to convincingly re-create the Swiss Matterhorn on paper, faithfully rendering its crags, clefts, and cliffs without actually visiting the location in person.

He had very little reference material to work with, only a photo layout from *National Geographic* magazine, another two page spread from *Life* magazine, the *Encyclopedia Britannica* as well as a handful of picture postcards Walt had sent from Zermatt.

Imagineer Harriet Burns turned Vic Greene's drawings into the first of a number of three-dimensional models, so that the Matterhorn design could be studied from every perspective.

She originated a technique of building the model in layers like a birthday cake. Constructing in layers enabled the model to be evaluated, structurally and aesthetically, as an assembly of components. One flawed layer could be replaced without scrapping the entire model.

Burns admitted that the Imagineers exaggerated the uppermost "hook" of the peak to dramatize the shadow it cast. The Disneyland Matterhorn is oriented exactly like the Swiss Matterhorn, relative to the compass-points, so that the sun over Anaheim casts authentic-looking shadows.

Burns remembered, "I said, 'Good grief a Matterhorn in the middle of Disneyland!' We just thought, well gosh, there's a *real* Matterhorn, so why would he want to bring it here?"

Running out of time and money (it would end up costing roughly a million and a half dollars to build the final attraction), Walt left the interior hollow and guests did not mind seeing the bare beams and catwalks because the final attraction moved so quickly and was so exciting.

"Nothing like the Matterhorn had ever been built before," Harriet Burns later said.

"The experts told Walt that there was no way we could build the Matterhorn with two separate toboggan runs on it, plus planters for the greenery, plus water flow systems to operate the waterfalls, plus openings for the Skyway.

"The experts said that after we had installed all of this machinery, the structure would no longer look anything like the original Swiss Matterhorn. They insisted that what Walt wanted to achieve was simply impossible. And Walt had a simple response: 'Just get it done'. So we put our heads together, solved all the engineering and design problems, and we got it done."

Disneyland's Matterhorn would be roughly 1/100th the height of the original or approximately 147 feet high compared to the actual 14,700 feet of the real thing. It would hide the steel support structure for the Skyway.

The Matterhorn was built in ten months out of 2,175 individual steel girders, each a different weight and length. These beams were covered by hundreds of plywood shapes from enough pieces of lumber to build 27 track homes to help create the contour.

Then the entire form was covered with tons of concrete that was sculpted and covered with 800 gallons of paint to resemble the majestic mountain.

Imagineer John Hench wrote, "That guests accept the notion of a miniature Alpine peak covered with snow in the middle of Southern California is a triumph of the Imagineer's art. The key effect that makes it so persuasive is the astonishingly realistic silvery-white, blue-shadowed snow."

The cap was completed first because it didn't house any of the ride mechanisms so that external access was not necessary. If it had been built from the ground up, previously finished areas might have been damaged during the continuing construction.

The steel skeleton was done by American Bridge, a major steel fabrication company. The company hung signs from the beams with its name to promote its business that specialized in bridge and high-rise structures.

Once the skeleton was in place, then the two tracks were installed. The track utilized for the first time tubular pipe rails allowing it to twist and turn beyond anything done in the past. The hollow steel pipe track could also be pressurized.

Karl Bacon of Arrow Development added, "We had to miss the other track with proper crossover points. There was not a lot of room for two tracks. To get enough hourly capacity to be viable, the sleds needed to be dispatched at a fairly close interval. We needed to design a block system to keep them separated."

Ed Morgan of Arrow Development recalled, "In a Wild Mouse ride, the people are sitting high above the rails. We said that we can't have that; it was not safe if you have a lot of forces that are not controlled. We wanted it nested by the rails. We built the bogies on the sleds so that the rails are at mid-section, and the rails encapsulate the car so it looks like you are going through the snow, not on top of it.

"Disney was going to design the sled but nothing happened. I decided to mock it up and they just accepted it. I never actually got anything but a preliminary sketch. It really didn't show the shape. The only reason our car was accepted is because Walt saw it and liked it.

"I felt we needed safety bumpers that would absorb a lot of energy if they bump each other. So the nose was two feet long and that could absorb a lot of energy. We also had a back bumper made out of a resilient foam cushion with a boot over it probably about six inches thick.

"We chose polyurethane for the wheels because we weren't going to run steel wheels on a steel rail. The noise being the biggest factor. Polyurethane rolls with a lot less effort than rubber does. A rubber tire deforms differently and loses more energy to heat than polyurethane. We had DuPont's assurance of the record that they would help us. They had the rights to polyurethane."

Fiberglass bodies were used because they were light, flexible and could be molded into a pleasing aerodynamic shape. The bobsleds connected to the track in three different places restricting the vertical movement of the car.

The vehicles were not motorized in any way, relying largely on gravity for momentum and pressurized air brakes for additional safety in key zones.

Equally challenging was making the building look like a mountain. Landscaper Bill Evans had to determine what should be a "timberline" for a fourteen story building. He finally decided it should be halfway up the summit, approximately sixty-five to seventy-five feet up with the snow level above that mark.

He planted full-sized live spruce trees on the lower levels and then progressively smaller trees at the higher elevations to create a sense of forced perspective so it looked taller. Thousands of plants native to Switzerland like edelweiss were planted in profusion around the base of the mountain as well as near the waterfalls and glacial pools.

As Evans told me when I interviewed him in 1985: "Let me tell you the prescription for planting a reproduction of a Matterhorn. The formula is to fill a cement bucket on the edge of a 125 foot boom, with some planter mix and fir bark for the ball roots of the trees, and then plop down a few plants and a tree and on top of the pile plop down a gardener on top of the plants and then hoist the whole thing up in the air about a hundred feet.

"Find some pad to dump the soil and plants and stomp them into place. And go back down for another load. That's how the planting was done. The area was equipped with a plastic irrigation and drip system and some rather conventional plumbing to make sure that everything drained.

"We had a sophisticated system of feeding those plants. (laughs) We had an old 50 foot gallon oil drum on the top of the Matterhorn connected to the irrigation system and we dumped some fertilizer in that and periodically it dribbled down on the plants.

"I think the Matterhorn was about 1/100th scale so it wouldn't do to put California fir trees or pine trees up there because they would be totally out of scale. We found some old stunted pinon pines on the edge of the Colorado Desert and brought those in. They were three to six feet high but much more in keeping with the scale. Very short needles. But in intervals of every three or four years they get replaced."

The Matterhorn straddles the boundary of Tomorrowland and Fantasyland just as the real Matterhorn does the borders of Switzerland and Italy. The ride has always had two tracks, commonly called the "A" side or the Tomorrowland side (2,126 feet of track) and the "B" side or Fantasyland side (2,238 feet of track) but the ride really doesn't belong in the Land of Classic Stories of Childhood or the World of Tomorrow.

For the most part up to 1970 the Matterhorn was listed under Tomorrowland because it was part of the 1959 rehab of Tomorrowland.

By 1972, the Matterhorn had moved on official park literature to Fantasyland, where it remains on current Disneyland guide maps today.

The Matterhorn mountain climbers would begin their first accent in 1959 using members of the Sierra Club who continued to do so for awhile until Disneyland hired its own climbing team. The climbers would typically scale the mountain in groups of two or three and were required to wear bright red Lederhosen and had to climb the mountain several times throughout each day.

There are forty different routes to take up the Matterhorn. The climbers would consistently climb the exterior until 1979 after which it would only be done sproradically.

There is a one-third court with a basketball hoop located in an empty space in the upper two-thirds of the mountain. However, despite urban legend, the basketball court was not built to get around a City of Anaheim ordinance about tall buildings. Walt himself gave his okay for its installation for the mountain climbers on their breaks to entertain themselves.

According to Disneyland lore, the visiting King Baudouin of Belgium asked his host Walt why the mountain had so many holes in it. "Because it is a Swiss mountain," Walt laughed referencing the many holes in Swiss cheese.

From the mid- to late-1960s, the Anaheim Police Department positioned a patrol officer on top of the Matterhorn to help direct traffic flow. From that high point, he could see for three miles in every direction. Using a two-way radio, he would help other police officers down below direct traffic and reduce congestion on the surrounding streets. The improved traffic flow was especially helpful for peak attendance days at Disneyland.

From 1961 until around 1972, a giant, twenty-four foot tall Christmas star that lit up at night was installed at the top of the mountain each December for the holiday season. In its early years, it also rotated but the mechanism kept breaking down and in later years it was just stationary. A large crane had to be used to place the star on top of the Matterhorn.

Shortly before the Matterhorn opened, Joe Fowler told Walt, "I think we'll have it finished on time but next time, when we have to build a mountain, let's let God do it!"

Submarine Voyage

Imagineer Bob Gurr recalls it was an offhand remark by Truman Woodworth ("Walt's got everything here except for a submarine.")

that Roger Broggie communicated to Walt that might have spurred the development of the ride.

Another motivating factor was that Pacific Ocean Park, a rival theme park supported by CBS, was soon to open with some attractions that mimicked the ones at Disneyland.

However, something new that the park was publicizing was a submarine-themed walk-through of the USS Nautilus, the world's first nuclear-powered vessel. Being fiercely competitive, Walt may have wanted to out-do that new park.

A July 23, 1958, memo from Irvine to Walt Disney listed the creative team handling the project: Claude Coats would work with Bob Sewell on the overall design and Bill Martin worked on the track layout and architectural planning.

Broggie and Wathel Rogers were to engineer and design the animation and effects. Ub Iwerks would work on projections. Gurr would design the submarine vehicles and the drive system with "technical data and advice" from General Dynamics Corporation.

So an investigation began to use the same type of cable system used in San Francisco for the famous cable cars instead of using individual engines. However, the Imagineers, including Broggie and Gurr after a visit to the city and a discussion with the operators, were concerned among other challenges about what would happen if the cables broke about how they would be able to get the guests back up to the surface and back to the shore.

The original concept was that the sub would actually be six feet or more underwater. That problem was solved by having a ride vehicle that didn't actually descend below the surface, but moved by a diesel engine with two guide trunks front and rear with flanged wheels along a rail.

Most of the adventure takes place in a huge concrete and steel box of a show building that, thanks to the landscaping genius of Bill Evans, was effectively disguised to look more like a forest behind a waterfall.

The United States Navy expressed an interest in becoming involved in the project, but retired Admiral Joe Fowler, a former Navy man himself and in charge of Disneyland operations, knew that could become a nightmare with all the paperwork and red tape and approvals and regulations. Walt hated being held accountable or overruled by someone else on any project.

There is the popular and often told story, sometimes by Fowler himself, that when several top ranking naval officers did ride the final attraction, despite being told by Fowler that the vehicle never submerged, the naval officers were completely fooled by the illusion.

The Disneyland Submarine Voyage was inspired in part by the August 3, 1958, voyage of the U.S.S. Nautilus as the first ship to navigate under the North Pole.. Of course, this being Disneyland, guests also got to encounter mermaids, Atlantis and even a friendly, cross-eyed sea serpent, so it wasn't completely scientifically accurate although it was indicated that some of these fantasy elements might just be hallucinations from oxygen deprivation.

Setting Your Course on the Submarines: Story Guide and Operations Procedures was prepared by the University of Disneyland for Submarine Operators at the park.

It was a seventeen page manual that included information behind the story, operating procedures (including emergency procedures like handling guests experiencing claustrophobia or a broken porthole or power failure), facts about the Disney submarines that can be shared with guests (including that each one cost approximately $80,625 or that there was nine million gallons of water in the lagoon), history of submarines, glossary of terms, suggested further reading and more. In addition, there were diagrams and photos (including behind-the-scenes shots of Walt himself).

Here is an excerpt from the introduction written by Fowler himself:

"This attraction is not just a ride on a submarine; it is Walt Disney's re-creation of a living experience and depicts one of America's most dramatic achievements—the nuclear powered submarine. Our fleet closely parallels its ocean-going counterpart in exterior design.

"Here in Disneyland, Walt has made it possible for everyone to experience the events that men of the United States Nuclear Powered Submarine Fleet have been experiencing during the past decade."

The Submarine Voyage was dedicated June 14, 1959 at 3:30 p.m. for a special media preview. It would open to the general public the following day.

The first real mermaids appeared in the lagoon in the summer of 1959 to promote the attraction as the brainchild of Disneyland's Entertainment Director Tommy Walker who held auditions for the role at the Disneyland Hotel pool. The living mermaids were brought back in the summer of 1965 for Disneyland's Tencennial celebration and were a summer attraction through the end of summer 1967.

When in the lagoon, they frolicked underwater to the delight of eager guests peering from the submarine portholes. The mermaids could not see inside the vessels but heard the music clearly so could time their appearances accordingly. There was a rock outcropping in the middle of the lagoon where they could bask and wave at guests.

Participants in the dedication ceremony included Chief Machinist Mate, Stuart M. Nelson of the U.S.S. Nautilus and his first wife Mildred Nelson, a former WAVE, who would formally christen the fleet; Rear Admiral Charles C. Kirkpatrick; Walt Disney and Art Linkletter.

Mrs. Nelson christened the Disneyland Submarine D-301 shouting "I christen thee Nautilus".

The Disneyland fleet included the same names as the actual U.S. submarine fleet: Nautilus, Seawolf, Skate, Skipjack, Triton, George Washington, Patrick Henry and Ethan Allen, and the training manual gave information about each of the real life counterparts. A total of 38 guests sat in the cramped quarters of each of the 52-foot long submarines.

The eight original aluminum vessels chugged along at 1.8 miles per hour along 1,635 linear feet of track for a ride that lasted eight minutes and 15 seconds. Guests saw 126 animated figures and 180 static figures, as well as approximately 10,000 artificial plants.

Construction of the Disneyland Submarine Voyage began in the fall of 1958. The eight submarine hulls were built by the Todd Shipyards of San Pedro. The submarines were then completed at the Disneyland Naval Yard in Anaheim under the supervision of Fowler who had built naval ships during World War II. The vehicles were painted a military gray giving them an added cache of authenticity.

The first summer the attraction was open, to add an air of reality, two real naval cadets were assigned to stand outside by the lagoon to interact with the guests. It turned out that they were more interested in interacting just with attractive young women as Fowler discovered when he went to check out the attraction one day. He reprimanded the cadets for their behavior, but the cadets had no idea who Fowler was and told the "old man to mind his own business."

"Hold that thought," smiled Fowler as he left and got dressed in his full Admiral regalia. When he returned, the cadets immediately snapped to attention and Fowler claimed that there was no further trouble for the rest of the summer as Fowler told me in a phone interview about a decade before he died.

Walt had originally wanted real sea life to live within the lagoon. But the lagoon's need for massive amounts of chlorine, as well as the logistics of rotating vehicles, and the need for a consistency of experience for each guest to see the fish, caused that idea to be abandoned. WED Imagineers used real "specimen" fish and created plaster cast molds to quickly produce the wide variety of sea life needed.

The fish performed simple repetitive movements and some were connected to overhead rotating turntables. Amazingly, these scenes were built twice as a mirror image so that a complete set of the same actions were on display for the guests on both the port and starboard side of the ship.

The guests saw sea turtles, moray eels, lobsters, crabs, sharks, giant clams, an octopus and more until a surface storm caused the sub to dive to 250 feet where it encountered the Graveyard of Lost Ships including examples of Greek, Roman and Viking craft. There was also a glimpse of a pair of deep-sea divers struggling to recover some sunken treasure from the vessels.

Nearing a polar ice cap, the sub dives underneath the North Pole to an area where sunlight has never penetrated and strange luminescent sea creatures live. Then three swimming mermaids and three more enjoying golden treasures on the ocean's floor are seen as the sub enters the ruined remains of the lost island of Atlantis that sunk beneath the waves as a result of an underwater volcano.

Imagineers Blaine Gibson and Jack Fergus sculpted the mermaids for the attraction over several weeks.

That volcano is still active and springs back to life forcing the vessel to move into an area where guests saw the long curved humps of a green sea serpent with a comical face.

The captain feels that perhaps a lack of oxygen and being underwater too long is causing hallucinations so orders the sub to return to the surface.

Monorail

Monorail Red had been assembled on the beam way at the park just two weeks prior to the dedication ceremony on June 14 on a spur line behind Fantasyland. Monorail Blue would not be ready for another two weeks or so until July 3, 1959. The two trains were identical.

Monorail Red had broken down every day after its assembly, so Imagineer Bob Gurr and Conrad Deller, the chief designer at Alweg, would spend time each night talking over the problems and drawing sketches for replacement parts.

The drawings were taken to the machine shop at the Disney Studios in Burbank where replacement parts would be made overnight and delivered the next morning, where they would be installed in the train. Monorail Red finally made a successful loop around Tomorrowland without breaking down the night before the dedication.

There was no time to train the newly hired Monorail drivers, so Disneyland wardrobe during the night shift made Bob Gurr a uniform and fitted him with it in the early morning. Gurr had eased Monorail Red carefully into the Tomorrowland station with the understanding that he only needed to drive it away after the ribbon cutting ceremony.

The idea was that even if the Monorail once again broke down once it was out of the station, the cameras would have seen it leaving and think it was up and running.

The Richard Nixon family would dedicate Walt Disney's Highway in the Sky. They had stayed at the Disneyland Hotel Saturday night in owner Jack Wrather's personal suite thanks to personal arrangements by Walt himself.

They arrived at the Monorail station at 9:15 a.m. on Sunday morning June 14 to pose for press photos for newspapers east of the Rocky Mountains who needed them for their Monday editions. The actual dedication with the family would take place later in the afternoon around 4 p.m. after the dedication of the Submarine Voyage. That is why photos of the dedication show the Nixon family in different clothing in different photos.

At the photo shoot, Gurr told me in an interview, "Walt wanted to show Nixon the inside of the Monorail cab. We turned on the 600-volt DC power so I could get the air conditioning to cool down the cab. In a few minutes, Walt had the entire Nixon family in the cab. The security personnel were still on the platform.

"Now Walt could get very twinkly-eyed and excited when he was showing off something new, and he told everyone about his dream for modern transportation in America.

"Walt was having a good time. When there's something that he's got, and nobody else has got it, he's like a very proud papa. He was in an extremely good mood. The eyebrows were up, and he was in one of those moods. He turned to me and said, 'Let's go!' and when Walt tells you something you don't hesitate or question it. You do it.

"I worried the thing might only have one good lap in it and I was saving that for later that day for the ceremony but off we went. When we passed over the Submarine Voyage waterfall, Nixon let out a four letter exclamation because all the White House Secret Service people were back on the station platform and they were all scrambling around. I had kidnapped the vice president of the United States!

"I was so grateful when we finally were heading back to the station but Nixon's two daughters eagerly wanted to go around again and Walt said, 'Bobby, give 'em another ride!' So I did but I had visions of the Monorail bursting into flames and we hadn't developed any rescue procedures. As we zoomed through the station, we didn't slow down and the Secret Service tried to jump into the train but didn't make it.

"Nixon just roared with laughter. Apparently, he was sometimes irritated by all the security he had around him. I didn't find any of it funny at all. When we pulled back into the station, Walt and the Nixon family all walked down the ramp and looked back up and the Secret Service were all in the train. They hadn't even noticed we had left and walked down. That made Nixon laugh as well.

"[Alweg's Chief Designer Conrad] Deller ran up to me shouting in a thick German accent, 'You crazy Disney people! Just because you get the train to run once, you put your vice president on this thing without knowing how it really works! You are a crazy person!' I agreed but you don't say 'no' to Walt."

Nixon laughed at his head of security, "You should have seen the expressions on your faces!" Then he left to take his mother to church while his wife and daughters stayed and enjoyed some of the attractions.

Gurr said: "Up to Disneyland, the word 'monorail' usually referred to the Wuppertal Monorail in the town of Wuppertal, Germany. It was a mountain town with a curving river and the monorail was built because it was the easiest way to go up and down through this little town.

"They had pylons built on both banks of the river and the track hung down and the train swung freely underneath. It was very simple and practical. It was like a railroad car with the wheels above it, hanging on a rail. It had been running over 50 years by the time the Alweg Company started to do their work."

What made the Disneyland-Alweg system unique was that instead of being suspended by an overhead rail, the monorails straddle a beam and are supported and stabilized by vertical and horizontal wheels. It was referred to as a "saddle bag" system recalling the bags that cowboys would sling over the saddles of their horses.

According to Disney legend, after leaving the set after watching some filming of the live action feature movie *Third Man on the Mountain* in June 1958, Walt Disney and his wife Lillian ventured into Cologne, Germany, where, while driving along a country road, saw the test track and test train for the Alweg monorail.

As the story goes, Walt and Lillian had visited Germany years earlier and ridden the Wuppertal Suspension Railway that made Lillian feel queasy because of the swaying motion and sharp turns. As they were driving along this road, Walt rounded the bend into a clearing just as the Alweg monorail train passed above the road right in front of him.

He followed the train beams and found the offices of the small research group called "Alweg" based on the initials of its founder, Axel L. Wenner-Gren, who was a Swedish scientist who had his money "frozen" so it could only be spent in Germany after World War II to aid in the rebuilding of the country.

Angry, he used it to experiment with a prototype for future transportation that would make the Wuppertal monorail look archaic.

Walt took photos and got as much information as he could since he did not speak German and then returned to California and gave it all to Imagineer Roger Broggie to bring the monorail to Disneyland.

The Alweg Company had been operating their test monorail since 1952. Its beam way was on a long curve approximately one mile in length, without grades. However, if someone mapped out the test site and the road for that year, it is clear that the test track never went over any road and the only road nearby was a small old country road so Walt would have had to have been very lost to be on it ... or knew exactly where he was going and why.

There had been two articles in the *Los Angeles Times* the previous year that extensively talked about the Alweg monorail and the possible building of an extensive monorail in Brazil. These articles were well placed in the newspaper, so it is reasonable that someone at WED, and perhaps even Walt himself, could have seen them.

Joe Fowler recalled, "Well, in 1957, I went to Europe and met Walt at the Octoberfest. I had four of the most wonderful days of my life there with Walt and Lilly and my wife and myself. I told him that I had heard of this monorail in Cologne, Germany, which was running on an experimental basis on a mile long track, and I was going to look at it.

"He said, 'Fine.' I did and I got all the data [I had all the pictures and everything] and I came back to the Studio and I told Dick [Irvine], 'Dick, if we show these to Walt, we're sunk. He's going to build it, I'm sure.' And he did. And that was the beginning of the monorail."

That trip would be about April 1958, which sets up Walt's trip to Europe in June of 1958 to see (or accidentally discover) the Alweg test site pretty nicely.

The story of Walt discovering the monorail by "accident" probably began with Roger Broggie, who was maybe remembering a visit Walt made to the German site to see Fowler's recommendation and got a little lost trying to find the place. Gurr often tells the story of Walt "discovering" the monorail but said he got it from Broggie not Walt.

Like the Disneyland Railroad, the Monorail was owned and operated by Walt's personal company, Retlaw ("Walter" spelled backwards). As a legal concession to Alweg, for several years the monorails were boldly identified as the Disneyland-Alweg Monorail System until 1976, even though they were being sponsored like the Disneyland railroad by the Santa Fe.

There had only been three people from Alweg involved in helping with the Monorail, but most people thought that the company had built the entire system.

Alweg Chief Designer Conrad Deller worked with Gurr, and two other Alweg employees worked with Disneyland's Chief Structural Engineer John Wise on the beam way. Gurr has mentioned many times that he was appreciative of the expertise of Deller.

For Alweg, the publicity served as a double-edged sword. On the one hand, it received publicity and accolades for the monorail system at Disneyland. On the other hand, critics used it as an example that the system was only good for "kiddie amusement parks," and not as a serious alternative to transportation.

In October 1958, Bob Gurr's first drawing of the design for the Disneyland Monorail, then tentatively called "Monorail Viewliner," was submitted. The Viewliner, designed by Gurr, was a futuristic looking train made from car parts, but ran on railroad wheels that ran from a Tomorrowland station to a Fantasyland station from June 1957 to September 1958.

As Gurr recalled, "The German engineers were extremely upset that Americans who were not engineers and had no experience with monorails should have the arrogance to show up with their own design. At the meeting was a subcontractor from a car building company in Mannheim who thought he had it all wrapped up that they would build the Disney trains. There was a week's worth of heated discussions and at the end we had agreed that we would proceed with my design without their technology. Disney would build the cars in California."

The job of building the Monorail was originally assigned to the Standard Carriage Works of East Los Angeles, but, in late 1958, Walt Disney, pressured for time, moved it to his Burbank studios where the two Monorails were built on soundstages that had previously been used for the live-action feature film *20,000 Leagues Under the Sea*.

Teams at the Disney Studio worked night and day, seven days a week to meet the deadline. To avoid distractions, the area was roped off and even Walt respected that boundary and did not cross over despite his curiosity.

As Gurr recalled: "The Alweg version looked like a loaf of bread. I made it sleek and graceful, like a Buck Rogers rocket ship I remembered seeing from when I was younger. I figured I could distract people from looking at the rail and hide the wheels by making it look like that kind of a spaceship with the point in the back and a sled runner in the front.

"It hides the fact that it's an ugly rectangle shape and since it looks like those 1939 arrow-shaped cylinder rocket ships, it seems futuristic. Walt liked it immediately. It was truly like the world of tomorrow with this sleek vehicle zipping along that beam high in the air with the sky behind it."

The first Monorail vehicles were known as Mark I models. They had two separate cars (red and blue because those were the colors of the two previous Viewliner trains) followed by three cabins.

Each car could carry 82 passengers who had to surrender an "E" Ticket worth fifty cents to ride. The monorail circled Tomorrowland along eight-tenths of a mile of elevated track higher than the surrounding berm and climbing to a height of 31 feet near the Autopia.

Guests could see the still remaining orange groves and vegetable farms outside the park.

Each front car had a bubble-like windshield to provide a panoramic view. They also featured a bubble dome for the driver since Walt did not want guests looking at the back of the neck of the driver. The bubble dome had been inspired by the Boeing B47 Bomber.

Disney saved money because the chief electrical engineer at the Disney studios was able to get some inexpensive used Westinghouse DC motors, the same kind Disney was using for its film cameras. The driver simply needed to push the power arm forward to go and pull it back to stop. The vehicles were equipped with automatic air brakes.

There were various "speed zones" around the track from 18 to 43 miles per hour, although, in general, drivers tried to hold the speed to an average of 20 mph in the park and 35 in the parking lot area. The beam way is about 20 inches wide and 35 inches in depth. Imagineer Bill Martin laid out the track configuration that was similar to the one for the Viewliner.

Imagineer Roger Broggie remembered, "It was a delicate balancing act because the engineers wanted it to go in a straight line with no grades because it would operate with fewer problems. The Disney art directors wanted it to have twists and tight turns and climb maximum grades so that it would be a better show for the guests. It is no surprise that Walt agreed."

The rubber tires on the vehicles are about the same size as on a family minivan. The tires are arranged in pairs at the front and back of each car, and follow the top of the beam. They are guided by another set of smaller tires which ride along each side of the track, one at the top and one at the bottom.

The purpose of these tires is to keep the train upright through the use of heavy springs that hold the tires tight against the beam. Otherwise, the vehicle would have the tendency to lean.

A series of direct current electric motors power the train, picking up 600 volts through a pair of "bus bars" running along the side of the track.

1960

- Attendance: 4.9 million
- Employment: 3,693
- Payroll: $12.2 million
- Highlights
  - Art of Animation exhibit opens
  - Circarama debuts
  - Disneyland hosted its first Private Party for outside groups in May

Disneyland's fifth birthday in 1960 was a bit anti-climatic since, less than a year before, in 1959, the park experienced such sweeping changes. It has all been well documented with a huge summer celebration that included a television special and theatrical documentary featurette released in 1960, *Gala Day at Disneyland.*

Walt and his team were also deeply involved with the 1960 Winter Olympics held in February 1960. Walt wasn't just responsible for all the glamour and glitz, like the opening and closing ceremonies, nighttime entertainment for athletes and officials, as well as decorating the venue. He was also asked to provide help with tickets, parking, and security.

Disney officially bought out the Western Printing and Lithographing investment that gave them 13.8 percent of Disneyland. The buy-out actually gave the company the impetus to break away from Dell that was distributing its comic books and activity books and start its own comic book line called Gold Key.

In July, just before the anniversary, American Broadcasting Paramount Theaters Inc. sold its 35 percent interest in Disneyland for $7.5 million. ABC's interest in Disneyland was originally purchased in 1954 for $500,000.

However, despite all this non-stop activity, under Walt's watch, Disneyland always had something new every year and new milestones were always being made and 1960 was no different.

Disneyland held its first private party on Friday, May 13, when 5,042 Knights of Columbus enjoyed exclusive use of Disneyland. The New Year's Eve Party that year was attended by over 14,000 guests showing that more and more local residents were considering Disneyland as a location to celebrate on that evening.

Of course, some things disappeared like the Kaiser Hall of Aluminum Fame in July 1960. Kaiser had convinced Walt that aluminum was truly going to be the metal of the future which is why it supposedly fit into Tomorrowland.

The Kaiser pavilion was a self-guided walk-through exhibit showcasing the history of aluminum products "past, present and future." Most impressive was at the entrance, a polished 40-foot aluminum telescope shown on the opening day television special.

Dixieland at Disneyland

The "Dixieland at Disneyland" event debuted on the Rivers of America in Frontierland on October 1 for one night only from 8 p.m. to 1 a.m. The show started with a floating Mardi Gras parade accompanied by fireworks. A floating raft was created for each of the six bands, complete with multicolored spotlights that lighted up the musicians.

And, for the grand finale, all six bands gathered aboard the Mark Twain Riverboat and sailed past the audience, swinging in time to the song *When the Saints Come Marching In.*

When the Mark Twain docked, the bands each marched off to six separate locations throughout Disneyland to perform for the crowd during the remainder of the night. At the stroke of midnight, the bands once again assembled and were in a foot-tapping parade down Main Street that culminated at the railroad station. It took operations by surprise when over 9,000 jazz fans showed up for the special one-night party. Tickets, which included admission to the park, were $4.50.

Bands included Bob Crosby and the Bob Cats, The Elliott Brothers and the Dixie Dandies, Disneyland Strawhatters, Joe Darensbourg and the Dixie Flyers, Albert McNeil Choir, and Young Men from New Orleans. Louis Armstrong and the Firehouse Five didn't start appearing until the second year. The event proved so instantly popular that it expanded and continued until 1970. It was held in the fall because that was the "off season" and was used to generate attendance.

Nature's Wonderland

In June 1960, Walt Disney spent $1.8 million to expand the area devoted to the Rainbow Ridge Mine Train into Nature's Wonderland. The new seven acre wilderness was touted as having 156 types of plant life and over 200 amazing animals, many electric-mechanical that would perform simple repetitive movements like a bear scratching its back on a tree.

The expansion had sections to represent Disney's True-Life Adventure nature films like *The Living Desert* (1953), *Beaver Valley* (1950), *Olympic Elk* (1951), and *Bear Country* (1953). Cascade Peak now towered seventy five feet in the air with its three waterfalls.

The engine cab and cars were repainted a bright yellow with an additional ore car added to each train and the ride was extended another two minutes. In the redesign, all seats now faced forward.

Guests went under a big waterfall, over creaking trestle bridges, passed by four spouting geysers and more. Many items from the original attraction were retained including the almost human cactii, the Devil's Paint Pots, and the Rainbow Caverns.

The last train ride was on New Year's Day 1977 and the attraction was closed to make room for Big Thunder Mountain Railroad. Several items were retained and used in the new attraction.

Cascade Peak that had been built for Nature's Wonderland, remained until 1998. Cascade Peak actually looked taller than seven stories, because of the little pine trees that had been selected to surround its base. Its main purpose was to block the sight of Beaver Valley and Bear Country from all the traffic on the Rivers of America that included the Mark Twain, the Sailing Ship Columbia, the Mike Fink Keel Boats and the Indian War canoes.

Its waterfall, named Big Thunder, also helped aerate the water in the river. Cascade Peak, of course, was not a real mountain, but a building of steel beams and wooden frames built by the same Disney team that had built the Matterhorn a year earlier. Lack of maintenance over the years resulted in severe water damage and termite issues. In addition, work was needed on the faux rock façade. The needed repairs were deemed too expensive and the entire structure became the victim of bulldozers in 1998.

Of course, the name Big Thunder later inspired the name of the Big Thunder Mountain Railroad that replaced the area in 1979. One of the original mine trains and two ore cars were incorporated into a curving length of track near the largest waterfall, where it had appeared to have been derailed. In 2016, after many years of sitting abandoned backstage, they were officially donated to the Los Angeles Live Steamers Railroad Museum in Griffith Park, where they will be restored and displayed next to Walt Disney's Carolwood barn.

An October 2017 Mickey Mouse short titled *Rainbow Caverns* had Mickey taking Minnie on a romantic vacation to Nature's Wonderland and the Rainbow Caverns, but someone had "dropped a big thundering mountain" in its place. Mickey finds an abandoned mine shaft and mine train that is the exact model and color of the original attraction and uses it to locate the original area utilizing his vintage Disneyland souvenir map, that is an exact replica of the large promotional poster Walt used to advertise the new addition to guests. They encounter some of the icons of the original attraction including twisting caves, Balancing Rock Canyon, the Devil's Paintpots and the Old Unfaithful Geyser, even Marc Davis' bear repeatedly scratching its rear on a tree and, finally, the fabled dayglow Rainbow Caverns.

Skull Rock Cove

One of the most dramatic scenes in Disney's animated feature *Peter Pan* (1953) takes place at Skull Rock in Neverland Lagoon. Captain Hook and Mr. Smee take the Indian princess Tiger Lily to the location and threaten to drown her at high tide if she does not reveal the whereabouts of Peter Pan. Fortunately, Pan rescues her just in the nick of time after a battle with the villainous Hook.

Skull Rock does not exist in the original James Barrie novel, but was the creation of the Disney artists for the film's story.

For the first five years of the park, the Chicken of the Sea Pirate Ship Restaurant, that was meant to represent Captain Hook's infamous ship, was anchored in a shallow pool. The surrounding area was devoid of any landscaping. It looked unfinished next to some of the other attractions. It seemed natural to put it into an appropriate setting from the film.

In December 1960, Skull Rock Cove was added to the area and included sandy beaches, an outdoor dining area with tables and chairs made of the ship's kegs, palm trees and a pathway leading to volcanic rock outcropping.

Rockwork stood 30-feet tall and curved around the northeastern shore of the lagoon. The massive rock that resembled a skull was designed by Imagineer Ken Anderson. The new addition not only added to the atmosphere of the pirate ship, but screened the Casey Jr. train from view and helped the transition to the rocks that surrounded Monstro the whale just around the corner.

From the skull's open mouth, a waterfall poured out over the craggy lower teeth. Several smaller waterfalls at various heights cascaded down from either side. The skull featured huge, hollow eyes that at night were lit by an eerie green light. A huge crack squiggled down the top of the forehead.

Skull Rock and the Pirate Ship became the unintentional victims of the New Fantasyland project in 1982. During the renovation, several rides like Dumbo and King Arthur's Carrousel were relocated. The intention was to do the same with the ship and Skull Rock and move them to the queue area for the Storybook Land Canal Boats.

However, damage to the ship prevented that from happening and removal of Skull Rock was already in progress and too late to stop. Some of the lower rockwork still remains.

Art of Animation Exhibit

The Art of Animation exhibit was located between Circarama and The Art Corner in Tomorrowland. Previously, the space had been occupied by the Satellite View of America that had opened with the park.

When Walt Disney was producing the animated feature film *Sleeping Beauty* (1959), he realized that a great way to publicize the "high art" approach of the film, as well as address all the letters that flooded into the studio from young artists interested in animation, would be to put together a traveling exhibit showcasing the history of animation and how animation was done.

The traveling exhibit was titled *The Art of Animation: A Walt Disney Retrospective*.

There were three versions of this exhibit, and each featured different original art. In fact, a 24-page exhibit souvenir guidebook with a white cover was produced featuring material from the Bob Thomas book *The Art of Animation* (1958) also meant to publicize the film *Sleeping Beauty*.

One of the exhibits was showcased in Tomorrowland at Disneyland and it was natural to be placed next to The Art Corner that sold animation related material in May 1960. The exhibit featured early optical devices, like thaumatropes and a zoetrope, as well as displays explaining not only the history of animation, but the process along the perimeter of the circular room.

The interior of the room had plastic chairs, potted plants and ashtrays so guests could smoke. Television monitors showed segments from the Disneyland weekly television show episode *The Art of the Animated Drawing*, first shown on November 11, 1955.

There were two other traveling versions of the exhibit that toured the United States beginning in 1958 and then one was sent to be shown in Europe and the other to Japan in 1960 to once again promote the release of *Sleeping Beauty* in those countries.

The famous attraction poster done by Paul Hartley also promoted that this was part of the "international exhibit" seen around the world. It was a popular exhibit because, at the time, very little was known about animation. It also served to help drive sales at The Art Corner next door. The expansion of the CircleVision theater next door in 1967 resulted in its removal.

Circarama

Inspired by seeing a Cinerama presentation where three large screens were synchronized to show a motion picture, Walt Disney had Ub Iwerks develop a process where a movie could be presented on a series of screens that completely surrounded the audience. The two men share the patent on the process.

It was called Circarama, not only as an allusion to Cinerama, but also because the film was sponsored by the American Motors Corporation, who produced cars like the Rambler. The building was located just to the left of the entrance of Tomorrowland.

The audience stood in an asphalt paved circular area 40-feet in diameter with the 8-foot high screens elevated about 8 feet off the floor. There were no "lean" rails in those early days.

A Tour of the West presented a journey beginning on Sunset Boulevard in front of the Beverly Hills Hotel, then a high-speed trip down Wilshire Boulevard and then along the Los Angeles Freeways to Monument Valley, Arizona, and then off to Las Vegas and the Grand Canyon.

In 1958, Walt created a brand new Circarama film for the Brussels World's Fair, *America the Beautiful*. The new film showcased portions of the entire United States. It was then shown at the American National Exhibition in Moscow, Russia in 1959. In June of 1960 the new film debuted at Disneyland, sponsored by Bell Telephone, as a free attraction.

Sunkist Citrus House

Nearly 160 acres of citrus trees had to be cleared to build Disneyland. The oranges grown on the property over the years were sold to Sunkist, the largest shipper of fresh produce in the United States. Sunkist marketed its fresh-squeezed fruit juice as a healthy alternative to artificial beverages like Coca-Cola.

The Sunkist Citrus House took over the former location of the Puffin Bakery in July 1960. The former bakery's dining room was enlarged by taking over the adjacent space that had been previously operated by Sunny-View Farms Jams and Jellies. While the interior space was now one large dining area with tables and chairs and the counter on the far left, the exterior still looked like two separate businesses. It was later replaced by the Blue Ribbon Bakery and, eventually, the Gibson Girl Ice Cream Parlor.

The shop was owned by the Perricone Citrus Company (Sam Perricone) and run by B.C. "Bo" Foster. Guests could have fresh citrus shipped anywhere in the United States in a special Disneyland box.

Orange juice was fresh squeezed every day at Disneyland for the Citrus House as well as distributed to all the restaurants in the park.

In addition to fresh squeezed orange juice from oranges and lemonade from concentrate, as well as frozen fruit juice bars, the shop sold lemon tarts, lemon meringue pie and orange cheesecake from Marcheta's Bakery in Garden Grove.

Every day, employees drove to Yorba Linda to get the oranges, to Corona to pick up the large containers of frozen lemonade concentrate, and to Garden Grove for the pastries. The shop also made the non-alcoholic Mint Julep (orange juice, lemonade, mint flavoring, sugar and grenadine syrup) sold on the Mark Twain at the time.

The main attraction of the Citrus House was the semi-automatic juice squeezers, where an employee had to constantly feed the oranges one at a time into the chute on top of the squeezer. They used size 138 oranges, meaning an average size so that 138 oranges fit into a single carton. Only Valencia oranges were used, never navel oranges.

The machine automatically cut them in half and squeezed the juice with six reamers on one side and six on the other. The reamers slowly rotated around, picked up an orange half, squeezed it, and dumped the peel in a circular motion with a continuous stream of juice trickling out.

Walt was fascinated by the machine and often in the early morning hours, before the park opened, he would unlock the shop and make himself a glass of orange juice, often inviting workmen he found on the street to join him so he could keep using the machine. Eventually, he was given a small version by Sunkist for his Disneyland apartment.

1961

- Attendance: 4.7 million
- Employment: 3,819
- Payroll: $12.5 million
- Candlelight Processional Narrator: Dennis Morgan
- Highlights:
  - Disneyland-Alweg Monorail system expands to connect with Disneyland Hotel
  - Flying Saucers debut
  - First all-night Grad Nite Party held in June
  - Tinker Bell begins summer flights from peak of Matterhorn to set off "Fantasy In the Sky" fireworks
  - With Santa Claus standing on top of the mountain giving directions, a huge crane placed a rotating twenty-four foot tall star atop the Matterhorn for the holiday season. After the first two years, the star stopped rotating and was eventually removed after 1972.

By 1961, Anaheim was the fastest growing city in the United States, and Orange County the fastest growing county in the nation thanks to Disneyland. The Disneyland Hotel was the largest hotel in Orange County.

It was calculated in the July issue of *The Disneylander* that during the summer season guests "were pouring through the Main Gate of Disneyland at the average of thirty-three people every minute".

However, it was not as active during the rest of the year. Disneyland had not yet developed into a year-round attraction. When kids went back to school after summer vacation, attendance dropped significantly.

In order to try to rectify this situation, Disneyland became involved in establishing the Anaheim Visitor and Convention Bureau to help promote all of Anaheim as a major tourist destination. Disney gave the bureau interest-free loans to help get the organization started. Disney was already publishing the quarterly *Vacationland* magazine given away in local hotels to promote all entertainment venues including Knott's Berry Farm.

Disneyland welcomed its 25 millionth guest Dr. Glenn C. Franklin on April 19. Along with his wife, Helen, their three children, and his mother, the lucky Franklin family received a private guided tour of the Park, a table of honor at a luncheon and unlimited use of attractions all day long.

Vice President Richard Nixon visited on September 2 with his daughter Tricia; and President Dwight Eisenhower and his wife Mamie were guests at the park December 26. Actor Leslie Nielsen, who was filming *Swamp Fox* for Disney, visited the park and posed with the submarines.

In September, the Holidayland picnic area would close as would Don DeFore's Silver Banjo Barbeque restaurant.

A 16-piece Navy band was on hand in Tomorrowland June 17 as television cameras and photographers covered the ceremony of 17-year-old Timothy Townsend as the five millionth guest to ride the Submarine Voyage.

Officiating at the ceremony was Joe Fowler, described as the Admiral of the Magic Kingdom's Navy, who read a letter from Walt Disney and presented Townsend with a Disneyland Submarine pin and cap making him an Honorary Captain of the Disneyland Submarine fleet.

Walt intended to take author P. L. Travers to Disneyland on her first full day in Los Angeles, which was Easter Sunday, but it was much different than depicted in the film *Saving Mr. Banks* (2013).

In a letter dated March 31, 1961, Walt Disney wrote to the author: "I'm sorry I can't be on hand to greet you on your arrival in Los Angeles, but I have been fighting a cold for some time and have been spending as much time as possible in the dry desert air hoping to shake it...It was my thought that you might like to go to Disneyland on Sunday. Mr. Dover will take you down there—perhaps going down to the Park in time for lunch and spending the afternoon there. He will discuss the details with you."

Storyman Bill Dover had been assigned to "babysit" Travers. Walt gave them full access to his apartment above the firehouse on Main Street, use of his little personal electric car, and the assistance of a guest relations hostess. Despite later claims by Travers that she was not pleased with her one and only time at Disneyland, according to Dover's trip notes she seemed to have enjoyed the experience.

The first all-night Grad Nite Party was held at Disneyland Thursday June 15, bringing 8,500 young guests from 28 Los Angeles area schools for the biggest high school graduation party ever held in the United States.

The students transported to the Park on buses were accompanied by chaperones from their schools. The party lasted from 11 p.m.-5 a.m. and included admission to Disneyland, free admission to all rides, attractions, entertainment and more.

However, food and the shooting galleries were not included. Students were required to meet dress code standards. Popular music groups played live to the excited crowd. Cost of ticket was six dollars.

Snow White Grotto

Imagineer John Hench retold the story of Snow White Grotto in his book *Designing Disney: Imagineering and the Art of the Show* (Disney Editions 2003).

"We encountered a special challenge when Walt unexpectedly received a gift of statues of Snow White and the Seven Dwarfs carved from pure-white Carrara marble, which arrived in wooden crates from Italy with no return address or any other indication of who might have made and sent them. Walt called me down to the studio warehouse to look at them, and told me he wanted them somewhere in Disneyland. I had to tell him that we would have a perspective problem with the figures. The sculptor had carved Snow White the same size as the dwarfs. 'Just figure it out', said Walt."

Hench's clever solution was to put the Snow White figure at the top of a cascading waterfall, next to an undersized deer and bird, and the dwarfs much lower and closer to the guests so it created a forced perspective situation where Snow White seemed in the right proportion. Hench's vision for the fountain was inspired by one he had seen in the small town of Brie, north of France.

On April 9, 1961, Walt Disney dedicated the Snow White Grotto, and the illusion that Hench had created was enjoyed for decades by guests who never noticed his sleight-of-hand maneuvering. The Wishing Well was Walt's idea—so the coins could be easily collected and donated to charity and to discourage Park guests from tossing coins into the Castle moat.

One persistent addition to the story over the years was that the statues were a gift from an Italian sculptor who used a set of hand soap bars of the characters released in Europe as his reference and Snow White was the same size as the dwarfs in the set so she could fit in the box.

However, after Hench's death, paperwork was discovered that the sculptures were actually commissioned by Walt Disney. Milan based sculptor Leonida Parma fashioned the figures from pure Carrara marble and had sent a message that there had been a mistake in the measurements due to a mistake in translation.

Each of the dwarfs were 31 inches tall, which was fine, but Snow White was only 39 inches tall. It would cost $2,000 to re-sculpt Snow White. However, it was only $611 to carve some small animals.

When Tokyo Disneyland wanted a duplicate of the Snow White Grotto, the sculptures were removed from Disneyland and copied in fiberglass. Since they had suffered in the weather over the years, they were warehoused with the duplicates taking their place in the park.

Then, Disney forgot they had the originals stored away until, during some moving, the Snow White figure was dropped and was damaged. The little princess did get repaired, the other figures rescued and all of them are now safely housed at Imagineering in California. Some guests on the Adventures by Disney Backstage Magic tour get to have a glimpse of these Disneyland treasures.

Flying Saucers

Opening on August 8, 1961, because of mechanical difficulties, the Flying Saucers was the first announced Disneyland attraction that failed to debut on schedule.

The Flying Saucer attraction did provide great fun for the over five million guests fortunate enough to ride this modern version of carnival bumper cars or the Midwest "duck bump" attraction that Walt was familiar with where a guest in a larger inner tube maneuvered around a pond and could bump into other guests.

A guest would board one of the 64 one-person saucer vehicles designed by Bob Gurr and would be lifted by pressurized air from valves on the 16,000 square foot metal arena floor and could hover. Gurr described it to me as "a human air hockey rink". Each saucer had a lap belt like the ones on the Autopia.

By leaning, the guest could control the direction but not the speed of the vehicle. As the pilot leaned, the saucer would tip slightly in that direction, decreasing the gap between it and the floor and allowing air to escape in the opposite direction thus propelling the craft.

The blue-floored arena had two sides that operated somewhat independently. A large boom would sweep across half the circle, collecting saucers and maneuvering them back to the loading area while the just-loaded saucers started their ride. It operated continuously so a group was always loading or unloading while another was gliding and bumping into each other on the floor.

Hovercraft vehicles were very popular at the time and a German inventor brought one of his versions to the Disney Studios to try and sell it to Walt Disney. Gurr who had become responsible for all moving Disneyland vehicles took it for test run on the backlot. While it handled well, Gurr worried the high speed razor-sharp blades were not safe in the general public and the individual motor might fail under the demands of constant use.

Gurr created a design that was basically an overturned bowl with no moving parts. He added two handles by the seat for guests to grip but they had no effect on the movement. Arrow Development who had built many Disneyland attractions including the Matterhorn Bobsleds developed the arena.

Four 100 HP motors supplied 300,000 cubic feet of air per minute pressure underneath the arena that was covered with thousands of damper baffles that would open and close to control the air flow to different sections of the floor. As a saucer approached a given area, the air pressure under the saucer would increase, lifting the saucer by inches.

There were difficulties with the attraction from the start and, as mentioned, it did not even open on schedule. The dynamics of this scale pneumatic system were pretty much unknown so the constant bouncing sometimes introduced a vibration, like an echo upsetting the flow of air, and caused the system to stop.

The sudden drop in air pressure would create a sound like a sonic boom heard throughout the park. Guests who were too heavy had difficulty lifting the vehicle and guests who were too light could not properly move it.

Lack of dependability, limited capacity and the plans for the remodeling of the new Tomorrowland to open in 1967 with new attractions resulted in the attraction being closed. Space Mountain later occupied the same space.

Monorail Extension

Until June 1961, the only ways to go between the Disneyland Hotel and Disneyland Park were to take the tram, or to walk across the parking lot, or to drive your own car, or—if you were a VIP—to be driven in one of the hotel's VIP station wagons.

Then the Disneyland Alweg Monorail was extended. The monorail station was adjacent to the lobby. Tram service was still available, but the cool way to go to Disneyland was to take the monorail.

Walt did this because he was upset that no one was considering the monorail as a serious transportation alternative. Las Vegas has turned down his proposal to have a monorail going down its strip corridor to the casinos. With this extension, Walt hoped that the monorail would stop being considered an amusement park ride but a legitimate form of transportation.

The monorail beam was expanded so the Monorail could leave Disneyland Park and stop at the Disneyland Hotel, now making it the first permanent operating Monorail transportation system, rather than just a sight-seeing attraction, in the Western hemisphere. It was the first operating Monorail to cross a public street.

The beam was extended into the 2.5 mile "highway in the sky" that Disneyland still uses today at a cost of $1.9 million (or roughly a half-million dollars more than the total cost of the original system). That year also saw the introduction of the Disneyland Monorail Mark II models that featured four cars to try to better accommodate the demand, as well as the addition of a new yellow car version called Monorail Gold.

In a letter dated May 12, 1961, Walt invited the Nixon family to return for the dedication of the new extension.

"Almost two years ago, Julie and Tricia dedicated our first Monorail Trains at Disneyland. Since that time, these trains have traveled 54,013 miles and carried more than 4,500,000 passengers. For this summer, our Monorail system has been greatly expanded to more than two and a half miles from inside the Park all the way over to the Disneyland Hotel and return. We even have a new station at the Hotel.

"I thought that you and your family might enjoy being our honored guests for the day, which is Sunday, June 11th and inasmuch as your young ladies dedicated the original system, it would be appropriate for them to dedicate the new extension. I can even assure you that the scissors will be sharp this time!"

Unfortunately, Richard Nixon sent his regrets that he wouldn't be able to be there at that time.

Although all other guests entered Disneyland at Main Street Station, Disneyland Hotel guests who arrived by monorail train entered the park in the back corner of Tomorrowland. It operated at a top speed of twenty-five miles per hour.

The Mark I trains (Red and Blue) consisted of three cars each. In 1961 it became a true transportation system when Tomorrowland station was lengthened to accommodate the debut of the four-car Mark II and the additional new Yellow train. The monorails were now longer at 112 feet and each train could carry up to 108 guests since it had an additional car.

At Walt's suggestion, the front cab was changed with an enlarged bubble dome so that more guests could view the scenery. The electrical system was upgraded as well as the air conditioning. The track was extended two and a half miles outside the park and a second platform was constructed at the Disneyland Hotel station.

The new link went over the berm, ran south along Harbor Boulevard to the auto entrance, turned west across the parking lot and went over West Street to the Disneyland Hotel. When it left that location, it returned by passing Holidayland and the Park's main entrance, went over the employee entrance and back into Tomorrowland where it completed its trip over the original route.

It was the first passenger-carrying monorail in America to run adjacent to a major highway and cross a street. A Disneyland survey found that 99.6 percent of the passengers felt that the experience was superior.

The construction required more than 118,000 man hours of labor, 10,760 tons of sand, 66,700 bags of cement, and 702 tons of steel with over two hundred new pylons added.

The addition of the monorail strengthened the Disneyland Hotel's competitive advantage and during the summer months the hotel's 306 rooms were operating at one hundred percent capacity.

The Disneyland Hotel made plans to expand all areas, including rooms, restaurants, convention facilities and entertainment/recreation. Ground breaking was done for the eleven story high Sierra Tower that would open the following year in September 1962. The high-rise tower would become Orange County's tallest building at 118 feet.

The year 1961 did see the hotel open a new 40-acre golf complex consisting of an 18 hole course, a 250 yard (50 tee) driving range and a miniature golf course named the Magic Kingdom Golf Course, where each hole was themed to a different Disneyland attraction. It was illuminated for night playing. Disney Studios art director Al Applegate was the construction supervisor of Disneyland personnel Andy Anderson, Larry Smith and Bud Washo.

Hole one was a replica of the Main Street train station. Hole three was Sleeping Beauty Castle with a draw bridge and courtyard. Hole five was the Matterhorn mountain. Other holes were themed to the TWA Moonliner, an Octopus lair from the Submarine Voyage, the Frontierland Painted Desert, the Frontierland fort, Skull Rock from Fantasyland, Tom Sawyer's Island, and Monstro the whale.

The final hole was titled Mickey's Lagoon and featured a large fountain with a sculpture on top of Mickey Mouse holding a golf club. Mickey's figure, like the other statues on the course, were originally all white to suggest Greek or Roman statuary, but at multiple requests from the guests, they were eventually painted.

Tinker Bell's Flight

The popular weekly Disney television show opened each week with Tinker Bell introducing audiences to the four lands of Disneyland. She became closely associated with the new theme park especially with some Park specific merchandise like a glow-in-the-dark wand and a little bell that one of the most frequently asked questions of cast members was "Where is Tinker Bell?"

Disneyland sponsored "Disney Night" at the Hollywood Bowl on August 1, 1958. One of the highlights of the evening entertainment was a 1,000-foot glide over the audience by aerialist Helen "Tiny" Kline dressed as Tinker Bell and that gave Walt an idea.

The first Tinker Bell to fly at Disneyland in the summer of 1961 was Tiny Kline. She was 4-feet, 10-inches tall and weighed 98 pounds. Tiny Kline came to America as a Hungarian immigrant at the age of 14. She became a well-known and popular burlesque dancer.

She also worked off-Broadway in theater productions and caught the attention of a well-known Wild West trick rider whom she married shortly thereafter. Five weeks after the wedding, he fell off of his horse and died, leaving Kline to begin her own career in the circus.

Starting at the bottom as a virtually nude, painted "statue girl," she worked her way up to "Roman rider" which meant she stood atop a charging steed in the chariot races at the end of the show and eventually became the queen of the aerial iron jaw act. That act became her trademark when she performed for Ringling Brothers.

Kline, at age 70, became the very first Tinker Bell at Disneyland. Suspended 146 feet up in the air, she glided down a long wire from the Matterhorn to Sleeping Beauty's castle to signal the beginning of the fireworks.

She was on a wire but most high wire acts in the circus are done no more than 50 feet above the ground. She was put into a harness, her wings attached and then hooked up to the cable. The entire flight took approximately thirty seconds.

Disney Legend Bob Matheison remembered:

"The first woman to do it at Disneyland was Tiny Kline, who was a grandmother in her 70s and had worked in the circus doing an Iron Jaw act. That is where she grabbed this ball with her mouth and twirled and slid down the cable and such. However, since she grabbed the thing with her mouth, she was always looking up, not down. So sometimes when she looked down off the Matterhorn she froze up for a moment and we had to give her a little push.

"At the other end were these two big guys with mattresses, padding and the like and even though she was this tiny little thing, she built up so much momentum that she would knock these guys over. Then she had to rush to wardrobe to change and run to catch the last bus leaving for Los Angeles, which was at 10:30 p.m. so we would all be there shouting and cheer her along as she ran on these tiny legs to catch the bus."

Her "Catching Tower" was behind the Fantasyland Theater. Kline performed for the next two summers but in 1964, she succumbed to cancer and the wand (and harness) went to 19-year old French circus acrobat Mimi Zerbini. Zerbini was also a circus family veteran but only performed as Tinker Bell for that one summer. In 1965, Judy Kaye began a career of almost two decades of flying across the night sky at Disneyland.

1962

- Attendance: 5.1 million
- Employment: 3,880
- Payroll: $13 million
- Candlelight Processional Narrator: Dennis Morgan
- Admission: Adults ($1.60), Junior ($1.20) Child (sixty cents)
- Highlights:
  - Additions to Adventureland
  - The Spring Fling night-time event is first held at Disneyland on April 14. For a single entrance fee, guests have unlimited use of all rides.
  - The KTTV TV station in Los Angeles, California, airs the weekly series *Meet Me at Disneyland* from June 9 – September 8
  - Frank Sinatra, Jr. makes his public singing debut with the Elliott Brothers band at Plaza Gardens on July 28, 1962.
  - Dixieland at Disneyland September 28-29
  - The walls were put up for the construction of the exterior of the Haunted Mansion
  - 17,000 guests celebrated the New Year at Disneyland's New Year's Eve Party
  - The Chicken Plantation Restaurant was torn down to make way for New Orleans Square area. However, the fried chicken was so popular, Disneyland set up pass-through windows in the construction fence to appease guests

Meet Me at Disneyland

From June 1962 to September 8, 1962, Disneyland produced a Saturday-only show (airing at 7:30 p.m. PST and proclaimed as "Live from Disneyland Town Square") titled *Meet Me At Disneyland* in a an attempt to drive up attendance during the summer weeknights.

It was a live broadcast directly from the park each week so it was pretty frantic. Sponsors included Stouffer's, Fritos, Chicken of the Sea, and Hills Brothers Coffee, who were all involved as lessees in Disneyland at the time.

The show ran on a local Los Angeles channel, KTTV which was Channel 11. The producer was Tommy Walker who was assisted by Chuck Corson. The master of ceremonies host was Johnny Jacobs (later a well-known announcer for many television shows), who would introduce the performers and interview guests in the park. Disney writer Larry Clemmons wrote most if not all of the scripts and Buck Pennington (from KTTV) was the director. Bob Matheison was listed as doing sound.

The Osmond Brothers appeared on the show broadcast July 7 along with the Vonnair Sisters, Owen Pope, Frank DeVol and others. It was episode No. 5 titled *There is Something About a Band*. Other shows included everyone from Fred MacMurray to the Firehouse Five to Annette Funicello to Benny Goodman to Frank Sinatra Jr.

Corson claims it was Andy Williams' brother, Don, who watched the Osmonds on that television show and convinced Andy to use them on his weekly television show. Most biographies claim it was Jay Williams, Andy's father, who saw the talented boys and recommended them to his son. Supposedly, they reminded Jay of how Andy and his brothers sang as young boys.

Meet Me at Disneyland Episode Guide:

- June 9: Main Street U.S.A.
- June 16: Plaza Gardens
- June 23: Rhythm on the River
- June 30: Swingin' Through Space
- July 7: There's Something About a Band
- July 14: Tahitian Terrace Show
- July 21: Fun in Frontierland
- July 28: Music on the Mall
- August 4: Fun in Fantasyland
- August 11: This Was the West
- August 25: Swingin' at the Magic Kingdom
- September 1: Dixie on the Delta
- September 8: Talent on Parade

La Coquette. On April 22, to celebrate Easter Sunday, a giant hot-air balloon from the 1956 film *Around the World in 80 Days* lifted off from the Hub with balloonists Peter Pellegrine and Francis Shields, it rode to an altitude of 2,000 feet and landed 45 minutes later in an orange grove ten miles away.

The balloon was named *La Coquette* and was built by Goodyear for the U.S. Navy and originally used during World War II for the training of blimp pilots. For the movie, it was painted silver with various mythological figures to evoke a 19th century "Jules Verne" aesthetic.

It proved to be so popular with Disneyland guests that it made an annual appearance at Easter through 1967.

Moonliner and Rocket to the Moon

The Moonliner rocket was 72 feet tall (80 feet with the legs) and was estimated to be one-third what the actual size of the rocket might be to hold 102 passengers. The exterior featured 15,000 square feet of aluminum.

The sponsorship shifted in 1962 to McDonnell Douglas when TWA owner Howard Hughes sold his interest in TWA and that company decided to end its sponsorship of the Tomorrowland attraction.

The dedication ceremony took place June 8 where Donald Douglas spoke to an audience that included Walt Disney, Joe Fowler and the Tomorrowland spaceman. The new business relationship resulted in changed signs, the uniforms of the attendants, and an updated briefing film with Douglas images for the pre-show area under the direction of Claude Coats. New speakers and projection systems were installed.

The Moonliner was renamed the McDonnell-Douglas DC-78. McDonnell Douglas painted its name on the rocket and replaced the horizontal red stripes with vertical blue ones, destroying the forced perspective Imagineer John Hench had originally created that made the rocket look taller.

The Rocket to the Moon attraction had guests enter a double hemisphere building where they supposedly boarded the Star of Polaris spaceship piloted by Captain Collins. Roughly 104 guests filled a three-tiered circular theater that was meant to be the passenger compartment of the spacecraft.

At the center of both the ceiling and floor of the theater were large, round "scanner screens" where film of the flight to the moon and back were projected as if they were portholes. At appropriate times, the seats vibrated and air jacks under the seats helped with the sense of losing gravity.

Adventureland

Vacationland magazine for Summer 1962 stated: "For Disneyland's brand new Jungle River Cruise — part of another $7 million expansion at Walt Disney's Anaheim wonderland — has been designed as a combination 'you are there' exploration and fun-filled laugh provoking adventure whose 'actors' are elephants, tigers and many more beasts of the jungle.

"Starting with a proven success — the true-life jungle cruise has been one of Disneyland's most popular attractions since opening — Walt Disney is adding a jungle-full of animated animals — startlingly life-like — and making the explorer's voyage longer and full of humor.

"Top highlight is sure to be the Indian elephants — big ones and 'little squirts' — who will frolic, splash and swim in a unique 'elephant bathing pool'. Their trunks loaded with watery surprises (for unwary animals *and* explorers), nearly two dozen of the full-size elephants will eventually call Disneyland 'home', all brought to life through the marvels of Disneyland animation.

"The emphasis in new attractions is on Adventureland, with (1) the 'world's largest Tree House, (2) a 'Big Game Safari' shooting gallery, (3) a colorful African motif for portions of the bazaar shops and stores in Adventureland, and (4) the fabulous 'Stouffer's in Disneyland' dinner-show restaurants. Stouffer's Tahitian Terrace will feature nightly dancing and South Seas entertainment."

In preparation for the upcoming installation of Imagineer Marc Davis' Elephant Bathing Pool and African Veldt scenes both advertised in 1962 as "newly discovered territory", the river was extended to 1,920 feet. The two-story boathouse was removed and rebuilt as a single-story structure.

Swiss Family Treehouse

In 1960, Disney released a popular live action adventure film titled *Swiss Family Robinson*, based on the 1812 novel of the same name by Johann David Wyss. However, Disney made some significant additions to make the story more exciting and amusing.

Directed by Ken Annakin (whose name inspired George Lucas to create an Anakin Skywalker character) and shot in Tobago (in the Caribbean) and Pinewood Studios (outside London), the film recounts a large Swiss family on their way to New Guinea whose ship is attacked by pirates.

Shipwrecked on an uninhabited island, the father and his two eldest sons salvage material from the ship, including furniture, supplies, and ship parts, like the steering wheel and construct a treehouse on the island.

The treehouse (designed primarily by Disney animator and director Wolfgang Reitherman with input from John Hench) was built in a 200-foot spread samaan in the Goldsborough Bay area. Samaan is a wide-canopied flowering tree with a large symmetrical crown native to tropic regions.

Director Annakin said that the treehouse "was really solid - capable of holding 20 crew and cast, and constructed in sections so that it could be taken apart and rebuilt on film by the family." Unfortunately the surrounding dense foliage only allowed three hours a day when there was enough sunlight to shoot on that particular set.

After the filming was completed, the locals begged Disney to let the treehouse remain (without the interior furnishings) and it became a popular tourist attraction, but was finally destroyed in 1963 by Hurricane Flora. While the treehouse was destroyed, the tree itself remained, but fell into obscurity as new generations are now unaware that the Disney film (which has also fallen into obscurity) was ever filmed there.

Walt Disney felt that children of all ages wanted a treehouse of their own and decided using the centerpiece from the film would be a great addition to Adventureland because, at the time there was only one attraction: the Jungle Cruise.

Imagineers thought that it would be a waste of time, space, and money, because guests would never want to climb all the way up only to have to walk all the way back down. When the attraction opened, adult climbers outnumbered kids three to one.

They studied the gnarled roots of the mammoth Moreton Bay Fig Tree planted in the 1800s by Anaheim horticulturist Tim Carroll to aid in authentically creating details of the Disneyland version. Imagineer Bill Martin was in charge of the ultimate design with input from those people who had worked on the tree for the movie.

The 62 concrete banyan-like roots go down roughly 42 feet and were installed on January 17, 1962. Ten months later at 2 p.m. on November 18 (just in time for the extended Christmas hours), the tree was unveiled. Actor John Mills (who played Father Robinson in the movie) and his daughter, actress Hayley Mills who had appeared in several Disney films, were there for the dedication, along with the rest of their family.

Landscaper and Disney Legend Bill Evans, with tongue-firmly-in-cheek, dubbed the original tree "Disneyodendron Semperflorens Grandis" which means "large, ever-blooming Disney tree" and the new version as Tarzan's Treehouse retains that same designation.

The tree's final cost was $254,900. It utilized six tons of reinforced steel and 110 cubic yards of concrete. The smaller branches were taken from real manzanita trees and were adorned with vinyl leaves fiber-glassed onto each branch.

The steel limbs had an 80-foot span and supported a network of 1,000 branches with 300,000 handmade vinyl leaves and floral blooms that all had to be attached by hand.

The Swiss flag flew from the top of the treehouse, which sparked a comment from a confused, but still irate, visitor from Switzerland who told the hosts at the attraction that "the Swiss people do not really live in trees!"

When the attraction opened on November 18, Disney guests had to climb up 68 steps to see all the different rooms and areas like the kitchen, library, Mother and Father's master bedroom, the boys' room and more. Interestingly, they had to walk down 69 steps (one extra step) to return to the ground.

The Swiss Family Treehouse had a quaint, but effective, plumbing system that actually worked and provided kinetic entertainment for the guests. A huge, river driven water wheel at the tree's base provided the power for a mini-bamboo-bucket brigade that scooped up the water and transported it to the uppermost room, where it flowed into a bamboo canal system.

From there, gravity would rush and twist water through each tree-house section to an eventual return to the river below. Disney claimed it cycled through 200 gallons an hour from the river.

Throughout the attractions guests could hear Mrs. Robinson's shipwrecked pump organ playing Buddy Baker's buoyant composition, the *Swisskapolka*.

Tahitian Terrace

Tapping into the same love for South Seas culture that inspired the Enchanted Tiki Room, the Tahitian Terrace restaurant simply reformatted and expanded part of the Plaza Pavilion restaurant that already had a Hawaiian themed patio facing toward the Jungle Cruise attraction and was known as the Pavilion Lanai.

Until the opening of the Blue Bayou restaurant, the Tahitian Terrace was considered the fanciest dining location at Disneyland. It was primarily just open during the summer and during busy seasons for lunch and dinner. The food and entertainment reflected the islands of Polynesia like Tahiti, Samoa, and Hawaii.

It was an outdoor seating area with tables and chairs and a higher level with a roof all facing the stage and served by waiters and waitresses. Unlike other restaurants, there were set times to dine because of the show. It was an approximate thirty minute experience with a live band providing the appropriate Polynesian rhythms.

Originally it was sponsored by Stouffer's but was later taken over by Kikkoman. During construction, Walt Disney felt the tree was too short and suggested cutting it in half and adding a section of concrete in the center. When he told Admiral Joe Fowler he wanted a curtain of water to part and then close again, Fowler immediately replied "Can do!" which earned him his famous nickname.

From the back of the menu: "Walt Disney has opened wide the portals to an enchanting island world across the blue Pacific...a world of romance, beauty, and exciting entertainment!

"Towering high above you is an amazing tree, a tree that grew (in less than a year) to a height of 35 feet through a secret formula of Walt Disney and his 'imagineers'! The branches of this 'species Disney-dendron' are laden with more than 14, 075 hand-grafted leaves and fiery-colored flowers that bloom perpetually. Today this tree is Disneyland's second largest of this rare, unnatural species, exceeded only by the Swiss Family Treehouse.

"Nestled beneath the tumbling waterfall is a matchless stage setting...a stage whose 'curtain' is a cascade of water, and whose 'foot-lights' are a leaping flame of fire burning on the water itself! For your summer evening entertainment, the falls magically draw aside . . . and out from behind the waters, sarong-clad natives appear to perform the swaying rhythms and amazing rituals of the islands . . . the hypnotic bare-foot fire walk and thrilling fire-knife dance, and the traditional grass-skirted hula of Samoa, Tahiti and Hawaii."

Men were brought up from the audience to have an embarassing hula lesson. All the guests were given complimentary artificial leis.

At the time, the menu was considered exotic for typical American tastes with Barbecued Pineapple Ribs, Skewered Chicken (with soy sauce), broiled teriyaki steak, coconut shrimp and coconut pineapple ice cream although the highlight for many was the (non-alcoholic) Planters Punch Tahitian, a blend of all the exotic fresh fruits of the Islands in a tall frosted cylindrical glass with faux flower memento.

In the 1960s, "Stouffer's in Disneyland" as the brand was labeled sponsored three restaurants in Disneyland: Plaza Pavilion, Tahitian Terrace, and French Market Restaurant. Originally, they were going to sponsor The Enchanted Tiki Room when it was proposed as a restaurant.

Big Game Safari Shooting Gallery

This attraction had several different names during its existence: Big Game Safari Shooting Game, Safari Shooting Gallery, and Big Game Safari. While the name changed, everything else about the actual attraction remained exactly the same.

It was the largest of the three shooting galleries at Disneyland. It had a larger variety of targets than any other shooting gallery in the United States and the artwork was designed by Imagineer Sam McKim. It had sixteen air rifles called "elephant guns".

The summer 1962 edition of *Vacationland* magazine proclaimed, "If you're a marksman, the new Big Game Safari is for you. While it's based on a time-tested shooting gallery tradition, this jungle hunt is an authentic Disney creation — a one-of-a-kind rapid-fire adventure where you'll shoot at all kinds of jungle animals and birds, each hand-crafted for Disneyland."

It was located in the area that previously housed the Cantina between the Guatemalan Weavers shop and the bazaar shopping area. It required a "C" ticket or twenty-five cents for one round. It had a thatched roof and was decorated liberally with bamboo.

Leaning up against the bamboo laced counter, shooters stared across a stretch of water to see the tropical jungle background and hear animal sounds. The proscenium was framed with cut plywood green jungle foliage.

The moving targets included lions, tigers, elephants, rhinos, hippos, snakes, apes and other exotic animals as well as tikis and natives. They were traditional chain-driven targets that moved back and forth in front of the African backdrop.

MacGlashan Enterprises had been producing lead shot shooting galleries like this one since 1935 including the ones in Frontierland and in the Penny Arcade on Main Street that was removed because Walt decided the sound interferred with the ambiance of turn-of-the-century America. Disney bought the company in 1969 and it continued to operate independently.

An attendant would come along with a plastic tube to load each rifle. This gallery used MacGlashan air guns and fired .22 caliber lead pellets that were still powerful and dangerous. They had no gunpowder charge at all, relying on the energy from the compressor alone for propellant.

A full round of ammunition cost just 25¢ or a "C" coupon. The game had 16 guns total, allowing for a maximum capacity of 16 guests at the same time. The average shooting time per guest was estimated at 56 seconds, allowing for 53 guests per gun, per hour.

The estimated two million lead pellets yearly were so abrasive that they caused severe dings on the targets and the surrounding artwork. As a result, the attraction required new hand painting every night using roughly forty gallons of paint every week. Sometimes it would take up to eight hours to repaint.

Usually the painters tried to do most of the work within the two hours from seven am to nine am. They had a special trailer designed specifically for the shooting gallery with paint buckets on the sides and special rollers and brushes. Eight times a year, the repainting built up so much that the surfaces had to be burned clean and completely repainted.

Backstage Disneyland magazine (Winter/1965) stated the attraction required eleven different colors of paint. The article stated:

"The paint they use on everything is vinyl except for the water targets, and these are painted with colored shellac.

"Occasionally funny things happen, especially when a new man is working. For instance the Adventureland gallery has several giraffes and if the eyes are accidentally touched, they move and scare whoever is painting them. It takes only one shot and one piece of lead, and the paint job is on its way to being done again."

Paint shop supervisor Ray Schwartz said, "The painters have to be artists as well as good brush and roller men. Several of the targets have intricate patterns like bark on the trees, spots on the giraffes, etc. and the fellows have to make them look real. Authenticity and realism are an important part of every Disneyland attraction."

The pellets would sometimes richochet off the targets, even flying into the guest area behind the shooter. The U.S. government began regulating lead exposure and companies stopped manufacturing the ammunition used at the galleries as demand dwindled. The guns at shooting galleries were later replaced by rifles that utilized infrared beams of lights rather than pellets.

Adventureland Bazaar

Imagineer Rolly Crump was given a six week deadline and a budget of $38,000 to remodel the Adventureland Bazaar covering roughly 2,800 square feet. It was Crump's first opportunity to be an Imagineering Art Director.

He pulled items from Disneyland's boneyard. He used some of the old ticket booths as cash register stations. He used mirrors on the walls to make the space look bigger. He used columns from the Chicken Plantation restaurant that was just torn down. He also bought some things and built some things. It became a popular merchandise location.

1963

- Attendance: 5.6 million
- Employment: 4,106
- Payroll: $13.8 million
- Candlelight Processional Narrator: Dennis Morgan
- Highlights:
  - Walt Disney's The Enchanted Tiki Room opens
  - Presented by People-to-People and Mexican Tourist Association, "Salute to Mexico" opens July 29 presenting dance, music, history and crafts. It ends in November.
  - Following the assassination of President John Kennedy, Disneyland is closed for the National Day of Mourning on November 23
  - In late June, Count Basie and his internationally famous orchestra opened a six night engagement at Disneyland on Friday in an explosive jazz salute to the upcoming Independence Day Holiday.
  - Another swinging chapter of the big band era began early August with the appearance of the Tommy Dorsey Orchestra featuring Frank Sinatra Jr., the Pied Pipers and Helen Forrest.
  - *National Geographic* magazine photographer Thomas Nebbia took the photo of Walt, Lillian and their grandchildren inside their apartment over the Main Street Firehouse giving the public its first look at the secret hideaway.

Dixieland at Disneyland

The event debuted at the park October 1, 1960 on water craft on the Rivers of America including barges, keel boats, canoes and the Mark Twain Riverboat. In 1963, Walt had Imagineer Rolly Crump build an impressive backdrop and stage on the edge of Tom Sawyer Island. The event was held Friday September 27 and Saturday September 28 from 8:00pm to 2:00am.

It was staged and directed by Tommy Walker. Narrated by Frank Bull. "The story of Dixieland brought to life by the men who made musical history. A musical Mardi Gras!"

Performers included Al Hirt and his Band, Kid Ory and the Young Men from New Orleans, Firehouse Five Plus Two, Dukes of Disneyland, Burch Mann Dancers, Calvary Baptist Singers and more. Following the performances on the river, these groups and more performed at different venues throughout the park including the Golden Horseshoe, Plaza Gardens, Fantasyland Theater, the Mark Twain Riverboat and more.

Autopia

The cars on the Autopia attraction kept breaking down. Arrow installed a center control rail like the one they used at Six Flags Over Texas since 1960. By doing so, it eliminated the need for a side bumper.

Introduced was the new Mark VI car. Arrow Development designed and built what they felt was the "ultimate car" that wouldn't break up the curbs and roadways. In 1963, 160 all-new Mark VI cars (80 for each Autopia) debuted at the Park. They had Kohler engines, Mercury clutches and lightweight frames. Bob Gurr worked on the body design but did not work on the mechanics.

The Mark VI had fenders and fins like the Mark V but had an oval front end like the Mark IV. They each weighed 600 pounds.

However, they proved to be a disaster with frequent break downs. The light frame would get bent or break from crashing in the front and back. The clutch blew up on a regular basis. Since they were from an outside vendor, maintenance became a nightmare.

Topiaries

As Landscaper Bill Evans told me, "Walt had been to Europe [including Tivoli Gardens] and had seen some fine topiary and he was suitably impressed. Conventional topiary goes back some 3,000 years. The plant material customarily employed to produce topiary figures was very, very slow growing. It takes years and years to respond to the desired effect.

"Walt was a bit too impatient for that. 'Let's get some topiaries in the park in a year or two,' he said. He didn't see any point in waiting 20 years. The artists would do illustrations that they wanted. We blew them up to full size and then took a lot of reinforcing rods and warped it around into the shapes we needed. In effect, we built a kind of skeleton out of steel.

"We persuaded these plants that they should grow to correspond to that skeleton. You bend them a little bit in January and a little bit more in February and a little bit more in March until you get the bones of the plant around the basic shape and finally you get to what you want.

'The difference in doing this short order topiary is that this stuff grows fast. That is a great advantage for the opening but it is a great disadvantage in the long haul. That European topiary is hundreds of years old. This stuff isn't going to last a hundred years. We can get maybe ten years out of it.

"We have to have stand-ins behind the scenes ready to come aboard because this stuff outgrows and we can't hold it down indefinitely. At one time, Walt was even thinking of putting them (the animal topiaries) on turntables that rotated (in front of It's A Small World) so it would look like they were dancing."

That idea didn't develop for several reasons including the weight factor as well as the added maintenance required.

Disney cast member Joe Delfin, who worked on the landscaping of the Jungle Cruise and Storybook Land Canal Boats recalled, "I used to make turkeys out of plants for Thanksgiving for fun [at Disneyland], and once, in my spare time, I had one going behind the Skyway and I got caught by Ray Miller."

Miller, who was Delfin's supervisor, didn't say anything then, but, a short time later, Miller and Disney Legend Ken Anderson invited Joe to go out for lunch. That lunch ended in a car ride as they began discussing how Walt had seen examples of topiaries while on a trip to England and Belgium, and how he wanted the same type of thing.

The ride ended at a museum that housed topiary figures in Beverly Hills and, from behind a protective rope, Delfin got a somewhat distant look at what were considered traditional topiary figures.

"The next Monday they put me into it, and I stayed in it for two years."

By 1963, there were roughly two-dozen topiaries inside Disneyland. They included a waltzing hippo, a poodle, a pig, bears, elephants, seals, and giraffes. They were generic animals that were easy to make out of the material available rather than a specific Disney animated character.

"Although viewed best only from the excursion train [that circles the park], a topiary garden is properly part of Fantasyland," wrote Evans in 1965. "Here you will find giraffes, camels, elephants, and waltzing hippos, motionless, but alive and well.

"This inanimate zoological garden is made up of thuyas, junipers, cypress, ficus and African boxwood. A laughing pachyderm, fashioned from golden thuya, a relative of the juniper family, sitting on a grass ball with its trunk raised high in the air and growing in a green wooden box brings joy to many visitors."

That laughing elephant along with a two-humped camel, a giraffe and an elephant doing a hand stand were uprooted to take up residence in the front of It's A Small World when it opened in May 1966.

Evans wrote. "For example, a camel with four feet on the ground requires four individual trees, and you draw straws to see who gets the neck. On the other hand, if the hippopotamus is poised on one toe the problem is simplified, providing you can produce enough plant above that point.

"Now that our chlorophyll circus is past its growing pains, the gardeners who bent, tied, clipped, and manicured the troupe can relax a bit, but only a bit, because these animals lead a somewhat precarious existence. It is possible to kill these plants with kindness. Over-watering is quite as dangerous as under-watering.

"Having in mind that beauty is only skin deep, we are understandably concerned with the welfare of our animal charges. Too much water, too little water, too much fertilizer, too little pest control, could materially damage or destroy 24 months of hard work in making them."

The real "Disneynifcation" of topiaries with an emphasis on specific Disney characters, like Mickey Mouse, rather than generic animals became possible when Evans developed a new system of stuffing a rebar skeleton with Sphagnum Moss and an internal watering system. That is the process used today.

The Enchanted Tiki Room 1963

"Wahine e o keonimana. Ladies and gentlemen, a small reminder before entering the Tiki Room. We ask you to refrain from smoking inside, and please, do not carry any food or drink into the Tiki Room.

"And, oh yes, no flash bulbs, please! Our performers are temperamental and easily upset. Thank you for your cooperation. And now ladies and gentlemen, United Airlines invites you to come with us, to a world of joyous song and wondrous miracles - Walt Disney's Enchanted Tiki Room."

Walt Disney and his wife Lillian loved going to New Orleans and browsing the antique shops where they picked up several items, including some that ended up at Disneyland including in the Disney apartment over the firehouse as well as antique mirrors for the Plaza Inn and items in Club 33.

On one of these trips in 1946, Walt Disney discovered an antique mechanical bird in a gilded cage and instantly became fascinated by this little bird sitting on a perch that could turn its head, flap its wings and tail, and open its beak to whistle.

As Imagineer Harriet Burns recalled, Walt said, "It's amazing that you can get such interesting movement from a very simple mechanism. He said 'You know, they've done this in Europe for hundreds of years – if they've done this this well, we can do things now much better'."

He gave the intricate moving bird to his Imagineers including Lee Adams, an electrician at the Burbank studio, Roger Broggie and Wathel Rogers and a few others to deconstruct the figure to see how it worked. It is still in working condition today in the Walt Disney Archives.

In 1959, Walt had considered a Chinese restaurant off on Center Street to be sponsored by Chun King that would include Chinese philosopher Confucius as a mechanical figure entertaining guests.

He would be surrounded by dozens of mechanical singing nightingales in cages, as a reference to the story *The Emperor's Nightingale*. The dining experience and show were planned to last an hour. While some mockups were done including a Confucius head, it was all cancelled by June 1960.

Imagineer Rolly Crump recalled one meeting: "Walt called us in one day—this is when we were re-doing Adventureland; Adventureland was getting a whole facelift – and he said 'I wanna do a little tea room, a little Tiki tea room.' Just a little thing for... sandwiches and tea and coffee."

Imagineer John Hench was assigned and came up with concept art that he labeled "Tiki Tea Room". It had colorful birds in cages hanging over the diners.

As Crump recalled, "Walt looked at John's drawings and said, 'John, we can't have birds in this restaurant'. John said, 'Why not?' Walt said, 'Because birds will poop in the food!'."

"That pretty much killed that, except that John replied, 'No, no, Walt, those aren't real birds, those are fake birds'. Walt replied, 'Disney doesn't stuff birds, John'. John said, 'No, no they're not stuffed birds! They're little mechanical birds'. And Walt perked up and said, 'Oh, little mechanical birds', and he loved that idea and that's how the whole thing got started!"

The idea of a dining experience with mechanical characters had always been firmly in Walt's mind as something he wanted to do.

A breakthrough came when the U.S. government declassified information about a process that NASA had developed to control the launching of space rockets via sound impulses recorded on magnetic tape. This technology became the basis of what Disney would soon call Audio-Animatronics, whereby the movements of life-size human and animal figures could be manipulated by sound frequencies.

The process worked like this: Tones recorded on magnetic tape would cause a metal reed to vibrate during playback; the vibrating reed would close a circuit causing a relay; and the relay sent a pulse of energy causing a pneumatic valve to operate a simple action such as a bird's beak opening.

Figures had a natural "resting or neutral position" like a closed beak when no electronic pulse was present. Basically, when there was a pulse the mouth would open and when the pulse was stopped the mouth would close. The only challenge was to synchronize that action with the soundtrack.

When the final attraction opened, Disney advertised it as "Performed using a tape recorder of the same type used in the Polaris Missile. Space Age electronic wonders of audio-animatronics."

Disney used a one-inch wide fourteen channel magnetic tape that produced 438 individual actions. While the final Enchanted Tiki Room attraction included over 200 figures including 12 tiki drummers, 4 totem poles, 54 singing orchards, 24 singing masks, 7 birds of paradise (the plant variety), 8 macaws, 12 toucans, 9 forktails, 6 cockatoos and 20 other assorted tropical birds, only 120 audio-animatronics actually sang and/or spoke.

Walt Disney supposedly coined the term "audio-animatronics" himself. In an interview Imagineer Harriet Burns recalled being in a meeting with Walt, John Hench, Fred Joerger and herself where Walt was playing around with words to define the new process. They sat around saying Walt's new word out loud and thinking how funny it sounded but that it did describe what was happening.

The term was first used commercially by Disney in 1961, filed as a trademark in 1964, and registered in 1967.

Besides the small valving used in rocket motors, an inertial navigation computer used in submarines in the 1960's was also used to control some of the animatronics all before servo valves, analog or digital controls, servo motors, solenoids, air pistons or torque tubes.

"Audio" referred to the sound tones that triggered the actions of the earliest audio-animatronics. By playing back a sequence of audio tones off a high-speed magnetic tape, the varying frequencies of the tones were transformed into electronic signals, each one triggering a specific piece of animation.

"Anima" referred to animation which was not just movement but the subtle extras of how that movement was achieved like using eye blinks, anticipation with movement, etc.

"Tronics" referred to electronics. When all three elements (sound, animation and electronics) were finally brought together and synchronized, figures amazingly seemed to spring to realistic life or at least the illusion of life.

With Hawaii becoming a state in 1959 and the surge in popularity of Tiki Bars and military personnel who had been stationed in the South Pacific during World War II returning home with an affection for South Seas culture, a Polynesian-themed restaurant at Disneyland was a natural choice for 1960's especially since Adventureland needed something more than just the Jungle Cruise to entertain guests.

Walt knew that Stouffer's was interested in sponsoring another restaurant in Disneyland so in 1961 he met with Vernon Stouffer in Cleveland. Vernon was the founder and president of Stouffer Hotels, Stouffer Frozen Foods and Stouffer Restaurants that all operated under The Stouffer Corporation.

In the 1960s, "Stouffer's in Disneyland" as the brand was labeled sponsored three restaurants in Disneyland: Plaza Pavilion, Tahitian Terrace, and French Market Restaurant.

According to the Summer 1962 issue of *Vacationland* magazine published by Disney for local Orange County hotels and motels, Stouffer's was set to sponsor another dining location:

"Walt Disney's Enchanted Tiki Room, one of three new restaurants at 'Stouffer's in Disneyland' and Disney's first 'by reservation only' dining spa, may steal the spotlight from the other new attractions. For Walt Disney is bringing together all the talents of his 'imagineers' to create a complete dinner show performed by an exotic collection of birds, flowers and Polynesian Tikis that actually sing, talk and act!

"Many new animation techniques, developed exclusively for Disneyland, will 'bring to life' the birds, idols and flowers. And, lest you should think it's not possible for inanimate objects to sing and act, just remember that this dinner-show is based upon legends and myths treasured for centuries by the natives of the South Pacific.

"Stouffer's, one of America's foremost restaurateurs, will also open European and American Kitchens in its Plaza Pavilion (facing Main Street) and a Tahitian Terrace overlooking Adventureland. The latter will feature nightly dancing and South Seas entertainment."

The Adventureland side of the Plaza Pavilion became the Tahitian Terrace and the Plaza Pavilion, Tahitian Terrace and the Enchanted Tiki Room would all have utilized the same kitchen space since they were all in the same building.

When the restaurant became an attraction, several elements survived. A small bathroom had been built to the left of front of the entrance door for restaurant patrons making it the only attraction to have such a facility. The original restaurant chairs were welded together into rows and used for the show's seating for the first few decades until someone realized that installing benches would increase capacity.

The Magic Fountain at the room's center was designed as a bussing station and still contained storage compartments for silverware and other items in its base.

John Hench said, "My assignment was to design the Enchanted Tiki Room. My proposed room was cross shaped with four wings and a central open space. I located the service center for the tables in the central area, allowing unobstructed viewing of the show from the tables in the wings.

"My show concept began with a single Audio-Animatronics bird singing to a beat picked up by another bird, then by groups of birds, creating a lively avian jam session. The volume grew as singing flowers joined in, followed by the carved tiki gods that adorned the columns throughout the space.

"More tiki figures intensified the rhythm with drums as they sang of the mountain gods' anger and announced a coming storm. Rain sound effects and strokes of lightning created still more uproar. With a final crescendo, the gods spent their anger and a chandelier full of singing birds descended from the ceiling, introducing the lighter, happier song that closed the show."

It was determined that utilizing the small restaurant space would limit audience capacity too much to cover the costs of the show. When it was transformed into an attraction and the tables were removed, it provided room for an additional one hundred seats.

Hench said, "When we decided to include more guests and eliminate the food service, I took out the service center, added theater-in-the-round seating and set an elaborately carved fountain in the central area, whose central jet of water reached eight feet in the air, touching the birds' chandelier to trigger its descent.

"The engineer who reviewed my detail illustration for the fountain's climatic action told me that it couldn't be done: a small column of water would break in the middle before reaching eight feet.

"So I asked Roger Broggie if the water could be lifted in a hollow glass tube that would rise from the fountain at the right moment. He said, 'Yes, if we can have a hole deep enough to recess the tube and a lifting machine'. So we did it. The overflowing water hid the glass tube perfectly."

Stouffer's had signed a lucrative contract and Walt had to personally talk the company out of it persuading them that the adjacent Tahitian Terrace would be a much better and more profitable experience for them.

The show was often just called just the "Bird Show" and later "Walt Disney's Legends of the Enchanted Tiki" and "Walt Disney's Legends of the Enchanted Island" before the Sherman Brothers wrote the memorable "Tiki, Tiki, Tiki Room" theme song.

When the attraction was built at Disneyland, massive rows of sensitive electronic equipment were installed to run the show. In order to keep this equipment from overheating, air conditioning had to be used making the Enchanted Tiki Room the first air-conditioned attraction at Disneyland.

Walt decided he wanted a pre-show forecourt area to get the guests in the mood for the show and to help alleviate the wait time for the next show. He assigned Crump to design the area. Crump found the book *Voices on the Wind: Polynesian Myths and Chants* written by missionary Katherine Luomala.

He used the myths and legends in it as his primary resource for his sketches of the various gods, many of which came from traditional island stories like that of Tangaroa, the Māori god of the sea from which all things were created, who proudly says "from my limbs let new life fall."

However, as Crump admitted, he often just played around with some ideas that amused him.

Crump said, "In Japan, they have where the water will drip into a bamboo tube and when it fills, the back end of it tips and it hits a log to make a sound to keep the deer and the rabbits out of the gardens. So I thought, 'Well, I'm going to that idea into one of my tikis'.

"I was looking up in the books about Polynesian art, I found this one beautiful little drawing, actually it was a sculpture of a tiki and he had a little weenie laying on top of someone else's head that was between his legs. And I found out later that was his wife.

"But anyways, I went ahead and built this little tiki like that and John Hench saw it and said, 'We can't put something like that in Disneyland, Rolly!'. And I said, 'No, no John, I won't have anything that looks like a weenie, I'll just have a bamboo tube', so I built the thing and that's the first piece of sculpture I did for the Tiki Room. But I never gave it a name.

"Walt looked at the one without a name and asked, 'What does this one do?' Thankfully, John who was also there responded quickly: 'It's the god of tapa cloth beating.' Walt just kind of looked at it and said 'Clock?' Not missing a beat, John shook his head [in agreement] and said, 'It's the guy that tells the time.' When the meeting was over, John said, 'Rolly, you better go find out who the hell the god is that tells the time!' I did, and it was Maui. It was just a happy accident that worked out well."

Walt approved it, and the Māori trickster god Maui suddenly became the keeper of "Tropic Standard Time." Crump designed all the others including Hina, the goddess of mist and rain who has water come out from underneath the brim of her hat and Pele the goddess of volcanoes and fire whose has little flames shoot out of her.

Crump said, "I did the drummers in the Tiki Room, up at the top there. When the attraction opened and I went in there and watched it, I saw the drummers up there beating the drums. They really looked dead. What the drummers were saying was 'Rolly, do a little something more to make us come to life'.

"So I got those little Sparkletts truck shiny things like we used in some dark rides, and I put them in the eyes of the drummers. So all of a sudden, when the drummers were beating their eyes were flashing because of the vibrations. All of a sudden, it really brought them to life. It really enhanced the entire show".

The rain effect at the end of the show was the creation of Imagineer Yale Gracey who used thin ribbon strips of Mylar attached to a little motor at the top so when it vibrated it looked like it was raining.

Invited press saw the finished production on the Disney Studio lot in Burbank in April 1963. The official press preview was held at Disneyland on June 29. Officially, the attraction opened to the public on June 23, 1963.

Bob Sewell and Marc Davis researched bird study collections at the Natural History Museum. Briefly, Sewell collected a large number of tropical bird skins but Walt decided to discard them because he didn't want Disneyland to get a reputation of killing wild birds for an attraction.

Davis designed many of the anthropomorphized birds, flowers, and tikis including the singing tiki poles.

Sculptor Blaine Gibson produced the bird shape and the expressive face. "Walt didn't want an absolutely realistic parrot," Blaine remembered, "but one with a little bit of cheek on it, something you could get some expression out of."

Gibson made clay models that looked like real birds but with slightly exaggerated faces so the audience could see their expressions.

Walt told Imagineer Harriet Burns who would feather the figures, "He said, 'I want these birds to be so real you can see them breathe'. He spared no expense in trying to capture a sense of reality to the extent of buying an expensive set of exotic bird skins sent to him from South America. He paid a fortune for them but they just looked like a pile of dead birds. They had no charm at all."

Burns along with Leota Toombs and Glendra Von Kessel, created and attached all of the plumage for the birds. The personally applied thousands of feathers to them.

Burns was having difficulty finding the right material for the birds' chests that would realistically stretch and expand as they "breathed" and return to its original shape. At a planning meeting she noticed Walt wearing his favorite blue cashmere sweater and its movement over his elbows was the perfect solution. Burns created a custom woven fabric that mimicked Walt's sweater.

Singer Norma Zimmer was the voice of the orchards and the soprano part in the Hawaiian War Chant. The *Barcarolle* featured Maurice Marcellino. Marcellino also provided some of the bird calls along with

Beverly Ford, Dorothy Lloyd, Clarence Nash (voice of Donald Duck) and A. Purvis Pullen. Singer Bill Lee provided the imitation of Bing Crosby.

The lovely white cockatoos including Collette, Suzette, Mimi, Gigi, Fifi, and Josephine were voiced by Sue Allen, Sue Lewis, Sally Sweetland, Betty Wand and Bruns' wife Jeanne (Gayle). Walt insisted that the cockatoos on the Birdmobile not sing with bird chirps but try to imitate multi-octaved Peruvian singer Yma Sumac.

Imagineer Rolly Crump recalled, "Walt told me he wanted me to design a bird mobile that came out of the ceiling with about a hundred birds on it. I did some sketches and found there was no way you could put a hundred birds on that thing.

"The system we would be using to lower the mobile into the room and power all the birds ran off of compressed air. There wouldn't be enough room for all those power lines in the mobile itself, so I had to cut it back to thirty birds. It turned out just fine, though.

"I made the birds into showgirls. I designed them with white feathers and added little sequins to their breasts so when the whole Tiki Room lit up, they would sparkle. I managed to put a little touch of Las Vegas on those girls.

""I sculpted a good bit of the interior of the Tiki Room as well. We based our designs for the Tiki Room on the Sepik River regions of New Guinea."

The Sherman Brothers were invited to attend one of the early full mock-up presentations for the show.

Richard Sherman later recalled, "Walt said 'Okay, start it,' and the next thing we know, the birds were coming down singing *Let's All Sing Like the Birdies Sing*, the orchids were singing... and then the Tiki torches were chanting. When it was all over, nobody knew what it was...

"We asked what it was we'd just witnessed, and Walt replied, 'That's what you're gonna tell us. You're gonna write a song that explains it and Larry [Clemmons], you're gonna write some gags to go with the song, 'cause I wanna have fun with this thing.

"We had to think fast. Luckily we remembered that about two years earlier we had written a lengthy calypso to cover a lot of boring footage showing how the Disney crew had carted tons and tons of equipment to Tobago to film *Swiss Family Robinson* (1960).

"We suggested that an articulate parrot could sing a song to set up the show. In fact, we continued, he could even act as the emcee! The song could be done in a calypso beat—'The Tiki, Tiki, Tiki, Tiki, Tiki Room.' It had a sound you could remember. And Walt bought the idea, just like that, adding: 'Instead of one parrot emcee, we'll have four, with French, Spanish, German, and Irish accents.' He always had a way of plusing a good idea."

The Sherman Brothers had suggested a parrot because an audience would accept the fact that a parrot could "talk". Larry Clemons was an animator and a writer at the presentation and had made the mistake of asking Walt, "Walt, what is it?"

Wally Boag, the performer at the Golden Horseshoe Revue, had done specialty comedy writing for Disneyland so was brought in to punch up the script. The writing team also included Fulton Burley who also performed at the Golden Horseshoe Revue, and Marty Sklar, Bill Cottrell (then the head of WED) along with Clemmons.

The four parrot hosts evolved into macaws, amusingly dubbed by the Imagineers as "the MacAudios." The primary host was named José, a Spanish-accented fowl fellow, voiced by Wally Boag.

Michael was the done in an Irish brogue by Fulton Burley. Pierre with the French accent was the voice of Ernie Newton who provided the thick German accent for the decapitated knight in the Haunted Mansion attraction. His appearance by the opera ghosts was a visual gag based on the expression "A night at the opera".

Fritz who had a German accent was voiced by Thurl Ravenscroft who also supplied voices for the Haunted Mansion, Pirates of the Carribbean and Country Bear Jamboree.

They were recorded February 1963. "They all fell into it and had a great time. We always had a ball with these guys." recalled Richard Sherman.

Originally in 1963, each bird's plumage matched the flags of their implied countries of origin. José was red, white, and green for the Mexican flag, Michael was white and green, Pierre was blue, white, and red and Fritz was red, black and white. These main birds have changed the color of their plummage over the years.

Imagineer Wathel Rogers developed a control system that used a joy stick.

Unlike most of the attractions at Disneyland at that time, the Tiki Room was owned and operated by Walt Disney himself through his WED Enterprises (Imagineering) organization. That meant admission was not included as a ticket in the Disneyland ticket books.

Guests had to purchase a separate seventy-five cent ticket (fifty cent for children) until sponsorship of the attraction changed over to United Airlines in 1964 who wanted to use it to market their new flights to Hawaii.

At that time the Enchanted Tiki Room became an "E ticket" attraction that at the time cost only sixty cents for an adult. United Airlines maintained sponsorship until 1973. Dole took over sponsorship in 1976.

However, because this was innovative technology, guests did not understand what the attraction was and often just walked by. Even cast members had difficulty explaining it since nothing like it had been done previously with which to compare it.

Boardwalk barkers have always been a mainstay of carnivals to encourage guests to visit their attraction. A "barker bird" was placed on a bamboo perch by the attraction marquee near the Adventureland entrance.

It was to give guests a brief demonstration of what was happening inside the theater and to get them to come in to see the show. It was originally known as the Tiki Room Ballyhoo Parrot but is most commonly referred to as the Barker Bird. It was Juan, the cousin of Jose, and the figure used the same mold as Jose so it was another macaw and not a parrot.

Boag wrote the dialog and voiced the character in a similar comical accent as Jose in several different spiels: "Amigos, Romans, and Disneylanders! Stop walking while I'm squawking. Walt Disney's Enchanted Tiki Room . . . is Disney entertainment at its most exciting, best kind. The show is on the inside, not the outside—that would be silly. In the Enchanted Tiki Room you sit down on your feather dusters inside an air conditioned theater."

The bird had to be removed because large amounts of guests were stopping to watch its spiel and they were clogging the pathway into Adventureland and to the entrance of the attraction itself. The weather also took its toll on the unprotected figure. However, thanks to the Barker Bird enough guests saw the attraction so that word-of-mouth made it a success.

1964

- Attendance: 5.9 million
- Employment: 4,190
- Payroll: $15 million
- Candlelight Processional Narrator: Dennis Morgan
- Highlights:
  - Below deck museum quarters on Columbia Sailing Ship opens and Trapped Safari/African Veldt added to Jungle Cruise
  - "Fantasy On Parade" Christmas parade debuts
  - Thirty-six Disneyland cast members create an "official certificate of membership in the Order of the Red Handkerchief". Eligible members were those who had operated the Mine Train Thru Rainbow Caverns.
  - First death in Disneyland recorded: Mark Maples, a 15-year-old Long Beach student on the monorail
  - The name of the Mickey Mouse Club Theater is changed to Fantasyland Theater. Astro-Jets renamed to Tomorrowland Jets. Circarama theater renamed Circle-Vision.
  - The first transcontinental Picturephone call is made between Disneyland and the New York World's Fair
  - Disneyland hosted more than 400 American athletes heading to Japan for the 1964 Summer Olympics. Events included a tribute show on the shores of the Rivers of America, featuring Bob Hope and a cast of Hollywood stars.
  - Mimi Zerbini takes over from Tiny Kline as the Tinker Bell who flies during the nightly fireworks.
  - Much of the attention and financial resources were focused on the opening of the 1964 New York World's Fair where the Walt Disney Company had produced four of its most popular pavilions that would later be moved to Disneyland.

Sailing Ship *Columbia* Below Decks Museum

Passengers boarded the full-scale replica of the original sailing ship *Columbia* by climbing steps up onto the main deck when it first debuted at the park in 1958.

Once they were on board, they could now visit a nautical museum below deck, which showed what life was like for the 1787 crew. In addition to the galley, pantry, dry stores and sick bay, there were quarters for the crew, bosun, bosun's mate first mate, captain, and surgeon.

Emile Kuri, chief art director for Walt Disney Studios and Walt's personal interior decorator, also designed things for Disneyland including at Walt's request designing a "set" for "below decks" on the *Columbia*. It was Walt's aim to educate the public about America's mostly-forgotten rich maritime history.

Kuri came up with was a veritable maritime museum below *Columbia*'s main deck decorated with authentic maritime equipment and details.

As the flyer given out to guests at the park proclaimed, "Now Walt Disney brings to life the adventure, the thrills and the excitement of that dangerous journey (to carry the Stars and Stripes around the world in 1787). See replicas of the equipment and quarters used by the crew: the open-hearth galley and forge, officers' quarters, the Captain's Great Cabin, carpenter's bench and cooper's shop and much, much more. The Columbia between-decks area is one attraction you won't want to miss!"

"Below Decks" as it was originally called was accessed through the ship's main hatch, and the added attraction opened on February 22, 1964. Ray Wallace, designer of the ship, was again on hand for the ceremonies. "The *Columbia*'s realistic below decks accurately portray the life and lot of the seaman," he wrote at the time.

When the ship was docked in Fowler's Harbor, visitors could still board her and explore Below Decks, making the *Columbia* an attraction that was "open" even when it wasn't operating! To ride the attraction took an "E" Ticket but when it was docked, it only took a "D" Ticket to visit the museum.

All Night Grad Nite

The first time that Disneyland stayed open all night until five am the next morning was Grad Nite on June 18, 1964. It was also the first year that the Ford Mustang was introduced to the general public. To help market the car, Ford partnered with Disneyland to offer one of the vehicles as a giveaway to a high school student who attended Grad Nite.

The 1964 White Mustang ("fully equipped and raring to go") was displayed on a makeshift platform in front of the floral Mickey Mouse display at the entrance.

One young lady was extremely popular on the dance floor until security figured out that she had a long plastic straw protruding out of the back of neck, which the boys could "nuzzle" as they sipped long gulps of vodka from a flask attached to her bra.

Early in 1964, plans were being "laid for four Grad Nites with schools as far away as Lake Tahoe in Nevada scheduled." More than 50,000 High School seniors (from 130 high schools) attended all four Grad Nite Parties.

In just one night alone on June 18, 1964, thirty different schools attended: Arcadia, Aviation, Bell, Bell Gardens, Burbank, Burroughs, Centennial, Compton, Dominguez, Duarte, Eagle Rock, Edgewood, Granada Hills, Hawthorne, La Jolla, La Puente, Lawndale, Leuzinger, Los Altos, Lynwood, Manual Arts, Marshall High, Mayfair High, Mira Costa, Pasadena, Redlands, Redondo, Reseda, San Fernando and Verdugo Hills.

A student from Granada Hills High School who had been a member of the marching band won the car. Over thirty years later he donated it to the school to restore and raffled off at Homecoming with the proceeds being split between their Auto Shop program and the marching band.

The back of the ticket read: "According to Grad Nite Committee Rules: Date dress for girls and coats and ties for gentlemen are mandatory. Only those properly attired will be admitted. Only ticket holders arriving by authorized bus transportation will be admitted. No alcoholic beverages are allowed in Disneyland at any time." In the 1970s this last rule would be expanded to forbid marijuana or any other illegal drugs. The number of the front of the ticket was the identification number to confirm winning the Mustang.

Entertainers for the evenings included the Young Men From New Orleans (on the Mark Twain), Denny Brooks (Coke Corner), the Elliott Brothers (Plaza Gardens), the Strawhatters (Plaza Gardens), Hootenanny (20,000 Leagues stage), the Ward Singers (Golden Horseshoe), the Astronauts (Oak Tavern), the Mad Mountain Ramblers (Mine Train), the Spacemen with Kay Bell (Space Bar), and the Royal Tahitians (Tahitian Terrace). Local radio station KFWB channel 98 was live and on the air featuring interviews with the students who attended.

Tomorrowland Jets

The Astro-Jets attraction that opened in March 1956 was a popular amusement park spinner ride called The Super Roto-Jet built by the

Klaus Company in Memmigen, Bavaria. The rotating base was actually a converted World War II German artillery gun that could rotate 360 degrees and raise and lower the stubby little cylinders with tiny wings and an open cockpit.

Disney paid $200,000 for it. For the dedication ceremony, Disneyland invited jet pilots from El Toro Marine Air Station, the 11th Naval District Headquarters in San Diego and the Army Air Force Base at Long Beach to be the first pilots. Each pilot was accompanied by a child who was visiting Disneyland that day.

Each jet was on an arm extending out about twenty feet from the central column and guests could coax the height with a lever in the cockpit up to thirty-eight feet. The attraction was on the ground like the similar Dumbo attraction but it spun faster and higher.

The fleet of twelve ships each had a name selected by Imagineer John Hench: Canopus, Vega, Sirius, Castor, Regulus, Pica, Capella, Arcturus, Rigel, Spica, Proycon, Altair and Antares. They were painted white with red or blue trim.

The name and nothing else was changed to the Tomorrowland Jets in August 1964 because American Airlines was using the term "Astro Jets" for their new fleet of passenger planes.

It wasn't TWA who were still sponsoring the Moonliner and Rocket to the Moon attraction that complained but United Airlines who were spending quite a bit of money sponsoring The Enchanted Tiki Room while one of their competitors was receiving free publicity. Head of the park Dick Irvine agreed and authorized the name change. The name change was short lived because the attraction closed in 1966 in preparation for the New Tomorrowland.

Ruggles China and Glass Shop

The shop closed in March and was taken over by Disney and renamed the China Closet. Phil and Sophie Papel were the proprietors of the shop.

When asked to come up with a name, Phil recalled a favorite film entitled *If I Had A Million* (1932) where different characters were each given a million dollars by an anonymous benefactor. In one sequence, character actor Charlie Ruggles played a shy, accident prone employee of a china shop who is constantly being fined for breaking merchandise. He used part of his newfound wealth to smash all the expensive china and glass in his workplace with his cane. So Papel decided to use the Ruggles name.

Papel's shop did have a sign promising: "Relax. We do not charge for accidental breakage" unlike in the film where any breakage had to be paid for.

WED's Harry Johnson did the interior sketches for the design of the shop. The select merchandise would feature Wright Glass, Smith Glass, and a large selection of imports from England and West Germany. The Papels success with this shop led to a twenty store chain of retail gift shops in Southern California

Big Band Festival

Walt Disney himself and the people who were hired as Disneyland's Entertainment Directors over the years like Tommy Walker were fans of live entertainment, including Big Band music.

Walker spent $56,000 on talent for a "Big Band Festival" that began on June 13 and ran for five days. On Tuesday June 16, 50,505 people went through the amusement park's turnstiles to enjoy the music, which made that date the second most successful day in Disneyland's history up to that time.

Entertainers included Wayne King and His Orchestra (at Plaza Gardens), Count Basie and His Orchestra (at Tomorrowland), Benny Goodman and His Orchestra (20,000 Leagues stage), and Duke Ellington and His Orchestra (Frontierland's Golden Horseshoe Saloon).

Dixieland at Disneyland

The event was held September 25-26. The show was performed in front of the façade created by Imagineer Rolly Crump on the edge of Tom Sawyer's Island.

The program stated: "A musical mixture of the sights, the sounds, the feeling that were and still are Dixieland. Dixieland at Disneyland begins at 8pm on the Rivers of America between Adventureland and Frontierland with a swinging pre-show starring the Elliot brothers' Big Band Dixie and the Ward Singers.

"And then at 9pm, it's time for 'All That Jazz' narrated by Frank Ball and featuring Storyville Memories (Kid Ory and the Young Men from New Orleans), A New Orleans Fish Fry (Burch Mann Dancers), The Bourbon Street Beat (Sharkey Bonano and his Kings of Dixieland), New Orleans –Yesterday and Today (Sweet Emma Barrett and her New Orleans Jazz Band), Hot Sounds from the Windy City (Ben Pollack and his Pick-a-Rio Boys, Burch Mann Dancers), Puttin' Out the Fire (Firehouse Five + 2), The Legend of Louis (Louis Armstrong and his Band) and the Grand Finale."

And the music continued until 2am with Louis Armstrong and his Band (20,000 Leagues stage), Ben Pollack and His Pick-a-Rio Boys (Space Bar), The Elliot Brothers' Big Band Dixie (Plaza Gardens),

Firehouse Five Plus Two (Frontierland Riverside Stage), Sweet Emma Barret and Her New Orleans Jazz Band (Golden Horseshoe), Sharkey Bonano and His Kings of Dixieland (Tahitian Terrace), the Ward Singers (Fantasyland Theater) and Young Men From New Orleans (on the Mark Twain).

Death in Disneyland

The first death in Disneyland occurred on May 15. Student Mark Maples, a 15-year-old Long Beach, CA, resident, was killed when he tried to stand up on the Matterhorn Bobsleds.

After professing his love for a girl that had tagged along with his group but rejected his overtures, Maples attempted to jump out of a Skyway cabin hovering 60 feet over the ground. Restrained by friends, 15-year-old Maples was unsuccessful in his suicide attempt.

Later in the evening while on the Matterhorn Bobsleds, a still distraught Maples (or his companion) foolishly unbuckled his seatbeat and he attempted to stand up as their bobsled neared the peak of the mountain.

Maples lost his balance and was thrown from the sled to the track below, fracturing his skull and ribs and causing internal injuries. According to the police report, one of his companions heard a "thump" and noticed Maples was no longer in the ride. They reported his disappearance after the ride's conclusion, and authorities discovered Maples' unconscious body on a ledge about a third of the way down the Matterhorn's interior.

Maples was taken to the hospital in critical condition and officially died days later on May 19. Born April 1949 in Los Angeles, he was living in Garden Grove with his family and is buried in Forest Lawn Memorial Park Cypress, Orange County.

The Order of the Red Handkerchief

The Club first started in 1956, when the men on the Mine Train would go to the local watering hole to cool down after the attraction was closed for the night. Once a year the miners would meet at the Disneyland Hotel to eat, drink, and gamble all night long.

In February 1964 a charter formalized the club of those original mine train operators (and a few special members) into the prestigious organization called "The Order of the Red Handkerchief". A few of those 'special members' included Walt Disney, Ron Dominguez (later Vice President of Disneyland), writer Michael Broggie, Dick Nunis (director of park operations) and Ray McHugh, who kept 'the Order' together for many years.

The ride operators were all men and were proud that they spieled the entire trip themselves, without recorded audio. However as new cast members were added, the original team wanted to stand out so they began wearing red handkerchiefs as part of their costumes but were quickly told to stick to the approved costume. So they put the red handkerchiefs in their back-left pockets, being sure to let enough hang out to signal their distinct role among the cast.

1965

- Attendance: 6.4 million
- Employment: 4,590
- Payroll: $15,500,000
- Candlelight Processional Narrator: Dick Van Dyke
- Admission: Adult ($2.60), Junior ($1.80), Child ($1.10)
- Highlights: Celebration of Disneyland Tencennial
  - First Disneyland Ambassador: Julie Reihm who was also officially called "Miss Disneyland"
  - The Plaza Inn restaurant opens on the hub on July 18. It was formerly the Red Wagon Inn. A press party was held at the eatery where Walt, Reihm, and Mickey Mouse cut a ceremonial cake topped with a castle.
  - Great Moments with Mr. Lincoln opens
  - Disneyland welcomes its 50 millionth guest, Mary Adams
  - The Fantasy on Parade Christmas parade debuts
  - Shareholders of Walt Disney Productions approve the acquisition of WED Enterprises from Walt Disney
  - Walt holds a special anniversary celebration at the Magnolia Room of the Disneyland Hotel on July 15 for cast members
  - Judy Kaye becomes the new Tinker Bell who flies in the sky during the nightly fireworks and will continue to do it until Gina Rock took the role over in 1983.

The Walt Disney Company's attention and finances were still committed to the second year of the New York World's Fair and its four popular pavilions.

However, planning had begun on New Orleans Square and the New Tomorrowland that would open in 1967. Imagineer John Hench designed in February a Space Port that would evolve into Space Mountain. Construction began on the building to house It's A Small World attraction.

Walt told the press that "plans for Disneyland for the next three years amount to more than three times the original investment."

This year marked the tenth anniversary of the park so to help celebrate the Tencennial, Disneyland had a year long celebration.

According to the song written by the Sherman Brothers for the occasion: "Ten years of fantasy, ten years of fun, ten years of growing, and we've only just begun..."

As Disneyland Marketing director Jack Lindquist remembered, "To celebrate Disneyland's tenth anniversary, Pete Clark, Marty Sklar, Phil Bauer, Charles Boyer and I created, sold and produced a twenty-four-page color supplement. At the time it was one of the largest advertising supplements ever done and it was also the biggest advertising broadside that Disneyland ever launched.

"It went into all the Southern California newspapers, plus papers in San Francisco, Portland, Seattle, Las Vegas, Phoenix, Salt Lake City, Tucson and even Chicago. Our supplement contributed immensely to the overall success, image and identity of Disneyland's landmark Tencennial Celebration."

In fact, on March 10, Walt Disney flew to the California State Capitol to accept a resolution congratulating Disneyland on its tenth anniversary.

Musical Entertainment

Especially for the summer when the crowds were expected to be large, Disneyland featured not only famous Big Band names, but also folk artists, young recording stars, and much more. Newspapers reported that Disney spent over one million dollars for all the live entertainment.

During the day, guests could expect to find the Disneyland Band led by Vesey Walker, the Dapper Dans, the Gonzales Trio, Bud and Scott, Indian Village dancers, and the Golden Horseshoe Revue.

At night, the following groups performed: Bill Elliott and the Date Niters (at the Plaza Gardens Stage), the (Original) Clara Ward Singers, Kay Bell and Her Humdingers, the Yachtsmen Quartet, the Royal Tahitians dancers (at the Tahitian Terrace), the Young Men from New Orleans (on the Mark Twain), the Disneyland Mustangs, and the Firehouse Five Plus Two. The Park had nightly fireworks, of course with "Fantasy in the Sky" lighting up each night at 9 PM.

Disneyland hosted weekly themed music nights with Big Bands performing every night but Monday.

- June 19-June 26: Si Zentner and his Orchestra
- June 29-July 4: Stan Kenton and his Orchestra
- July 9-July 17: Wayne King and his Orchestra
- July 23-July 31: Harry James and his Orchestra (with drummer Buddy Rich and vocalists Ernie Andrews and Cathy Carter)

- August 6-August 14: Duke Ellington and his Orchestra
- August 20-August 28: Woody Herman and his Herd
- September 3-September 11: "Music Made Famous by Glenn Miller" with Tex Beneke and his Orchestra and Ray Eberle and the Modernaires

Monday was a night when the spotlight was on Hootenanny ("Disneyland's salute to folk music the world over. Featuring top names in the folk field brought to Disneyland for your enjoyment!" with a performance by 21 year old John Denver). The Yachtsmen Quartet acted as Disneyland hosts.

Tuesday nights the park hosted Humdinger at the Fantasyland Theater. "A 'Humdinger' of an event! Every week you can enjoy the sounds of swingin' young America. A young people's show to end them all! A musical variety show featuring teenage recording stars and the Humdinger dancers."

The Park's summer season ran from June 19 through September 11. It operated every day from 9 AM to midnight, with an additional hour each Friday and Saturday night. A Disneyland Holiday Swing over Memorial Day weekend and Dixieland at Disneyland in late September book ended this summertime entertainment.

On Saturday, May 29, and Sunday, May 30, Disneyland was open from 9 AM to midnight and featured The Tommy Dorsey Orchestra, directed by Sam Donahue, from 8 PM to midnight. Frank Sinatra, Jr., Helen Forrest, The Pied Pipers, Charlie Shavers on trumpet and Larry O'Brien on trombone accompanied the orchestra.

The sixth annual Dixieland at Disneyland, "one of the biggest musical events in Disneyland's ten-year history", took place on September 24 and 25 from 8 PM to 2 AM. Tickets cost $4.95 in advance or $5.95 on the night of the event. The event actually began at 6:30 PM with a Tailgate Ramble down Main Street, U.S.A. in "old-time Dixie freight wagons".

Louis Armstrong led the parade, which featured the night's performers: Sweet Emma Barrett, Turk Murphy and his Band, Bob Havens and the Dixieland All-Stars, including Matty Matlock, Eddie Miller, Nick Fatool, Stan Wrightsman and Ed Garland, The Firehouse Five Plus Two, Johnny St. Cyr, and the Young Men from New Orleans featuring trombonist Kid Ory.

Julie Reihm

The first Ambassador was a college student from Long Beach, California named Julie Reihm. She had been a tour guide at Disneyland during school vacations and weekends for the previous two years. Born in Galveston, Texas, Julie and her parents, Mr. and Mrs. Philip Reihm, moved to Long Beach when she was three months old. She lived there for twenty years before becoming "Miss Disneyland".

The term "Miss Disneyland" was used because Marketing Director Jack Lindquist conceived of the role as similar to Miss America but without the bathing suit competition. She was given a brand new 1965 Ford Crown Victoria car that was fully loaded. She was the only Disneyland Ambassador to be given a car.

After high school, she attended California State Long Beach to study speech. As a part-time job because of her background in public speaking, she became a Disneyland tour guide. Working weekends and summers in the Park, she met Walt Disney himself.

"I had first met him in the Park when I was a tour guide," Julie recalled. "He followed me up Main Street for awhile while I was giving a tour. I think he enjoyed taking you a little bit by surprise, and seeing your reaction to things. He delighted in seeing other people delighted."

After two years as a tour guide, Julie hesitantly applied for "Disneyland's Ambassador to the World" because she wasn't sure she wanted to take a year off from school.

Walt's commitments had increased and he found it hard to attend all the events to which he was invited especially during the Tencennial year. He needed a representative who could travel the world to represent him and the park when he could not be there in person.

After four weeks of interviews, she was chosen as "a personification of Disneyland's world-famous spirit of friendliness and happiness." It was only meant to be a one year role and not continue after the celebration but Reihm proved herself so valuable and charming that it became a permanent annual position.

She had a younger sister, Susie, and younger brother, Ryan, at the time. The official publicity declared that Julie was just over 5 feet tall, with hazel eyes and dark brown hair, and weighing 117 pounds. "In addition to her friend-making personality and smile, Julie has an excellent record in scholarship, music and public speaking. She hopes to become a teacher."

Julie studied piano for ten years and won a gold certificate of merit from the Music Teachers Association of California. She sang in school choruses and in the Disneyland Tour Guide Glee Club. According to the publicity release, she also loved "outdoor sports, such as swimming, tennis, surfing and bicycling."

Julie recalled, "I've learned so many fascinating things about so many places from the Disneyland tours My purpose was to share the joy, hope, and happiness of Disneyland to communities around the world."

She even appeared as a cut-out paper doll labeled Miss Disneyland in *Jack and Jill* magazine August 1965, something that has never happened for any other Disneyland Ambassador.

In 1965, Julie was a key part of the tenth anniversary festivities, helping Walt and his wife Lillian cut the ribbon for the opening of Great Moments With Mr. Lincoln and joining the press party for the opening of the Plaza Inn. She appeared on the *Wonderful World of Color* episode *The Disneyland Tenth Anniversary Show* where Walt introduced her to Disney Legends who gave her a preview of upcoming attractions.

"The highlight of my year was to see Walt smiling ear to ear about a new idea—a new project—and feeling his boyish excitement," she said.

Her travels took her to most of the United States and several foreign nations, where she often accepted awards and honors on behalf of Walt. She logged more than 52,000 miles in the United States, Europe, and Asia.

After a year serving as Ambassador, Julie returned to her studies. She would return on occasion to give tours to VIPs or attend special events, but eventually left California to raise a family in Virginia.

Grad Nite

The 1964 Grad Nite had been such a success that Disneyland tried to duplicate it on July 17 from 11pm to 5am. A ticket cost $7.00 for admission, unlimited use of all attractions (except shooting galleries), entertainment and the chance to win a 1965 Ford Mustang. This time instead of being white, the Mustang had a gold exterior and black vinyl top and the tag line "the modern Cinderella Coach".

Local radio station KFWB broadcast "live and direct from the hub of Disneyland" with DJ Genial Gene Ward and DJ Larry McCormick.

More than 50,000 celebrants from 138 High Schools attended four all-night Grad Nite parties.

Performers included Mel Carter with H.B. Barnum, Tina and the Mustangs, the Humdinger Dancers, and the Womenfolk (20,000 Leagues Stage), the Association (Golden Horseshoe Stage), the Royal Tahitians (at Tahitian Terrace), the Young Men From New Orleans (abroad the Mark Twain), Bill Elliot and the Disneyland Date Niters (at the Plaza Gardens), Deep Six (at the Oaks Tavern), the Clara Ward Singers (at the Fantasyland Theater), the Regents (at the Space Bar), Bud and Len (at Coke Corner), Hearts and Flowers (near the Mine Train), and the Port Royal Steel Drums (aboard the Pirate Ship).

Souvenir programs contained the following special message from Walt Disney:

"On this, one of your really big moments in your life, I want to wish each and every one of you all the best for the future. Today we live in uncertain times that really only offer a greater challenge for the future. Your generation has unlimited horizons to conquer and exploration of the universe may very well lay within your reach.

"Learn from the mistakes and disappointments of the past, but have confidence in your ability to build a better, happier tomorrow... because, after all, tomorrow is where you're going to spend the rest of your life.

"In the years to come I hope you'll look back on your Grad Nite at Disneyland with pleasant memories. We've enjoyed having you. When Disneyland opened in 1955, most of you were in the first or second grade. We've both come a long way since then. When your children attend Grad Nite at Disneyland (starting about 1983) I hope we're able to tell them that the wonderful world they live in is due to you."

Great Moments With Mr. Lincoln

Great Moments With Mr. Lincoln was an attraction sponsored by the state of Illinois for the 1964-65 New York World's Fair. Walt had originally wanted to do a Hall of Presidents show with all the U.S. presidents, a project he had earlier proposed for the never-built Liberty Street at Disneyland announced in 1958.

Sculptor BlaineGibson recalled: "We found out that Katherine Stuber, who owned a wax museum, had a copy of a life mask of Lincoln. I went over to talk with her and I started quizzing her. She said, 'If I tell you all this stuff, you're going to compete with me'. We convinced her otherwise and she sold us this life cast of Lincoln's head.

"It had originally been done in 1860 by Chicago-sculptor Leonard Volk, who was actually a brother-in-law of Stephen Douglas [a political opponent of Lincoln]. The mask was not something I could use directly. Instead, it was a thing that would give me ideas. It was the only accurate life mask of Lincoln made.

"Walt didn't want to use the death mask. When sculpting Lincoln, I made some exaggerated changes, based on my understanding of characters. For example, I probably increased the bone structure around the cheeks. However, I did conform to what was generally known about Lincoln.

"The first Lincoln head we did, we couldn't get all of the machinery in it. So I sculpted part of his hair on his head, so I raised it up a half an inch and then a wig went over that.

"I had one book that had all the heights of the presidents, including Lincoln. He was 6-foot-4 inches but I actually made him 6-foot-7 inches. We had to do that. He just didn't look tall. [Photographer] Matthew Brady always had other people in the photographs, so you could see that Lincoln was a head taller than normal. We didn't have anything to scale him to so we just made him taller."

Lincoln's skin over the mechanics was fiberglass and (where it could be seen by an audience) Duraflex which was a hot melt that had originally been developed for making the "hoochie-koochie hula-skirt dolls from the war" according to Imagineer Harriet Burns, who cooked up the mixture in a crock pot she brought from home. They purchased false teeth and glass eyes (which didn't look right so they had to make their own).

Imagineer Marc Davis was one of the Disney artists who came up with sketches on how the figure might move.

"I worked out on paper—word for word—head turns, head nods, arm moves, everything just like I would time out a scene in animation," Davis said.

During the animation of the figure, Walt would come down and act out Lincoln's speech, specifically pointing out how the cheeks should respond when the mouth moved in a certain way. Everyone agreed that the final figure and its animation had great dignity and that was the result of Walt's respect for the 16th president.

In April 1962 on a visit to the Disney Studios to see an update for the Ford and General Electric pavilions Disney was doing for the fair, New York World Fair's president Robert Moses was shown a rough demonstration of the Lincoln figure. Supposedly, the astonished and thrilled Moses said, "I won't open the Fair without this exhibit!"

Because of time deadlines, limits of technology, financial restrictions, and other speedbumps, the Hall of Presidents was trimmed to just Lincoln with the state of Illinois, "The Land of Lincoln," becoming the sponsor at its pavilion.

Despite some well-reported challenges, the figure and the show was one of the biggest successes of the New York World's Fair, so Walt arranged for a version to be installed in the Opera House on Main Street in Disneyland, where it also received acclaim.

Walt, his wife Lillian and Disneyland Ambassador Julie Reihm cut the ribbon to open the entrance to the attraction on July 18, 1965. The attraction was presented by Lincoln Savings and Loan Association.

While the main show remained exactly the same, making it the first time Disney had two similar attraction playing at the same time on both the East Coast and West Coast, it was the first of the World's Fair attraction to be installed at Disneyland.

The 500-seat theater was outfitted with hidden directional speakers to allow the voices of a choir to seem to move forward during the finale; automatically operated doors, which are a common place Disney theme park element today; walls that were lined with acoustical veneer for sound control; and 118 spotlights that created the lighting effects.

The lobby included a model of the U.S. Capitol that was thirteen feet long and four and a half feet tall. It was hand carved by sculptor George Lloyd using the original blueprints as well as photographs and drawings to achieve the intricate detail.

The dome was carved from a single piece of limestone and the entire building consists of more than 500 pieces of carved stone. Lloyd began the model in 1929 and it was completed in 1935 and toured the country. When it was exhibited in Los Angeles Walt Disney came across it in August 1955 and made arrangements to purchase it.

James Algar wrote a six minute autobiographical film presentation of Lincoln's life using full color murals painted by Sam McKim to be shown as the pre-show.

Walt was so committed that children would benefit greatly from the words of Lincoln, that he insisted that children should not need to use a ticket to see it, and sacrifice going on one of the other attractions because it would then seem like a punishment. Adults had to use an E ticket.

Every ticket book had a special child's complimentary ticket and on it was written: "So young people may have a better knowledge of the man who played such an important part in American History... Walt Disney Productions invites you to be their guest to spend a few.....GREAT MOMENTS WITH MR.LINCOLN Presented by Lincoln Savings and Loan Association Opera House Town Square Main Street U.S.A. Admit One Child."

Disney storyman Jim Algar patched together selections from a variety of Lincoln's writing to create the speech used in the presentation: Lincoln's address at Sanitary Fair, Baltimore, Maryland on April 18, 1864; his speech at Edwardsville, Illinois on September 11, 1858; his address before the Young Men's Lyceum in Springfield, Illinois on January 27, 1838; his eulogy to Henry Clay in Springfield on July 6, 1952; and his address at Cooper Institute in New York City on February 27, 1860.

Walt stated, "When we set out to select the speeches and writing for the monologue in the show, we decided to bypass the Gettysburg Address, even though its poetic qualities and poignant message are unexcelled. Because it is so familiar to nearly every American, we felt that it would not contribute significantly to our purpose—an in-depth fresh presentation of Lincoln's principles, ideals and philosophies."

1966

- Attendance: 6.7 million
- Employment: 4,580
- Payroll: $18,800,000
- Candlelight Processional Narrator: Dennis Morgan
- Disneyland Ambassador: Connie Swanson
- Admission: Adult ($2.50), Junior ($2.00), Child (seventy-five cents)
- Highlights:
    - Several closures in Tomorrowland after Labor Day weekend in anticipation of the New Tomorrowland to open next year. The land was boarded up on September 5.
    - Valentine's Dance, Youth Days and Spring Fling set new attendance records
    - Walt Disney is Grand Marshal of the Rose Parade, January 1
    - On December 15, Walt Disney died of lung cancer. His brother Roy insisted that Disneyland remain open because that is what Walt would have wanted
    - On December 22, the Anaheim City Council proclaims that every July 17 (Disneyland's anniversary opening) will now be declared "Walt Disney Day"

Walt's Last Visit

The last day Walt visited Disneyland Friday, October 14 at a special event saluting Medal of Honor recipients as part of the Congressional Medal of Honor Society National Convention being held at the Ambassador Hotel.

The attendees (the honorees and their families) viewed a presentation of Great Moments with Mr. Lincoln in the Main Street Opera House and then Walt talked wearing his familiar blue suit and dark tie and a huge smile. He gave each of them a ticket good for unlimited use of all attractions including the shooting galleries and a free dinner with multiple options at the Plaza Inn. He apologized that Tomorrowland was closed for renovations but promised they could all come back any time free of charge to see the New Tomorrowland.

"Around Disneyland," he said, "I'm the top kick. I run the show here. And I'm telling you that if they don't treat you right — you report it to me."

Medal of Honor recipient (and President of the Society), Sgt. Thomas J. Kelly then made a presentation to Walt: "This is something that was made up and arrived today... and it gives me great pleasure in presenting it to Mr. Walt Disney. It is the Seal of the Congressional Medal of Honor Society. It comes to you from all these fine men here; for all they have done for their country; and in deep appreciation for everything you did for this country.

"Presented to Walt Disney in grateful appreciation by the Congressional Medal of Honor Society of the United States. Dated Los Angeles, California, October 15, 1966."

The presentation date was actually moved up by one day to accommodate Walt's availability. After the presentation, Walt talked with the attendees and posed for photos and signed autographs. It would be the last time in his life that he would be on Disneyland property.

Second Death at Disneyland

On June 17, Thomas Guy Cleveland, a 19-year-old from Northridge, California was killed when he attempted to sneak into Disneyland along the Monorail track.

Cleveland scaled the park's sixteen-foot high outer fence on a Grad Nite and climbed onto the Monorail track, intending to jump or climb down once inside the park. Cleveland ignored a security guard's shouted warnings of an approaching Monorail train and failed to leap clear of the track.

He finally climbed down onto a fiberglass canopy three feet beneath the track, but the clearance wasn't enough. The oncoming train struck and killed him, dragging his body 30 to 40 feet down the track. He was the second and final fatality to occur at the park in Walt's lifetime.

Connie Swanson

The second Disneyland Ambassador was Connie Swanson. Walt and Disneyland management wanted Julie Reihm to stay in the role but Julie wanted to move on after traveling over 52,000 miles to represent the Park.

Swanson was a "twenty-one year old Anaheim girl who is a four year veteran of the Tour Guide corps at Disneyland. The five foot four inch Mormon Miss studied a year at Fullerton Junior College and plans to resume her collge career at the University of Hawaii or the University of Utah once her year long tenure as Disneyland's offical ambassador is competled.

"Miss Swanson began her career as a tour guide four days before Christmas in 1961. Since that time she has lead almost one thousand tours through the Magic Kingdom."

One of the reasons for her selection was her experience in school theater. She lived with her mother and grandmother in Anaheim. At the time, Swanson said, "I believe Disneyland is more than a park where people enjoy themselves. Disneyland is a little United Nations. People from the U.S. and all over the world meet here on a common ground which has no nationality. They learn to accept others here. There is no society structure her.

"Here they are not constantly reminded of society's demands. The same closeness may not be retained when they leave Disneyland but at least they have a little better understanding of others."

Last Photo of Walt

Renie Bardeau started working as a photographer at Disneyland in the summer of 1959. As Renie recalled, it was at the end of August 1966 that he took the last official photo of Walt Disney at Disneyland . Walt had been in the park shooting a commercial for Kodak.

This was all arranged by Disneyland's publicity supervisor Charlie Ridgeway who told me he had no idea Walt would pass away just over three months later. As he remembered, "It was late August. We didn't know how sick Walt was. We were told he had the flu, which seemed reasonable."

Walt was in front of Sleeping Beauty Castle sitting in the front seat of Disneyland Fire Department "Engine No. 1" vehicle with a costumed Mickey Mouse (performer Paul Castle).

Near the end of the shoot, Bardeau and Disneyland's chief photographer Charlie Nichols were called to take some photos: Charlie Nichols shot in black-and-white and Bardeau in color. When Charlie Nichols retired in 1968, Bardeau replaced him as chief photographer.

Walt was usually accompanied by two staff photographers. One photographer would handle black and white pictures meant for newspapers and the second would handle color for magazines and park marketing.

Bardeau recalled, "There is a little story of when I was shooting that particular picture. It was shot on a Rolleflex, and there are twelve pictures on a roll. I had shot eleven pictures of Walt at different angles...watching for his smile, watching to make sure Mickey was looking the right way, making sure the spires weren't hanging out of Mickey's ears. Anyway, I had shot eleven pictures, and I had said, 'Thank you, Walt, that's it.'

"He asks me if I was sure, and I told him I was. He then told me that at the studio we treat film like paper clips. You shoot, shoot, shoot all the film you need because if it's not in the can, you will never have it. So he asked me to shoot one more.... So, I shot one more, and he said, 'That's fine, thank you, Renie,' and he walked away."

Those multiple shots also explain why you might see occasional variations, especially in the position of Mickey's upraised hand.

Grad Nite

Approximately 60,000 Seniors of 33 High Schools attended five all-night Grad Nite '66 events, including Arcadia High School, Aviation High School, Bell Gardens High School, Burbank High School, John Burroughs High School, California High School, Colton Union High School, Compton High School, Corona Senior High School, Costa Mesa High School, Dominguez High School, Duarte High School, Edgewood High School, Hueneme High School, La Habra High School, La Jolla High School, Mayfair High School, Mira Costa High School, Orange High School, Palos Verdes High School, Pasadena High School, Poway High School, Redlands Sr. High School, Redondo Union High School, Reseda High School, Santa Ana Senior High School, Santa Ana Valley Senior High School, Santa Fe High School, Sierra High School, Thousand Oaks High School, Tustin High School, U.S. Grant High School, and Verdugo Hills High School.

Grand Canyon Diorama

The Grand Canyon Diorama was added to the Disneyland theme park on March 21, 1958. The Primeval World debuted July first as an addition to the Grand Canyon Diorama.

Immediately after viewing the Grand Canyon, guests saw the Primeval World that featured dinosaurs from Walt Disney's Ford Magic Skyway pavilion from the 1964-65 New York World's Fair.

During the journey, over two-dozen extinct creatures, including Brontosaurus, Pterodactyl's, Triceratops (including baby Triceratops hatching from their shells), Stegosaurus, a twenty-two-foot Tyrannosaurus Rex plus many more were showcased.

It depicts dinosaurs from all different time periods and places in the same habitat. Many of the dinosaurs are out of proportion to their actual size and there are many anatomical flaws.

Although the narration says that the dinosaurs are part of what the Grand Canyon was like millions of years ago, they were actually inspired by the dinosaurs in the *Rite of Spring* segment from the animated feature film *Fantasia* (1940). The background music is not from that film but from Bernard Hermann's score from *Mysterious Island*, a 1961 film made by Columbia Pictures.

Only the dinosaurs were brought to Disneyland since Ford declined to sponsor the entire pavilion being relocated. The New York attraction also featured humorous looking cavemen designed by Imagineer Marc Davis but Walt felt they were too crude, especially when compared to the President Lincoln audio-animatronics figure.

Changes

Disneyland pioneers Tommy Walker and Ed Ettinger left the Park's employ during the summer to seek employment elsewhere. Tommy spearheaded Disneyland's entertainment events and Ed had been director of Marketing. Donald Novis, an original star of the Golden Horseshoe Revue, and Johnny St. Cyr, a legendary Dixieland player who performed with Disneyland's Young Men from New Orleans, both passed away during the summer.

Music at the Park

The summer's musical entertainment kicked off with Big Band Holiday of the Memorial Day weekend, May 28 and 29 that was the only Big Band event of the summer. Unlike previous summers, there was less concentration on Big Bands and more on folk, country, and rock bands.

The Big Band Holiday featured Xavier Cugat making his first appearance at Disneyland (together with Charo); the fifth appearance of Harry James; Anita O'Day; and the first Disneyland appearance of Nelson Riddle. Some of Disneyland's own talent also performed at the event: The Elliott Brothers Orchestra, Tina and the Mustangs, the Young Men from New Orleans, and the Royal Tahitian Dancers.

Just like in 1965, each Monday Disneyland featured a folk Hootenanny, and each Tuesday a Humdinger geared toward the youth audience. Country Music Jubilee was held each Wednesday, and Thursday was reserved for Guest Band Nite, which spotlighted the band that generally performed Tuesday through Saturday of that week.

In addition to the guest talent, Disneyland had its regular talent scattered throughout the Park each day. On Friday and Saturday nights, the Firehouse Five Plus 2 after they finished their work week at the Disney Studio joined the roster (performing at the French Market when New Orleans Square opened), with the Glenn Kennedy Orchestra appearing on Sunday nights.

New Orleans Square brought new entertainment to Disneyland, including the Royal Street Bachelors and tap dancers Gene and Eddie leading the Delta Ramblers Dixieland Band.

It's a Small World

The New York World's Fair of 1964-1965 was an opportunity for Walt Disney to show that his approach to theme park entertainment was not just a California accident, but something that appealed even to the more supposedly sophisticated audiences of the East Coast.

It's a Small World opened April 22, 1964 and during its two years of operation it was determined that more than ten million people rode it, which meant it had a higher attendance than any of the other highly-rated Disney shows at the fair.

More amazingly, this was even though there was a special admission ticket (with funds going to UNICEF: United Nations International Children's Emergency Fund) required for this happiest cruise that was not charged at any of the other Disney shows.

The attraction was sponsored by the Pepsi-Cola Company that was working with the United Nations agency devoted to children's welfare to have a pavilion that would provide a "salute to UNICEF and the world's children."

It was Walt himself who came up with the concept of a little boat ride. Arrow Manufacturing, responsible for innovations like Disneyland's Matterhorn, was already working on a boat ride system based on some ideas by Imagineer Bob Gurr. It was an innovative vehicle that would allow boarding and disembarking at the same time and was later incorporated into Pirates of the Caribbean attraction.

Walt came up with the name for the attraction: "The Children of the World." Walt wanted it to be a pleasant experience for "children of all ages" showcasing a "wonderland where all the world's children live and play" where the boats would travel on the "FantaSea" although it would later be called the "Seven Seaways".

There were several meetings with the show designers and Imagineer Marc Davis who was the chief art director for the project came up with a sketch that really stood out. However, Walt wasn't satisfied and decided to get artist Mary Blair involved.

Blair started work on the show in June 1963. The first piece she did was the Siamese Dancing Girl and Walt loved it. He gave her the approval to continue doing all the children in that style.

Besides the basic design of the children, Blair's major contribution was the color styling helping to create instant mood changes as guests sailed around the world. All the colors showcased in the previous scenes combine into an all-white finale.

The audio-animatronics doll figures were known as "rubber heads," based on a notation that appeared on Marc Davis' drawings. Davis was supplying gags for the scenes and the flow of action of the figures including the dancing. Once, he had to improvise a can-can dance in the Imagineering machine shop to demonstrate how he wanted a particular movement.

The dolls were sculpted by Blaine Gibson and costumed by Alice Davis, Marc Davis' talented wife.

Letters were sent out to the consulate offices of the 26 countries depicted in the attraction to get information on the costumes. In addition, Alice went through copies of *National Geographic* magazine in the Disney Studio library as well as spending hours in museums and other libraries.

Not only did Alice make sure the designs were accurate but that the materials used to make the costumes were authentic to the specific country. That commitment often caused challenges because the costumes had to survive constant movement. During one of the early tests, the can-can dancers popped their pantaloons within the first two hours.

The Imagineers depleted the costume jewelry stores of Southern California, using more than 8,000 crystals, beads and sequins. Nearly 200 pounds of glitter was used on the sets. To keep all of this together along with the braids, feathers and tassels, five gallons of glue was required each week work was being done.

The "rubber head" children were not actually made out of rubber, but a special hot-melt vinyl and Duraflex for durability, because it was estimated that a singing child would open and close its mouth about a million times a month.

There were boy and girl dolls but the basic shape had to work for every culture. Blaine Gibson and Orlando Ferrante went to doll stores to get really large doll eyes. The ones they ended up getting were the ones that would shut when the doll went to sleep.

"So it was easy for the machine shop to come up with an air actuator that made them blink. That was important because blinking is the key part of keeping something alive," stated Gibson.

The dolls were broken up into three general categories: singers, dancers and instrument players. The dolls were all the same size, although there had been discussions about varying the sizes to create a greater sense of perspective.

Walt was personally involved with Gibson's and Greg S. Marinello development of the dolls' facial design with each animated doll's face completely identical in shape to emphasize that everyone despite skin color or costume is alike.

Imagineer Claude Coats laid out the pattern for the river that wound through the attraction. Imagineers Rolly Crump and Jack Ferges created all the "toys," the term that referred to everything that wasn't an animated children doll from props in the scene to skating penguins. Working with approximately thirty people, Crump used styrofoam and paper-mache, often gluing on Chem Wipes for additional support, to build more than 250 "toys."

Crump studied Blair's children's books for ideas and to help understand her style. The idea for the ice skating penquins came from a toy on Imagineer Yale Gracey's desk where a little ice skater would skate thanks to a hidden magnet underneath.

Originally, Walt had wanted the children to each sing their national anthems. However, when it was attempted, it was a cacophony that was insufferable when the songs overlapped as they frequently did.

Walt called in songwriters the Sherman Brothers who were hard at work on *Mary Poppins*. He told them he wanted "a simple little roundelay... like *Row, Row, Row Your Boat*" that would be melodious and was simple enough that it could be repeated over and over in different languages.

Richard Sherman suggested a counterpoint song – one containing two melodies which could be used both singly and simultaneously. The Sherman Brothers scrutinized all the different translations to make sure they communicated the same message. Other than a few translation adjustments (because they felt it sounded too "communistic" on the French version), there were no major problems.

Imagineer Harriet Burns remembered Walt talking to the Sherman Brothers at WED and using the phrase "it's a small world after all" to describe the feeling he wanted. Walt never meant the phrase to be a title or even a lyric but was just making a casual remark to try and capture the spirit of song that talked about the children of the world.

The voices of children from several countries recorded the song: A London church choir, television performers in Mexico, a school chorus in Rome, a group of kids in Burbank, California as well as a choir of adult singers for the grand finale.

To install the attraction, crews worked seven days a week to make the deadline. Walt constantly monitored the attraction and the only request he made was to add more balloons in the air in one section.

Walt always knew that he wanted to transplant either the attractions or parts of the attractions to Disneyland. In June 1965, as the New York World's Fair was preparing to close, construction had begun on the Small World show building at Disneyland for the attraction. Construction ran from June 9, 1965 to May 28, 1966.

Imagineer Roger Broggie remembered that there was so much work involved in moving and restoring the show that a new subsidiary company known as MAPO (named after the film *Mary Poppins*) had to be created.

When the attraction moved to Disneyland, it changed significantly from the New York presentation since the show building was one-third larger.

Crump said, "The New York sets were placed in the same order at Disneyland (although some were different, right or left side) but we added quite a lot. The European section was built at least a third larger than the World's Fair, so I had to 'piece' the sets to fill the space.

"We never had a North Pole area at the Fair, which I designed for Disneyland along with the Islands of the Pacific. We had to completely rebuild every set that was at the Fair…re-canvas them, re-paint them, re-flitter them, and then add another third to the ride."

In March 1966, Buddy Baker conducted additional music for the Disneyland attraction and its new sections including the music for the clock tower.

It was Crump who designed the façade for the Disneyland attraction after Blair's initial design was rejected by Walt. Her intent was it to look like it was a little girl playing with blocks.

Crump worked with Blair to get her style in the final façade as well as include stylized cutout turrets, towers and minarets which are vaguely reminiscent of world landmarks like the Leaning Tower of Pisa, Tower of Pisa, Eiffel Tower and more.

Blair's original rendering for the façade was so colorful it would have been a maintenance nightmare as well requiring constant repainting as the colors faded in the California sun so Crump made it white with gold accents to help with maintenance.

The structure required so much gold leaf that it used everything available in the United States and Disney had to get some from Germany to finish the job. That gold leaf later tarnished and was replaced by American supply. On some early blueprints, the structure is listed as "Small World Palace"

It was Walt himself who came up with the idea of the clock like a European Clock Glockenspiel that he was familiar with from his travels. Blair drew a small black-and white sketch on a napkin while on an airplane flight and Crump transformed it into the final thirty-foot high version.

Originally Crump had only nine figures coming out of the clock but it was Walt who said to have 24 characters since there are 24 hours in the day. The doors on the clock open every quarter hour showcasing a parade of character figures and ending with the time being shown before all the doors close again.

It is a functioning clock. The "TIC -TOC -TIC –TOC" sound was made by two metal rods that would alternately lift and drop hitting wooden blocks next to speakers that amplified the TIC-TOC sound to the exterior area by various output speakers. It was replaced by a recording of that sound in the 1980s.

Crump was also the one to come up with the idea of having a doll representing Mary Blair placed on the Eiffel Tower in the attraction.

It's A Small World opened at Disneyland on May 28, 1966 and was sponsored by Bank of America. Besides the Disney and Bank of America dignitaries, the press release declared there were 1,500 foreign consular officials, more than 800 members of the press, 500 youngsters in native costumes and the International Children's Choir of Long Beach. Walt Disney and Bank of America Chairman of the Board Louis Lundborg sat in the first boatload of children to inaugurate the journey.

In addition, a parade of local folk dancing groups and marching bands also participated. On a signal from Connie Swanson, ten thousand balloons, white peace doves and fireworks filled the sky overhead. Walt Disney joined "children from sixteen ethnic groups" to pour flasks filled with a liter of water from the "seven seas and nine major lagoons" into the waterway for the attraction.

The event was officially known as "Operation Water". Government and private representatives gathered the water and photographs were taken world-wide documenting that gathering for publicity purposes.

Denmark's O.B. Johnston got a flask from the Baltic Sea with the help of photographers, public relations people and a pretty model dressed in traditional costume and include a few drops of water from a bottle found in the sunken hull of a local warship. Gunnar Mansson in Sweden enlisted the aid of Harriet Carlsson, chief hostess of Stockholm's Skansen park who performed the task wearing her national costume.

In Durban, South Africa, Jack Small took off his socks and waded out up to his ankles to get water from the Indian Ocean. However as the date approached, the water from the Indian Ocean was missing. It was resolved by a confused call from TWA that discovered in its Lost and Found Department a small bottle of absolutely colorless water.

Antonio Bertini of the Disney office slipped down a rocky embankment to get a jug of water from the Mediterranean while being watched by costumed Mickey Mouse, Goofy and Pluto.

Frank Forsyth went to Huntington Beach, California and paid a couple of kids to wade out into the Pacific Ocean to get the water. To air freight a liter of water from Venezuela cost $21.86 according to a bill in the Disney files.

Walt himself poured a liter of water from Frontierland's Rivers of America into the flume from a Davy Crockett-style rustic canteen.

China was not officially recognized by the United States so was not represented in the attraction until the 1970s when it was added to both the Disneyland and Walt Disney World version. There were 24 original Disneyland Park topiaries premiering in 1963. They included a waltzing hippo, a poodle, a pig, bears, elephants, seals, and giraffes. In 1966, they were permanently planted at It's a Small World.

As Rolly Crump told *E Ticket* magazine, "Walt's intended audience with 'it's a small world' was everybody. He was always saying that there should be something in Disneyland for everybody. I used to sit outside the ride and watch people come out of 'small world.' They'd be smiling, and they'd be laughing, and there really wasn't another attraction where people came out and were happy like that."

New Orleans Square

Walt had always wanted there to be a New Orleans-themed section in Disneyland. Architectural elements from that city in the late 1800s were in evidence on buildings at the far end of Frontierland from when it first opened in 1955.

New Orleans Square was the first new land ever to be added to Disneyland. It was officially dedicated on July 24, 1966, by Walt and Victor Schiro, who served as mayor of the city of New Orleans from 1961-1969.

A reporter for a New Orleans newspaper at the event wrote that "it's the next best thing to being there" and repeated the information from the Disney publicity material that it was built for almost the exact amount paid for the entire Louisiana Purchase in 1803, roughly $15 million, just $2 million shy of the cost to build the entire Disneyland park roughly ten years earlier in 1955.

At the dedication, Walt said, "Disneyland has always had a Big River and a Mississippi sternwheeler. It made sense to build a new attraction at the bend of the river, and so New Orleans Square came into being - a New Orleans of a century ago when she was the 'Gay Paree' of the American frontier."

When Schiro repeated that the Disney version was just like the real thing to reporters, a playful Walt off to the side and in a soft voice said "only cleaner." Walt also joked that since the mayor had just made him an honorary citizen of New Orleans ("You know I am already a Louisiana Colonel," remarked Walt) that maybe he should make the mayor an "honorary dictator of the Magic Kingdom."

Unfortunately the Pirates of the Caribbean attraction was not ready to open since Walt had made major changes in the approach to the ride after he saw how successful and efficient the water vehicles were in the It's A Small World attraction at the New York World's Fair.

While most Disney fans think of New Orleans Square as primarily the location of the attractions Pirates of Caribbean and Haunted Mansion, Walt was particularly interested in the shopping and dining experience that could be created.

When New Orleans Square opened, there were chants and ringing bells of a voodoo queen living off a balcony on the backside of the Square near the bathrooms and the train station where guests can purchase a beignet and a non-alcoholic Mint Julep.

It was meant to suggest the infamous Marie Laveau who practiced voodoo in New Orleans in the 1700s and 1800s. After all, her portrait could be found in both Pirates of the Caribbean and the Haunted Mansion when those attractions first opened.

World famed mosaicist Hanns-Joachim Scharff did thirty table tops in the Creole Café, the mosaic thresholds for the French Market, and work on two of the quaint specialty shops. The threshold designs were based on original art work from mid-19th century New Orleans. His next job for Disney would be the murals in the breezeway of Walt Disney World's Cinderella Castle.

Robert Jackson and Frank Allnutt from WED (Walt Disney Imagineering) prepared a twelve page "profile" of the new land in 1966. It was obviously written prior to the opening of the land and notice how often Disneyland is referred to as the "Magic Kingdom." It was to be used by reporters who were writing for newspapers and magazines to better describe what guests would experience.

Here are some excerpts from that document:

"New Orleans, The 1850s

"She was the nation's most colorful and exciting city...a proud cosmopolitan center that had already established a lasting cultural heritage...America's capital of aristocracy...seat of commerce and industry...a bristling port exporting more commodities than New York. Cotton was king, and the Good Life was his decree.

"Walt Disney, the perennial innovator, has accomplished another 'first' with the charming shops in Disneyland's New Orleans Square. He has made the "Magic Kingdom," world famous for its family entertainment attractions, *the* destination for collectors of the finest creations by craftsmen and artists from many eras and nearly every area of the world.

"Merchandise to suit every taste and budget has made New Orleans Square truly an adventure in shopping.

"From mosaic thresholds to chandeliered ceilings, from nostalgic stain glass panels to delicate wrought-iron lace, from fine old furniture to delicate bric-a-brac, these shops offer visitors settings of unequalled luxury and atmosphere."

It was Disney's first attempt to control and theme the dining and shopping experience for guests that later evolved into areas like Walt Disney World's Disney Springs. Disney was trying to define an area not just by the attractions but by everything else that would contribute in creating an overall immersive feeling for the location.

The Death of Walt Disney

While Walt projected an image of stamina and a big smile, he was often in unbearable pain especially during the last year of his life. His desk calendar shows a series of doctor's appointments and hospital visits.

These problems ranged from dental issues to a severe sinus condition that required weekly treatments to a painful a form of arthritis to complaints about exhaustion. It was even suggested he had a bout with walking pneumonia.

The press conference for Mineral King on September 19, 1966 showed Walt's face drawn and pale and he had shortness of breath after minimal effort. It was explained that the high altitude had aversely affected him.

Family and associates had long been concerned about his excessive smoking that seemingly caused dramatic and constant coughing fits as well as an old polo injury from the 1930s where four of his cervical vertebrae had been crushed and not properly treated.

It resulted in a calcium deposit building up in the back of his neck that caused a pain in his lower back and legs that plagued Walt for the rest of his life. In his later years, Walt required a couple of shots of scotch and a massage from the studio nurse in order to get home at night.

Walt entered Saint Joseph's Hospital, right across the street from the Disney Studio, on November 2, 1966, roughly a week after appearing in the fabled short film where he explained the E.P.C.O.T. concept. He was there for a routine pre-operative X-ray to take care of the calcification of the old neck injury from his younger days playing polo.

The x-rays showed a spot the size of a walnut on his left lung. It was a tumor. He had exploratory surgery to remove it the following Monday, November 7, 1966.

The surgeon told the immediate Disney family that he had six months to two years at most left to live. Not all of Walt's family was told. His older brother Ray and his younger sister Ruth found out about the operation through the newspapers that downplayed any seriousness and made no mention of a malignancy.

The doctor told Walt they had removed all the cancerous lesions and that with a little rest, Walt should be "as good as new" in an attempt to keep Walt's spirits up, but it was obvious that Walt sensed his time was limited.

On Monday, November 21, Walt was released from the hospital and spent the next several days with his staff at the Disney Studio and WED, his family and at his vacation home in Palm Springs.

By November 30, he was so weak he returned to the hospital. His strength continued to wane. Cobalt treatments diminished his strength and robbed him of his appetite. The combination of drugs that he was given sometimes made him confused. He spent his 65th birthday on December fifth in the hospital.

Walt did not want people to see him in the hospital and so only the immediate family was allowed into his room to visit with few other exceptions. Very few people, even those closest to him knew how sick he actually was.

The story told to the public was that he was undergoing surgery for an old neck injury from playing polo that most people knew had troubled him for decades and had re-entered the hospital for a routine post-operative checkup.

On the night of December 14, 1966, Walt seemed to get renewed energy and spent the evening describing to his brother Roy and Admiral Joe Fowler his plans for the Epcot using the ceiling tiles of his hospital room as a grid for reference.

Walt Disney died under the name of "John Smith" at 9:35 a.m. on December 15,1966 in Room 529 of Saint Joseph's Hospital of "cardiac arrest due to Bronchogenic ca(rcinoma)" which basically meant his heart stopped because of lung cancer.

Walt's death was not immediately announced to the press until several hours after it occurred. Walt lay in his hospital bed for a few hours while his family arrived and said their farewells.

The private funeral was held at 5:00 pm the next day at Forest Lawn Memorial Park in Glendale, California at the Little Church of the Flowers. Only the immediate family attended the services. Walt was cremated at Forest Lawn on December 17, 1966.

Roy O. Disney wrote in the 1966 Annual Stockholders' Report: "It was Walt's wish that when the time came, he would have built an organization with the creative talents to carry on as he had established and directed it through the years. Today, this organization has been built, and we shall carry out this wish.

"Walt Disney's preparation for the future is a solid, creative foundation. All the plans for the future that Walt had begun – new motion pictures, the expansion of Disneyland, television production and our Florida and Mineral King projects as outlined in this report – will continue to move ahead."

1967

- Attendance: 7.8 million
- Employment: 4,910
- Payroll: $22,300, 000
- Candlelight Processional Narrator: Gregory Peck (Saturday), Dean Jones (Sunday)
- Disneyland Ambassador: Marcia Miner
- Admission: Adult ($3.00), Junior ($2.50), Child (seventy-five cents)
- Parking: Fifty cents
- Highlights:
  - The Pirate's Arcade Museum opens in New Orleans Square
  - The Blue Bayou and Club 33 restaurants open
  - The Circle-Vision 360 theater opens in Tomorrowland
  - Seventeen year old Ricky Lee Yama tries to jump between the PeopleMover cars as it passes through a tunnel. He slips and is wedged between the two cars with his head and upper body crushed on August 21.
  - More than 18,000 guests greeted the New Year and thousands more attended the second annual Valentine Dance. A capacity crowd celebrated "Spring Fling".
  - House of the Future dismantled
  - Vaudeville '67 was performed every Wednesday during the summer season featuring celebrities and variety acts including Rudy Vallee, Frankie Lane and the Andrews Sisters
  - During the summer, Sir Edmund Hillary and his wife visited Disneyland's Matterhorn and went onto the mountain, inspected the climbers' rope and watched them climb the overhang.
  - Some additions to the Jungle Cruise attraction with some new dancing natives and two new gorillas.

The year 1967 marked the first year that Disneyland and the Walt Disney Company had to adjust to not having Walt Disney around to make decisions. Disneyland was such a personal vision of Walt's that there were concerns whether the park would grow or even survive without its loving father.

Even the cast training program for Disneyland was re-named "Traditions," because both Dick Nunis and Van France worried that new hires to the company needed to be reminded of Walt's personal philosophy, since the "boss" was no longer there personally to model the proper attitude and behavior.

The introduction to the Disneyland Traditions Manual was from Roy O. Disney: "Walt Disney was an American father with two children. He'd dreamed of Disneyland for 20 years . . . as a place where parents and children could share pleasant times . . . a place dedicated to the ideal, the dreams and the hard facts that have created America. In everything he did, my brother had an intuitive way of reaching out and touching the hearts and minds of young and old alike. His entertainment was an international language. In Disneyland he created a revolutionary new concept of outdoor entertainment . . . a world-famous theme show without equal or precedent."

One new addition from the New York World's Fair that is usually overlooked was that Walt went to the Spanish pavilion and saw a display and demonstration by the Arribas brothers and invited them to open up a shop at Disneyland. Disneyland had a glass blower from 1955-1966 named Bill Rasmussen who left the park to open a series of shops in cities like San Francisco and Boston.

In 1967, the brothers came to Disneyland and opened a glass shop and now over a half century later have shops at a number of different Disney theme parks.

On November 20, 1967, Disneyland got permission from Anaheim to expand its borders both in the park and the parking lot. By end of December, it was estimated that since the park's opening in 1955 roughly 67 million guests had been in the park so there was a need to expand.

Anaheim Stadium opened in 1966 (home of the California Angels) and the Anaheim Convention Center opened July 12, 1967. Hotels/motels had grown from 60 rooms in 1955 to more than 6,500 rooms in 1967.

And sadly, 1967 was the last summer for mermaids to appear in the Submarine Lagoon. Fortunately, the changes in the summer of 1967 were documented in the *Wonderful World of Disney* television program *Disneyland: From the Pirates of the Caribbean to the World of Tomorrow* that aired on January 21, 1968.

Marcia Miner

At a ceremony on the Golden Horseshoe Revue stage, it was announced that the new Disneyland Ambassador would be twenty-two year old Marcia Miner who had been a VIP Disneyland Hostess at Disneyland for the last three years.

Born in Long Beach, California on November 21, 1944, she moved to Venezuela in 1947 because of her father, John, being an oil company executive who was relocated. The family returned to live in the United States in 1958 and following her father's death in 1959, she and her mother moved to Garden Grove. Marcia attended Rancho High School where she was a member of the National Spanish Honor Society and Pep Club.

One of her responsibilities was a twenty-day, eighteen city tour across the country promoting the fifth release of the animated feature *Snow White and the Seven Dwarfs* accompanied by the seven costumed dwarfs from Disneyland, a musician and three tour supervisors.

"It was a lot of hard and strenuous work, but one of the most rewarding experiences of my life," said Miner. "We also tried to visit at least one children's hospital in each city. I did about fifteen to sixteen hours of radio time just by myself."

Grad Nite

Because of the changes in Tomorrowland, the Fantasyland Theater had to be rehabbed for the event. Repairs were made on the old curtains, teaser, old blue cyclorama and upgrades to lighting. The theater was also being used for other shows including Humdinger (performances by Randy Sparks and the New Society, Tammi Terrell, The Aubrey Twins, The Young Rascals, Neil Diamond, Joey Paige, Lesley Gore and The Mustangs) and Vaudeville '67 so scheduling was tight.

On June 15, 1967, local radio station KFWB's Tom Murphy and Bill Taylor broadcast live from Disneyland's hub. One lucky Grad Niter would win his or her own "Grad Nite Special" - a brand new 1967 *Mercury Cougar* - "the car of the year"!

Performers included Coke Corner Duo (at Coke Corner), Dobie Gray and His Band (at the Oaks Tavern), Aunt Dina's Quilting Party (near the Mine Train), Bill Elliott and the Disneyland Date Niters (at the Plaza Gardens Stage), Ward Gospel Singers (at The Golden Horseshoe), The Regents (at Plaza Inn), The Royal Tahitians (at Tahitian Terrace), The Aggregation (at The French Market), The Young Men (on the Mark Twain), and The Individuals (in the Fantasyland Entertainment Area).

A flyer sent to students stated: "Our discussions with graduates, parents, and faculty members indicate the necessity to once again stress the importance of the following in regard to proper dress :

(1) Boys must wear coats and ties.

a. Only suit coats or sports coats permitted.

b. (Casual) sweaters or jackets are prohibited.

(2) Girls must wear date dresses.

a. No mini-skirts are permitted. It is felt that skirts should be no shorter than one inch above the knees.

ANYONE NOT DRESSED IN ACCORDANCE WITH THE ABOVE, WILL NOT BE PERMITTED."

For the five Grad Nite parties in June, some 250 high schools from "Needles to San Francisco" and their 76,000 high school seniors celebrated at Disneyland. That meant more than one of every three high school graduates in Southern California were inside Disneyland on these five evenings.

Spring

The Easter season began with a special Spring Fling Party on Saturday March 18 from eight pm to one am. It featured entertainment from rock groups, swing bands, Dixieland combos and Polynesian music. It offered an exciting Grand Prize: a 1967 Mercury Cougar. Other prizes included Honda sport cycles, Muntz auto stereos, and complete Pendleton sports wardrobes. Advance tickets were five dollars and included admission, all dance areas and attractions except shooting galleries.

On Easter Sunday, March 26, a grand finale to the week-long activities including thirty antique autos and more than two hundred paraders dressed in turn-of-the-century costumes strolling down Main Street U.S.A. The climax of the parade was the ascent from the Hub of a twenty-one foot balloon containing 20,000 cubic feet of helium carrying two "Aeronauts" high into the sky.

Pirates of the Caribbean

Walt Disney had wanted an attraction featuring pirates at Disneyland as early as 1954 to be part of the pre-Civil War New Orleans area of the park.

In 1958, artist Sam McKim further expanded on the concept on his Disneyland map design that included a haunted house and a Pirate Wax Museum featuring a Rogue's Gallery of famous pirates and a Thieves Market for merchandise.

In 1961, Walt approached artist Marc Davis. Davis studied the history of pirates and came up with some dramatic tableaus to tell the story in a walk-through attraction meant to be underneath the New

Orleans location. Up above would be an enormous enclosed area where it was always a moonlit twilight and guests could wander through a Pirate Alley shopping district and an elegant restaurant located outside of a plantation near a bayou.

Davis went through three different designs of the underground pirate presentation where guests in groups of 50-70 would walk through a harbor town, onto a pirate ship and then through a tavern and a cobblestone town square.

There were discussions about having simplified electro-mechanical pirates narrate the story as guests gazed into the various tableau scenes. Electro-mechanical figures, like the ones on the Jungle Cruise or the Rivers of America, could repeat two or three motions and were the forerunners of Audio-Animatronics.

At the World's Fair, Walt saw how successful the sophisticated Lincoln Audio-Animatronics figure was and how the boat system in It's a Small World was so efficient in transporting a large number of guests through an attraction. Even though a huge hole had been dug for the Pirate Wax Museum and concrete and steel already laid in anticipation of finishing shortly after the fair, Walt had it all torn out and he started over. The original hole dug for the museum is now the caves before the main show.

However, because of Walt's new vision influenced by the World's Fair, the Pirates of the Caribbean attraction would be delayed until 1967 along with the Blue Bayou restaurant and Club 33 (inspired by the VIP lounge Walt saw in operation on the second floor of the Tower of the Four Winds in front of It's a Small World).

During Davis' research, it turned out that real pirates were not as interesting and dramatic as people remembered, so the thrust of the new show was to create the world of pirates people knew from the movies and books.

Davis' specialty was humor, and his skill was utilized to take the edge off the nefarious behavior of characters who proudly admit that they "kidnap and ravage and don't give a hoot." Instead of being rough men who would take advantage of women, they became lonely bachelors desperately looking to "buy a wench for a bride" to fill their affection-starved lives.

Exaggerated facial features (especially since the figures would only be seen for a few seconds) and a light-hearted theme song also underscored that these were simply "boys will be boys" having some fun like a high school football team out of control after winning a game. That certainly doesn't excuse their actions, but it made it all a bit more understandable for guests and less offensive for almost thirty years when some changes were made.

Musician George Bruns, whose previous credits included co-writing the hugely popular song *The Ballad of Davy Crockett*, composed the attraction's score, with lyrics and script created by the Francis Xavier "X" Atencio, who later penned the narration script and song lyrics for The Haunted Mansion.

Atencio voice-directed the performers for the attraction, but had some help from Imagineer Marty Sklar. Paul Frees did the voice of the Auctioneer and some of the other pirates. He was the voice of the Ghost Host in the Haunted Mansion, Ludwig von Drake, Bullwinkle's foe Boris Badenov, and countless other credits.

Thurl Ravenscroft, best known as the voice of Kellogg's Tony the Tiger for decades and the singer of "You're A Mean One, Mr. Grinch" did several pirate voices, including the accordion playing one in the trio of minstrels by the donkey and the drunk pirate hanging on a lamppost. He also did the sound of the singing/howling dog with the minstrels as he had supplied dog sounds in Disney's animated feature *Lady and the Tramp* (1955).

J. Pat O'Malley who was a popular Disney animated voice artist, including Colonel Hathi in The Jungle Book (1967) also voiced several pirates.

The voice of the magistrate's wife pleading with Carlos not to be "cheeken" was supplied by June Foray, who has countless credits, including being Grandma Fa in *Mulan* (1998).

A long model of the attraction was built. The figures were each nine inches high and could be moved from place to place. It was put up in sections on sawhorses with rings for each scene, so that someone could get the same view that the audience would see. A desk chair with rollers was pushed through the path. Walt went through many times and made suggestions and changes.

Before Walt's death, a full-sized mock-up of the auction scene was set up in a WED (Imagineering) warehouse in Glendale. A dolly with a chair on it was rigged up so that Walt could be pushed through at two feet per second (the approximate speed of the boats). Walt also got to walk the unfilled flume of the attraction, but there was not much in place in terms of scenery and figures to see.

Several of the sculpted heads are re-used throughout the attraction. For instance the character in his chair outside his shack across from the Blue Bayou Restaurant was also used as the standing pirate in the jail cell trying to tempt the dog to give them the keys.

In September 1998, I also got to talk with Alice Davis, Marc's wife, who was responsible for doing the costumes on the attraction. In the early days, she and her team of four costumers would go through each morning and check the costumes and adjust the wigs and with their own make-up kits applied make-up to each of the human figures and then powdered them so they looked more realistic. Today, Disney merely paints the faces.

While the Blue Bayou (originally designated as the Blue Bayou Terrace) was ready to open months before the attraction, Walt refused to do so because he felt that part of the experience for the restaurant was to see the bateaux slowly drifting in the nearby bayou. Both Pirates and Blue Bayou restaurant opened in March 1967. Club 33 opened in June 1967.

The opening of the attraction had the media reporters on the Sailing Ship Columbia. Comedian Wally Boag (iconic for his performances in the Golden Horseshoe Revue) was dressed as a pirate captain in a row boat along with his pirate crew.

They climbed aboard the Columbia and took the reporters prisoner (and brought up some attractive and appropriately dressed young women from down below, sometimes slung over their shoulders) and celebrated with music and dancing on the deck. Then they herded everyone off the ship and marched them toward the attraction.

In front of the boarded up entrance were two armed soldiers guarding the place but they were quickly overcome. The pirates used a huge log to "smash" open the door and the media entered for the first time.

The attraction cost more than eight million dollars and was the longest attraction adventure at Disneyland.

In 1997, the original Pirates of the Caribbean attraction became the first recipient of the Classic Attraction award from the Themed Entertainment Association (THEA), an honor accepted by Disney Legend Marty Sklar.

New Tomorrowland

When Disneyland opened in 1955, the thing that most disappointed Walt Disney was Tomorrowland. He didn't have the time, money, or technology to construct it to match his vision. It became a collection of company-sponsored exhibits promoting dairy products, paint, and plumbing, among other things.

Guests enjoyed the land, especially the Autopia cars, but it was not as cohesive a storytelling experience as the other lands of the park.

In August of 1957, Imagineering prepared a document called "The Future of Disneyland" and emphasized a project called "Science Land." This would be a re-imagining of Tomorrowland that Walt had jokingly nicknamed "Todayland" when talking with his staff.

"Tomorrowland was something very dear to Walt's heart," stated Walt's older brother Roy. "The old Tomorrowland had always been a source of annoyance to him because he never really accomplished what he was trying to do...he was involved in great depth in the New Tomorrowland until the day he died."

In 1959, Walt had tried to "fix" Tomorrowland by introducing the Monorail, the Submarine Voyage and the Matterhorn Bobsleds, but despite the huge success of these "E Ticket" attractions, the land still didn't come close to Walt's original plans to provide a glimpse at "the future just around the corner."

While $15 million had been spent on New Orleans Square, more than $23 million was spent on "Disneyland's New Tomorrowland: Where the Dreams of the Future are Reality Today." It was expanded to twice the size of the original land.

Walt Disney intended the New Tomorrowland to be "a world on the move" with a variety of transportation conveyances in constant motion to give the land a kinetic feeling of excitement of always moving forward.

At the dedication, Walt's brother Roy, who was then president of Walt Disney Productions, said that the New Tomorrowland was another example of the company's determination to "move ahead" without interruption in the carrying out of Walt Disney's plans.

Walt had been deeply involved in the re-design of New Tomorrowland, with serious meetings beginning in June 1964, and had significant input into all the new additions.

Besides the previously popular attractions like Autopia (which got a 1967 upgrade to the Mark VII Stingray), the Skyway, Monorail, and Submarine Voyage (Imagineer Marc Davis re-staged some scenes for 1967), the New Tomorrowland featured:

- *America the Beautiful* in a new nine-screen "Circle-Vision 360" theater presented by the Bell System.

- Flight to the Moon, a totally updated space adventure featuring the Audio-Animatronics Mr. Tom Morrow talking about the impeding launch of Flight 92 presented by Douglas Aircraft.

- Carousel of Progress from the 1964-65 New York World's Fair presented by General Electric and, featured on the upper level, Walt Disney's plans for EPCOT in a massive model called "Progress City".

- Adventure Thru Inner Space aboard the very first version of an omnimover vehicle called an "Atomobile," where guests were shrunk down and sent into a mighty microscope to journey into a snowflake in a presentation of the Monsanto Company. Monsanto's House of the Future still stood out in front of Tomorrowland but would be demolished by the end of the year.

- The WEDWay PeopleMover, a versatile new continuously moving, intermediate-speed transportation system not dependent on an internal combustion engine but on silent electric motors in the track itself that Walt intended to use in EPCOT presented by Goodyear.

- A dining and dancing outdoor complex sponsored by Coca-Cola featuring a futuristic garden area that rose from ground level to become the canopy for an entertainment stage. It was originally named Coca-Cola Refreshment Gardens, but was quickly re-dubbed Tomorrowland Terrace before the official opening. With no exterior walls, guests enjoyed Tomorrowland's new panorama and, at the end of a performance by a musical group, the stage descended leaving only the stylistic planters designed by Rolly Crump. In order to accommodate the performers loading and unloading underneath the stage, Disneyland's first underground tunnel was built that connected with the Flight to the Moon and Circle Vision buildings.

According to the press release: "For six of America's largest industries, WED Enterprises, Inc. — the Disney architectural engineering, research and development firm — has designed unique attractions to demonstrate that tomorrow's world can be built now through the application of current technology."

When the New Tomorrowland officially opened in July 1967 (to tie in with Disneyland's original opening twelve years earlier), several things were missing, including the Moonliner, the Flying Saucers, and the Clock of the World, among others to make way for the future.

Mickey Mouse dressed as an astronaut, along with Disneyland Ambassador Marcia Miner, appeared at the dedication that included a person in a jet pack flying around, fireworks, balloons and much more.

PeopleMover

When Disneyland opened in 1955, the steam trains went non-stop around the entire perimeter of the park on a "Grand Circle Tour" to allow guests a glimpse at what was actually there.

For the New Tomorrowland, the PeopleMover system was to provide the same function of showing guests an inside glimpse of the new attractions in a leisurely 16-minute ride in 62 continuously moving four-car trains. However, it was not free and required a "D" ticket.

The term PeopleMover was simply a casual placeholder identification suggested by Walt himself, because the vehicle moved people. He assumed that his staff would eventually come up with a better name, but that never happened.

The attraction was an updated version of a system developed by Imagineering for the Ford Magic Skyway attraction at the 1964-65 New York World's Fair. Ford did not want to sponsor the ride at Disneyland, since it promoted a form of transportation that could replace Ford automobiles.

Roughly every nine feet, the vehicle passed over one of 517 electric motors in the three-quarter mile long track that would turn a tire. The tires turn against the bottom of the vehicle, propelling the vehicle forward up to a speed of six miles per hour. Guests boarded on a rotating platform moving at the same speed so the vehicles seemed almost motionless.

It was Walt's intention that the PeopleMover would eventually carry citizens of EPCOT from their homes to shopping areas, to their work in the centralized hub of the city and more, without having to use cars. Doing so would eliminate air and noise pollution, traffic jams, save energy and much more.

Goodyear, maker of tires including the ones used on the attraction, became the sponsor for the PeopleMover.

On either side of the train were two facing 54-foot-long tile murals on buildings depicting children done by artist Mary Blair, familiar for her similar work on the "it's a small world" attraction.

One mural was on the *CircleVision 360* building representing global communication. The other was on the *Adventure Thru Inner Space* building representing different types of energy (sun, sea, sky, and water). Collectively, they were known as "The Spirit of Creative Energies Among Children."

Imagineer John Hench was the major influence in the re-design of the exterior of the New Tomorrowland and, on the PeopleMover, he was attempting to create a more organic approach that would welcome guests to the future.

Carousel of Progress

Another transplant from the New York World's Fair was the great, big, beautiful tomorrow (as the Sherman Brothers' theme song reminded us) of the Carousel of Progress that had been hugely successful at the fair.

For the attraction, Walt was inspired by the play *Our Town* that featured the story of a small town and its residents over several decades that he saw at least three times when it was performed in Los Angeles.

While the Audio-Animatronics characters were simpler in movement than the President Lincoln at the Illinois pavilion, there were roughly 32 of them that had to be coordinated, each on its own separate recording track.

The new Hench-designed Disneyland building was two-storied and there were two major changes to the show: First, the final scene was revised and updated, eliminating references to dated products like color kitchen lighting, and adding new miracles like videotape recording of television programs.

In the background, the Christmastime night showed the skyline of Walt's vision for EPCOT with the Cosmopolitan Hotel towering in the center.

Second, as guests went up the speedramp, they no longer saw the *Skydome Spectacular* as they did at the fair, but an amazingly detailed miniature of Walt's dream for EPCOT.

Built 1/8th of an inch to a foot, it was 6,900-square feet, 115-feet wide, and 60-feet deep. It had 2,500 moving vehicles (monorails, peoplemovers, moving sidewalks, electric trains), 20,000 trees, 4,500 structures (Walt insisted the interior of each of the buildings be finished, furnished and lit), 1,400 working street lights, and it all came alive as the audiences moved from one side of the room to the other on a three-tiered audience viewing area.

A small part of that massive model can be seen on the PeopleMover at Walt Disney World.

Adventure Thru Inner Space

Adventure Thru Inner Space gave guests a chance to be miniaturized "beyond the limits of normal magnification."

Guests boarded vehicles and went through the "Mighty Microscope" (12-feet high, 37-feet long) into a microscopic world of a snowflake. The vehicles continued to diminish in size while guests heard the audio log of the first explorer (Paul Frees) helping them understand what they were seeing on the 682-foot loop of track.

Eventually, the guests were confronted by the nucleus of the atom (containing a strobe light inside) and had to quickly return to normal size as the snowflake began to melt to find themselves once again in a "world of comfort and convenience, made possible through miracles from molecules." This phrase inspired the theme song for the attraction written by the Sherman Brothers.

Even as early as 1957 and the episode of the Disney weekly television show "Our Friend, the Atom," Walt had considered some type of attraction at Disneyland dealing with exploring the world of atoms.

Working with Dr. Charles Allen Thomas, the chairman of the Monsanto Company (that manipulated molecules), the Imagineers decided that frozen water would be the easiest and most understandable concept for guests. Walt had lived long enough to actually see the omnimovers in operation.

The omnimovers not only moved people quickly and efficiently through the attraction, but controlled what the audience would see. The curving sides of the vehicle prevented the guests from looking anywhere else besides where the vehicle was facing, as well as creating an acoustical chamber so that the narration could be heard more clearly.

"We are hoping the excitement generated in our attraction by the creativity of many Disney artists will bring alive the excitement of Inner Space," Thomas said.

To make the attraction more intimate, the Imagineers placed objects within easy reach of the guests in the Atomobiles, which was a huge mistake. People grabbed at items and even tried to physically destroy them. So the Imagineers came up with the concept now called "Envelope of Protection" meaning to put things well out of easy reach of a ride vehicle.

The darkness and intimacy of the attraction encouraged everything from covert smoking of marijuana to amorous antics. When the attraction finally closed, an angry guest wrote a complaint letter that included the interesting statement: "My son was conceived on that ride!"

Flight to the Moon

The original Rocket to the Moon attraction that had opened in 1955 took guests on a round-trip voyage around the moon and back to Earth. For the New Tomorrowland, the attraction was updated to Flight to the Moon utilizing all the latest technological advances that had happened over the last decade.

The theater was expanded, the seats were wider and there was now a four minute pre-show with eight Audio-Animatronics figures in the Mission Control room. Director Tom Morrow carried on a conversation with the ride operator explaining factual information. The actual flight also included a segment where explorers from a moon colony on a big screen gathering ore samples talked to the guests.

Imagineers were disappointed because NASA refused to share any information about their newest designs, including a lunar landing module, so when the actual moon landing took place two years later, the attraction was already hopelessly out-of-date in some areas.

On August 12, 1969, the Apollo moon landing was shown live on TV at the Tomorrowland Stage, the current site for Space Mountain, so that guests who wanted to visit Disneyland that day and spend money wouldn't miss the historic moment.

America the Beautiful

There had been several versions of a circle vision film titled *America the Beautiful* but the 18-minute long one from 1967 was certainly the best. Instead of the previous eleven cameras, this was filmed with nine cameras in 35mm film giving the images a better clarity and was housed in a beautiful new show building that now included reinforced lean rails.

There were pre-show and post-show exhibits including Picture Phones and Chatter Phones (speaker phones where a family could gather in a booth and talk at the same time to someone they dialed), as well as an opportunity to pick up a phone and hear a Disney character talk to you. Although "hosted" by the Southern California Pacific Telephone, this free show was sponsored by the larger Bell System and AT&T.

The film which could be enjoyed by 3,000 guest per hour celebrated numerous locations in America from New York to Williamsburg to the Grand Canyon to even Hawaii and Alaska. The film was later shown at Walt Disney World.

The Rocket Jets

The Rocket Jets were the newest version of a Disneyland favorite, although they were relocated above the PeopleMover making them the tallest object at over three stories high in Disneyland. The center spire was now a replica of a Saturn V rocket designed by Imagineer George McGinnis.

Walt was never interested in science-fiction which may be surprising for a man who spent much of his life dealing in fantasy. He was interested in science fact and how new advancements in technology would improve the lives of people in the immediate future.

Walt wanted Tomorrowland to showcase the latest discoveries and to inspire people to make even greater accomplishments that he hoped would unify the world. Walt's New Tomorrowland of 1967 was one of the last things that reflected his philosophy that science was our friend and it would unite our world in peace and harmony.

Unfortunately, like many of his dreams, this one was never fully realized.

1968

- Attendance: 9.4 million
- Employment: 5,510
- Payroll: $ 25,400,000
- Candlelight Processional Narrator: Henry Fonda (Saturday), Rock Hudson (Sunday)
- Disneyland Ambassador: Sally Sherbin
- Highlights:
  - Disneyland holds its first St. Patrick's Day Parade
  - The Ken-L Land Pet Motel renamed Kennel Club and sponsored by Kal Kan
  - Dick Nunis becomes Vice President of Operations for Disneyland
  - Robert Kennedy visited on June 3
  - Disneyland holds its first *Cinco de Mayo* fiesta.
  - The new Mark III monorails (the last with the bubble head and with a newly designed interior) would officially debut in 1969 with five cars instead of four for each train. However, there was some testing done throughout the year on the tracks beginning in February 1968, primarily with the new Monorail Green to help among other things in the adjustment of the extension of the stations at both the Disneyland Hotel and in Tomorrowland for the new longer versions.
  - The Autopia attraction in Tomorrowland is redesigned.

The year 1968 was filled with turmoil. Anti-Vietnam War protests around the world. Civil Rights Act signed by President Lyndon Johnson, who announced he would not run for re-election. Richard Nixon elected President of the United States.

Martin Luther King, Jr. and Robert Kennedy assassinated. Jackie Kennedy married Aristotle Onassis. The manned spacecraft Apollo 8 orbited the moon.

Walt Disney's Wonderful World of Color was still running on NBC on Sunday nights, although a year later in September 1969 it would be renamed *The Wonderful World of Disney*. The show still ranked in the top 20 most watched shows in 1968 and would remain in that ranking for the next several years but there was no host for the show since the company felt no one could replace Walt Disney in that role.

Minimum wage was $1.60 an hour. An adult ticket book to Disneyland with admission and 10 tickets would have cost $4.75 (a $8.60 value claimed the book). A child ticket book (ages 3-11) was $3.50 (a $5.55 value).

A ticket: $0.10. B ticket: $0.25. C ticket: $0.35. D ticket: $0.60. E ticket: $0.75.

Disneyland in 1968 was a bubble frozen in time, a fantasy world removed from the unpleasantness outside the berm, and was taking a moment in time to catch its breath. Annual attendance would end up being 9.4 million guests making a grand total of 77 million paying guests since opening day in 1955.

Walt had died in December 1966, and in 1968, his iconic signature was no longer on the little blue welcome note at the front of the ticket book. It was now Walt Disney Productions that welcomed guests to the park.

With the massive capital investment one year earlier in 1967 with the opening of a new Tomorrowland (that included six new attractions) and Pirates of the Caribbean in New Orleans Square, no new additions to Disneyland were in the immediate future.

All the resources and finances were being directed to Walt Disney World in Florida, since the necessary legislative bills establishing the Reedy Creek Improvement District and other authority necessary had been signed on May 12, 1967, paving the way for the preparation of the land and the building.

Of course, Haunted Mansion would open in 1969, but one of the reasons for its completion was that an exact duplicate was built at the same time for WDW to save costs and was, in fact, completely installed there and operational by April 1971, more than six months before the rest of the park opened.

Yet for a quiet year, it was not an uneventful one.

While Civil Rights was a hot topic in 1968, I want to remind readers what entertainer Sammy Davis Jr. said in 1988 about early Disneyland: "Frank Sinatra and I went to a preview of Disneyland. We had a ball. Disneyland has never gotten any credit for integration. Walt never made an issue out of it. He just did it. He has blacks and Asians and Italians and everyone and it's no big deal. It shouldn't be an issue and it's not."

In fact, in videos of Disneyland beginning in 1955, there are images of children of all races enjoying the attractions together. In 1968 black cast members were not just performers or worked backstage, but were in on stage roles defined as "people contact positions". Akinola James

Owosekun, a Nigerian exchange student attending Cal State Fullerton, was working as a skipper on the Jungle Cruise.

More than 30,000 people applied to work in one of the 3,000 jobs available at Disneyland.

In 1968, the Disneyland Ambassador was 21-year-old Sally Sherbin originally from New York City, taking over from 1967 Disneyland Ambassador Marcia Miner. She grew up in California and eventually enrolled at UCLA where she was a Bruin Belle and freshman cheerleader. She started at Disneyland as a hostess at *Great Moments with Mr. Lincoln* and later became a tour guide before moving to the *Carousel of Progress* as a VIP hostess.

By the way, the 1968 Disneyland Tour Guide of the Year, voted on by all the 85 female Guest Relations tour guides on who they felt was most representative of the charm, knowledge and enthusiasm of the group, was 21-year-old Vicki Rue from Downey, who was attending USC as a senior. It was her second summer as a tour guide. These guides in their plaid outfits and riding crops (to point, direct and keep eager young male admirers at bay) hosted more than 200,000 guests during the year.

Since no new attractions would open during the year, more than $1.5 million dollars was invested for live entertainment like the Big Band Festival that ran from May 29 to June 1, featuring Lionel Hampton (Tomorrowland Terrace), Harry James (Tomorrowland stage), Stan Kenton (Golden Horseshoe stage), and Wayne King (Plaza Gardens). The Dixieland at Disneyland event took place that year on the weekend of September 27-28.

There was a Spring Fling Party with nightly performances in different areas of the park by Bill Elliott and his Disneyland DateNiters Orchestra (Plaza Gardens), the Young Men from New Orleans (Mark Twain steamboat) and The Royal Tahitians.

Live entertainment offerings throughout the park during the summer alone included: Dapper Dans, Coke Corner Pianist, Plaza Inn Strings (female violinists who serenaded diners in the Plaza Inn), Keystone Kop Sax Quartet, Strawhatters, Adventureland Safari Band, Royal Tahitians, Royal Street Bachelors, Shoeshine Boys (Kenny and Teddy tap dancing), Delta Ramblers, pianist Joyce Cook, Pirate Band, Blue Bayou Strings, New Orleans Banjo Kings, Firehouse Five Plus Two, Teddy Buckner and his Allstars, El Zocolo Duo, Indian Dancers, The American Brass, Clara Ward Gospel Singers (nightly at the Golden Horseshoe), Fantasyland Polka Band, Matterhorn Music (including a yodeler as well as a Swiss Chordabox player), Pearly Band, The New Establishment (a rock band at Tomorrowland Terrace), The Hager Twins, and The Mustangs (dance band in the "it's a small world" dance area).

All of this to entertain guests as well as the daily Golden Horseshoe Revue, the Disney costumed characters (more than 32 every day during the summer), the nightly fireworks show, and even more including some "name act" singers.

For the Fantasy on Parade, more than eighty Disney characters (including ones from the 1967 animated feature *The Jungle Book*) and new floats were in view.

The Disneyland Kids of the Kingdom first appeared in 1968, modeled after the Up with People! and Doodletown Piper singing groups. Fifteen perky, upbeat and clean-cut performers in their white outfits with red trim usually performed on the Tomorrowland Stage and sometimes the movable Tomorrowland Terrace stage. They also recorded a record album on Vista Records in 1968. Yes, they were integrated and there was an odd number so that if someone was ill or couldn't make it, there was always a spare back-up.

Choreographer for the group was a young Barnette Ricci who later went on to direct the original Disneyland's Main Street Electrical Parade in 1972; write/direct/choreograph *The Magical World of Disney* stage show at Radio City Music Hall with the Rockettes and 82 Disney costumed characters in 1985; and wrote the Disney Channel Christmas show *A Magical Kingdom Yuletide Special* that same year that featured Scrooge McDuck. Ricci also became the artistic creator and director of the original *Fantasmic!* in 1992 among many other credits.

She eventually became vice president/show director of Special Events.

In addition to all the entertainment, the year saw the debut of many special events, including the first St. Patrick's Day Parade and the first Cinco de Mayo Festival. On Easter Sunday, there was an Easter parade down Main Street with antique automobiles and more than 200 people dressed in turn-of-the-century finery. Easter week had 311,000 visitors.

Sixty private parties for companies like Bank of America, Pacific Telephone, and McDonnell Douglas during non-public hours filled up just about every Friday and Saturday evening up to the summer season. Fourteen of those were held on Sunday or weekday evenings. Attendance at some of these events exceeded 15,000 people.

By the way, the New Year's Eve Party that year saw 23,000 celebrating guests turn out. In 1967, there were only 18,000. Celebrity guests throughout the year included President Richard Nixon, Senator Robert F. Kennedy and Princess Magaretha of Sweden.

The eighth annual Grad Nite at Disneyland had more than 300 High Schools traveling by air from Northern California to Disneyland. Performers included the Joe Tex Orchestra Revue, the Levee Loungers,

Bill Elliott and the Disneyland Date Niters, the Five Americans, Sam the Sham Revue, the Clara Ward Gospel Singers, the Honey LTD., the Royal Tahitians, the Mustangs, the Young Men from New Orleans, the Spats, and the Enchilada Brass.

More than 76,000 high school seniors celebrated at five all night Grad Nite parties or approximately better than one of every three high school graduates in Southern California total that year.

The Disneyland/LAX Helicopter

Since July 6, 1954, people had been able to take a helicopter from the Burbank airport to Anaheim in about a third of the time it would take by automobile.

There were two Disneyland related major tragedies in 1968. The Disneyland/Los Angeles International Airport helicopter service suffered two of the worst civilian chopper crashes in U.S. history.

The first crash occurred on May 22, 1968, when N303Y was en route from Disneyland to LAX. At about 5:50 p.m., Flight 841 was flying near a Paramount dairy farm. A single missing bolt in the main rotor hub caused it to detach and struck the helicopter's fuselage and caused the other four rotor blades to go out of control. All 20 passengers who had spent the day enjoying Disneyland and the three-man crew were killed.

The second crash, on August 14, 1968, involved N300Y, operating as Flight 417 from LAX to Anaheim. One of the main rotor head spindles failed due to metal fatigue and the attached rotor blade separated completely. The resulting imbalance sent the helicopter out of control and it crashed in Leuders Park, killing all 18 passengers and three member crew.

The type of helicopter involved in both crashes was the Sikorsky S-61, operated by Los Angeles Airways, which had regular passenger service between Los Angeles International Airport and the Disneyland/Anaheim heliport. In 1963 the Disneyland Heliport was moved from the Disneyland Harbor Gate area to a parking lot annex on Winston Road, almost a mile away next to a golf drive range/parking lot. "Anaheim Disneyland Heliport" was a Transportation Center for buses/limos as well as L.A. Airways

The one-way fare was around $15 (although some airlines offered a massive discount to its passengers who wanted to add the service to their booked flight). Thousands used the service each year as well as private and military copters using the site as well.

However, local Anaheim motel owners had protested for years that the service was dangerous and the noise disturbed their guests. In

January 1968, they had petitioned the Anaheim City Council to limit the flights but the Council sided with Disney that the value far outweighed the "minor disadvantages" to residents.

Helicopter service ended in August 1972 and the bulldozed heliport became a parking lot for the Disneyland Hotel.

Mickey Mouse 40th Birthday

Disney Archivist Dave Smith determined through a program from the Colony Theater in New York that Mickey's first truly public appearance was in *Steamboat Willie* on November 18, 1928 and for the 50th birthday in 1978 that became the official birthday.

For the previous 50 years, the Disney Company selected any date from September through late November as Mickey Mouse's birthday primarily as a merchandising tool to encourage theaters to rent Mickey Mouse cartoons and to do special promotions like parties or to attract attention to a new film release.

Mickey's official birthday was celebrated at Disneyland on September 22, 1968 with nearly 35,000 guests in attendance including more than 11,000 of them being children.

There was a big birthday parade down Main Street with more than forty Disney characters and twelve of the original Mouseketeers from the original television *Mickey Mouse Club* show. Guest bands performed and there was the giant dancing birthday cake from Disneyland's Tencennial.

All children 11 years old and younger (the official Disneyland cutoff for a child's admission ticket) received some type of gift ranging from Schwinn bicycles, to Mickey Mouse 45 rpm singles and long playing (LP) records, half-gallons of Carnation ice cream, Revell Model Kits, Mattel Kola-Kiddle dolls, six pack cartons of Coca Cola, Whitman Tell-a-Tale books and Disneyland ticket books.

Many children had brought birthday cards and presents for Mickey, as well, primarily packages of cheese.

Disneyland Parking Lot

Six new parking lot trams replaced the old side seating trams that had been operating for over a decade. According to Bob MacKinnon, Manager of Main Street and Parking Lot Operations, the new trams were equipped with automatic shifts, air brakes, a public address (PA) system from driver to rear operator, a warning light buzzer system and improved mirrors for greater visibility for the driver.

The seating configuration was changed to forward seating with each car accommodating roughly 30 people and the entire tram now holding at least an additional 25 people total. Powered by a Clark tractor, the fiberglass five-string trams cost approximately $50,000 each.

In 1968, parking lot attendants parked 345,260 cars generally holding 3.7 people in each car. The cost for parking was fifty cents and surveys showed that eighty-one percent of the people that came to Disneyland came by car. On August 17, 1968 a record of 15,449 cars were parked in the 120 acre lot. Using a checkerboard rotation process, the crew was able to park more than 15,000 cars per day even though there were only 11,000 spaces.

Lighting

With all the added nighttime entertainment and later hours, especially for the summer, Dick Irvine worried about the lighting since Tomorrowland was way too bright while New Orleans Square with just its vintage light posts was way too dark. Imagineer Rolly Crump handled the changes in lighting for Frontierland and New Orleans Square. Imagineer Yale Gracey took on Main Street U.S.A., Tomorrowland and Fantasyland. Each night they would go out with a crew of electricians and make changes.

Decoration Department

In 1968, Disneyland had a Decorating Department with a staff of 21 men who were responsible for keeping the attention to detail up to Walt's high standards. Each trash can in the park was monitored and hand-painted at a cost of more than a $100 each.

The ones in Fantasyland were brightly colored while the ones in Frontierland had to resemble wood. They had extra trash cans back stage so they could pull ones from on stage to work on during the day.

They were also responsible for painting the park benches to keep them looking new, maintaining the awnings, curtains and banners. One person was assigned full time just to keeping the teepees, clothing, headdresses and more in the Indian Village always in shape.

They had extra shells and fish for the Submarine Voyage as well as extra awnings and curtains for all the shops. They had thousands of artificial flowers for use anywhere in the park. In spring 1968, the men voluntarily attended a series of classes in floral arrangement held after working hours.

1969

- Attendance: 9.3 million
- Employment: 5,510
- Payroll: $ $29,900,000
- Candlelight Processional Narrator: Cary Grant
- Disneyland Ambassador: Shari Bescos
- Admission: Adult ($3.50), Junior ($2.50), Child ($1.25)
- Highlights:
  - Herbie Day held March 23
  - Chicken of the Sea Pirate Ship renamed Captain Hook's Galley
  - On August 16, Disneyland hits a record attendance of 82,516 guests in one day.
  - The weekly television show *Walt Disney's Wonderful World of Color* ended in September to be replaced the following week with the *Wonderful World of Disney.*

The Monorail

The year introduced the new Mark III monorail train that ran on a brand new air-cushioned chassis, was lighter than its predecessors, had more power (four 100 horsepower traction motors) and offered a better view.

The trains were extended to 137 feet, allowing for five car trains with room to hold up to 127 guests. The two loading platforms also had to be extended to accommodate them. The entire upgrade cost $2.3 million.

The Mark III version of the Monorail began service at Disneyland in July 1969 and were red, blue, gold and green. The Mark III Monorails were replaced by Mark V models beginning in 1986. Mark IV Monorails were only at Walt Disney World.

Herbie Day

Dozens of Volkswagen Beetle cars drove down Main Street U.S.A. on March 23 as part of the Herbie Day celebration.

This special event was held to celebrate the release of Herbie's first movie *The Love Bug,* which premiered March 13, 1969. Complete with a creative contest and colorful parade, the event was a great success.

Volkswagen supported Love Bug Day at Disneyland, held March 23, 1969. Park attendance, according to Disney publicity went "up 10,000 from the estimated attendance and our marketing at the Park feel certain that much the same kind of contest will become an annual event, including all makes of cars and involving the Southern California Automobile Dealers Association as sponsor."

The cars were judged in four categories to simplify the judging: most psychedelic, toy-like, comical and best personality. There were 800 entries and 100 (25 finalists from each of the four categories) were selected to be paraded through Disneyland, led by Mickey Mouse and the Disneyland Band and costumed characters like the Big Bad Wolf, the Little Pigs and Alice in Wonderland scattered throughout the parade. Dean Jones sat on the curb in Town Square watching it all.

The decorating took place in the parking lot and then judged. The finalists then drove from the parking lot into Town Square and then up Main Street ending at It's a Small World. Most cars had faces, often with moving eyes (sometimes attached to the windshield wipers) and there were several rabbits because of Easter. One car was done up like Donald Duck, but didn't make it out of the parking lot.

Morton and Barbara Allen of Studio City, California, won the grand prize – a brand-new, fully-equipped 1969 Volkswagen Beetle (contributed by Volkswagen, along with $2,500 in gifts for the winners of the four categories and $25,000 in radio and newspaper advertising), with the keys presented by *The Love Bug* star Dean Jones. Jones joked he was going to keep the new car and started to put the keys in his pocket. Nearby were Goofy and Pluto.

The Sweepstakes-winning car was painted completely yellow and done up with a female face (eyes with eyelashes, slender nose, bright red lips) and a paisley-flowered skirt along the length on either side of the car. A sign on the side read: "Hi, I'm Li'l Squirt. I love Herbie but he don't love me. (Sob! Sob!) 'Cause look at all those sexy VWs he's flirting with."

One of the finalists did up their car to look like Mickey Mouse with huge black mouse ears on top and the eyes on the windshield. Several cars were done up like mice, and many others had Mickey Mouse drawings on them.

Other prizes included color televisions, Kodak Super-8 movie cameras and projectors, and new Polaroid cameras. In 1974, there was another Herbie Day at Disneyland and that was an hour-long special on local television KTTV Channel 11.

In the weekly *Wonderful World of Disney* television show episode *Disneyland Showtime* (March 1970), singer E.J. Peaker drives up to Disneyland in her decorated VW bug to be in the Love Bug parade and actor Kurt Russell tells her it was last year.

With the film a huge hit in theaters, Herbie was included in parades at Disneyland, as well as part of the new traveling show, *Disney on Parade*, starting December 25, 1969. At one point Herbie actually "walked" across a high wire as part of the show.

The top 100 finalists were allowed to park on Main Street U.S.A. during the day for guests to enjoy and ride through the park for a unique parade led by Herbie in the afternoon. A similar event was held June 30, 1974, to promote the release of *Herbie Rides Again*.

Moon Landing

While Disneyland premiered its new version of Tomorrowland in 1967, just two years later on July 20 real American astronauts walked on the moon for the first time.

The Apollo 11 moon landing was shown live to park guests in Tomorrowland on a special screen.

Apollo 11 landed the *Eagle* lunar module at roughly 1:15 pm Pacific time, and the moon walk began just before 8pm. Visitors swarmed the makeshift movie theater in the land's central plaza, almost exactly where Space Mountain would stand eight years later.

Captain Hook's Galley

The Chicken of the Sea Pirate Ship and Restaurant was a Disneyland landmark from 1955 until 1969, when the name changed to Captain Hook's Galley since Chicken of the Sea dropped its sponsorship of the location in 1969.

Imagineer Bruce Bushman came up with the original drawings for the eighty-foot tall wooden ship, intending it to be an exaggerated version of Captain Hook's vessel the *Jolly Roger* from the Disney animated feature *Peter Pan* (1953). Its striking black hull and red-striped sails made this Fantasyland icon very impressive as it sat in a small pond of water.

Instead of being an accurately scaled sailing ship, it was meant to be more fanciful with its oversized crow's nest on four tall masts and the red and white striped canvas sails to fit in with Fantasyland. The entire ship made of Douglas fir was built backstage at the Main Street Opera house mill and then lifted by a construction crane to be put in Fantasyland.

Grad Nite

Admission was now $9.00. Performers included The Righteous Brothers Starring Bobby Hatfield, Tommy Roe, Shango, Merrily Rush and The Turnabouts, The Willie Mitchell Soul Review, The Friends of Distinction, Pak, The Young Tahitians, Los Gallos, and The Sound Castle. A total of 58 Schools attended Grad Nite '69 on June 11th, 1969

The Haunted Mansion

"Ghosts, ghouls, witches and bats—all swaying and screaming to the eerie tune of "Grim Grinning Ghosts"—moved into Disneyland's new Haunted Mansion at midnight." —*Los Angeles Herald Examiner*, Tuesday August 12, 1969

Employee previews of the Mansion were held on the nights of August 7 and 8th from seven pm to midnight that ran so smoothly that it was followed by unannounced "soft" openings on Saturday August 9 and 10 where limited numbers of park guests were allowed to ride.

A "Midnight" Press Event was held on the evening of August 11 from 10:30 pm to midnight. Fifty members of the press were given a special press package upon their arrival at the park that included a "Press Ghost" pass attached to a small glow-in-the-dark skull (a "skeleton key") which would be worn throughout the evening. They began the late night by being wined and dined at Club 33 and then Disneyland Ambassador Shari Bescos escorted them to the attraction.

The mansion officially opened as advertised in the newspapers and the park to all guests the morning of August 12, 1969. However, today, the Walt Disney Company claims that August 9 was the real opening of the attraction since that was the first time that a handful of Disneyland guests experienced it.

Eerily, actress Sharon Tate was murdered along with others early Saturday morning, August 9, 1969 by the disciples of Charles Manson and that event overshadowed all other news that weekend.

While Walt reviewed many early concepts and previewed elements of the attraction on a 1965 episode entitled *Disneyland's Tenth Anniversary* on his weekly television show *The Wonderful World of Color*, he never saw the completed show and it was the first major Disney attraction to open without the direct supervision of Walt Disney.

More importantly, Walt was never quite satisfied with a storyline for the attraction and the final one that was presented when the attraction finally opened in 1969 was a hybrid of many different concepts that had been developed for over a decade.

Certainly, "haunted" dark ride experiences were popular in trolley parks and later amusement parks. The famous Haunted Preztel (because the ride track twisted back and forth like the shape of a pretzel) was built in 1927 for Bushkill Park in Pennsylvania. It featured scary heads popping up from the floor, a hallway of doors hiding who-knows-what, a body trying to get out of a coffin and more very similar experiences to what would later be in Disneyland's Haunted Mansion.

In 1958, Walt Disney gave an interview to the British Broadcasting Company to promote his upcoming changes to Disneyland. When Walt talked about the haunted house he mentioned that it would offer a home for all the ghosts displaced from Europe since their homes had been destroyed during World War II.

By 1959, Walt assigned Yale Gracey and Rolly Crump to the project and they started by looking at all the sketches, storylines and other ideas that had already been developed. Walt himself would drop by to visit them and see how the work was progressing. Gracey and Crump concentrated on effects and not necessarily developing a storyline for showcasing them.

The exterior façade was built at the park in 1962 at the urging of Disneyland art director Harvey T. Gillett who drew almost all of the technical drawings necessary for the structure and created a layout for the construction.

However, the exterior was merely a shell with some small workspaces, a large foyer and two enormous Otis elevators because it had been determined that the show building would be across the railroad tracks so guests needed to be lowered to be able to walk under the tracks.

In early 1962, although the final storyline and effects were still not determined and the attraction was still planned as a walking tour, a brochure distributed at the park gates to help explain the construction and walls for curious guests stated that Walt was intending to bring New Orleans to Anaheim.

It claimed that Walt already had "talent scouts" out gathering the "world's greatest collection of ghosts" for the attraction to open in 1963. However, those plans were fortunately interrupted because Walt and his staff turned all their attention to developing and building four attractions for the upcoming New York World's Fair.

It was fortunate because those attractions resulted in the development of human audio-animatronics figures and an omnimover ride system that would later be utilized in the final attraction making it more effective.

In the 1964 Disneyland souvenir book, Imagineer Marty Sklar wrote, "Overlooking the Rivers of America in Frontierland, the facade of an old southern-style plantation house has already been completed. It will be occupied several years hence. No frontier setting would be complete without its ghosts of another day.

"Disneyland's will not live in a ghost town; they will occupy a deluxe haunted mansion. Here, the lonely ghost who seeks the companionship of 1,001 restless spirits can live in a domain of illusion and imagination.

"There will be spine-tingling built-ins that are sure to provide new life for even the most sagging spirits: fresh cobwebs daily, wall-to-wall creaking floors, stereophonic screams, cold drafts and midnight lighting all day long - plus an endless supply of guests on whom the inventive spooks can practice individual talents, from simple scares to supernatural shockers!"

It was Walt who came up with the phase "1,001 ghosts" to reference the popular book *1,001 Arabian Nights* and on the aerial map of Disneyland in his working office at the Disney Studio the construction area for the attraction was identified as the home for 1,001 ghosts. It wasn't until later that the concept of 999 ghosts looking for a guest to become number one-thousand became the theme.

However, the empty building still sparked curiosity, especially when Sklar also wrote a plaque placed outside of the gates that stated: "Notice! All Ghosts and Restless Spirits. Post-lifetime leases are now available in this Haunted Mansion!... For reservations, send resume of past experience to: Ghost Relations Dept., Disneyland. Please! Do not apply in person!"

Ghost Relations was a reference to Disneyland's Guest Relations department. Disneyland was indeed flooded with applications from around the world and sometimes physical items like the mask head of a Japanese ghost.

After the New York World's Fair, completion of the Haunted Mansion was once again delayed by the installation of some of the fair's Disney attractions at the park, the opening of Pirates of the Caribbean attraction and the opening of the New Tomorrowland in 1967. In addition, the death of Walt Disney in 1966 and the commitment to the Florida Project were also involved in the delay.

Despite those many legitimate reasons, because the façade had been standing for years behind locked iron glad gates, rumors arose that the attraction was indeed finished but it was too horrifying and someone in a test audience had been scared to death and suffered a heart attack. Different versions listed the victim as a reporter, a woman or an elderly man. Supposedly, Disney was desperately trying to readjust the ride.

Imagineers Claude Coats, Marc Davis and X. Atencio who had all been integral in the creation of the Pirates of the Caribbean attraction were assigned to the Haunted Mansion but Coats and Davis had vastly opposing views as to the tone of the attraction.

Coats wanted a scary adventure, and produced renditions of moody surroundings like endless hallways, corridors of doors and numerous characterless environments. He felt that guests would expect something scary from an attraction that was supposedly haunted.

Davis was well known for adding humorous characters and scenes in Disneyland attractions like the Jungle Cruise and Pirates of the Caribbean. He sketched countless gags. He felt that Walt would have wanted a family attraction where the entire family could ride it together.

While writer Atencio was able to accommodate both approaches in his final script as well as the effects created by Gracey and Crump, the attraction still walked a thin tightrope between being darkly foreboding and silly-spirited. It was Atencio who came up with the idea that the ghosts were there to socialize rather than terrorize as they gathered for a swinging wake.

By April 1969, the storyline and what would be in the individual scenes was finally locked down. WED's public relations manager Frank Allnutt wrote a detailed confidential memo that named each character and scene that would appear.

A sign designed to look like a tombstone was placed in front of the iron gates to announce the impending opening of the Haunted Mansion in late summer of 1969. It read, in part... "999 Ghosts and Restless Spirits have chosen active retirement in the Haunted Mansion. Should you desire to become number 1000, visiting privileges begin late summer 1969..." At the bottom was the promise it would scare "the daylights out of you."

On August 5, 1969 just days before the opening of the attraction, a memo was sent to head of Imagineering Dick Irvine from Marty Sklar. Sklar worried that "we have not as yet given this car an appropriate name and I would like to send one to the Park as soon as possible."

Attached to the memo was a list, prepared by Imagineer Bob White, of possible names for the Omnimover that he had collected from other Imagineers at WED.

Some of the names listed were Ghostmobile, Ghost Coach, Phantomobile, Banshee Buggy, Seance Conveyance, and Ghostly Hostmobile. One suggestion got the highest number of votes: Doom Buggy.

As Sklar later explained, at the time California Beach surfing culture used a "dune buggy" as a form of transportation so it was felt the name would resonate with young people.

The narrator, or "Ghost Host," merely referred to the ride vehicle as a "carriage... carrying you to the boundless realm of the supernatural" because the name had not been locked down in time for the recording by Paul Frees.

Promotional articles and teaser photos were sent to newspapers all across the country, and the official storyline was centered around the theme that 999 famous and infamous ghosts had moved in to enjoy an active retirement but with every Disneyland guest having the potential of becoming the one-thousandth.

The final press release said the Haunted Mansion cost seven million dollars to build and took ten years to develop. It said the attraction had a potential ride capacity of 2,616 per hour (assuming two people per doom buggy).

Disneyland's publicity department created a strong advertising campaign, including outdoor advertising and radio spots in addition to the standard print advertising and reports from the newspaper press.

The radio ads included humor in effort to defuse any potential fears. They featured "in spirit interview" with residents of the manor including a flirtatious Granny Ghoul, Phineas Pock who had died in 1720 and Willie DeWisp, the dead Olympic "hide-and-seek champion".

Billboard advertising featured characters like a headless knight frightening an old property caretaker. Early marketing was designed to increase people's curiosity and emphasizing the characters in order to distinguish it as different than the typical spook house at carnivals and fairs.

Just one week after the Mansion opened, Disneyland set a one day attendance record on August 16 of 82,516 guests eager to enjoy the new experience. In general at that time, weekday attendance at the park was roughly 30,000 that increased to approximately 50,000 on the weekends.

It set a daily attendance record that was maintained for eighteen years. That second weekend there was a minimum three hour wait to ride the attraction and the line snaked all the way to the Hub.

Disneyland also celebrated the attraction with various promotions, souvenirs and mementos including the co-branded Carnation "I Scream" Sundae, which came complete with a little red plastic spoon picturing the heads of the three hitchhiking ghosts and the phrase "visit the Haunted Mansion" etched into the handle. It was only available during the early months the attraction was open and it was advertised by large silk-screened posters throughout the park.

Disneyland quickly stocked some imported tin lithographed haunted house banks (each with a battery-operated ghost to grab the coin) and slapped some decals on imported Japanese Ichimatsu puzzle boxes in three different sizes from a small company in Hikone, Japan.

The Randotti Company produced plaster skulls and customizable miniature (four inches wide, eight inches tall) plaster tombstones that could be customized with a guest's name while Disneyland's Main Street Magic Shop started selling all sorts of spooky items including a special booklet of simple magic tricks called *Magic from the Haunted Mansion*.

While these items and others were only available at the park, Disney produced records, coloring books, puzzles and even a game that could be purchased by the general public.

Knowing that Walt Disney World was to open in 1971, when Disneyland's Haunted Mansion was being built, to save money, duplicates of interior items were made at the same time and put in storage. As a result the Haunted Mansion at Walt Disney World was completed months before the official opening date for that park.

Dick Irvine said, "Walt's philosophy was that we would be reaching a different audience in each park so that anything new that was developed could go in both places."

For Disneyland's New Year's Eve party of 1969, the new Haunted Mansion was prominently featured on all publicity material, out shining the headliner band, the Everly Brothers.

The popularity of the attraction has proven timeless, enchanting new generations of audiences and generating new merchandise.

1970

- Attendance: 10.3 million
- Employment: 6,200
- Payroll: $31,300,00
- Candlelight Processional Narrator: Charlton Heston (Saturday), Dean Jones (Sunday)
- Disneyland Ambassador: Cathy Birk
- Highlights:
    - The Legacy of Walt Disney display opens on Main Street U.S.A.
    - The Aunt Jemima Kitchen restaurant closes
    - The tenth and final annual Dixieland at Disneyland show is held

The Walt Disney Company's attention and finances were focused on opening Walt Disney World in Florida in 1971. Imagineer Marty Sklar told me in an interview, "We just didn't have the manpower to work on Disneyland and it wasn't the focus of the company at that time. It later became a problem that our attention was so focused on Walt Disney World that we had to go back and clean up a lot of things that were happening at Disneyland."

For the summer to celebrate Disneyland's 15th anniversary, over 500 performers were booked and the park budgeted over $1.5 million dollars for entertainment. More than five million guests attended from late May through early September. By September 19, ten million guests had already visited the park.

Show Me America was a fast-paced musical comedy that combined favorite tunes and humor and was performed on the Tomorrowland stage. More than 120 lavish costumes were made and showcased against spectacular stage settings. It contained musical comedy combined with favorite tunes, old and new, and plenty of humor. At the premiere performance sixty members of the press gave it a standing ovation. It closed September 12 after 124 performances.

A new exhibit, *Walt Disney: A Legacy for the Future* was opened in the Wurlitzer shop on Main Street Town Square on January 15. The exhibit featured 208 awards given to Walt during his lifetime and a six minute film highlighting the California Institute of the Arts (CalArts) that was scheduled to open that fall. The exhibit remained until 1973.

The park described it as "a multi-screen film show and display presenting Walt Disney's endeavors in the fields of art and education. Included are plans for his cherished dream, California Institute of the Arts, and the first public display of all 29 Academy Awards received during his lifetime."

Cathy Birk

Twenty year old Cathy Birk was a former tour guide before being selected from among sixty candidates to be the new Disneyland Ambassador.

Born in Paris, France on March 23, 1949, it was stated that she enjoyed playing the piano, sewing, horseback riding and furniture antiquing. She lived in Anaheim with her parents and twin brother, Serge. Her first responsibility was a two week tour to promote the Fantasy on Parade holiday parade.

In early June, she did a two month tour of major European cities in Ireland, France, Denmark, Norway, Spain, Switzerland, Germany, Holland, England, Belgium and Sweden. She reconnected with relatives in Paris.

Primarily she promoted Mickey Mouse's Anniversary Show, a compilation of Mickey Mouse theatrical shorts that was released throughout Europe that summer.

She said, "It's one thing to travel through Europe as a tourist but it's another to travel as the official representative of a place like Disneyland. There's just an extra sense of pride in representing the world of Fantasy and Magic for thousands of people."

A Troubled Year

On July 17, one hundred and thirty of Disneyland's original staff were brought together for a special celebration. It was determined that their combined service to Disneyland guests totaled more than 1,950 years.

However it was a time of unrest.

Eighty members of the American Guild of Variety Artists and 48 members of the International Alliance of Theatrical Stage Employees stage a strike at the Disneyland gates, seeking higher wages. This was the first employee strike in the park's fifteen-year history. Strikers marched with picket signs paraded outside Disneyland seeking higher wages and better working conditions. The strike lasted twenty-two days.

On September 6, stagehands, projectionists and sound equipment workers struck at Disneyland, but supervisory personnel took over and all attractions remained open. The strike, by members of Local 504 of the International Alliance of theatrical Stage Employes, was over the need for higher wages.

Yippie Invasion

According to the *Los Angeles Times* newspaper:

"ANAHEIM, Calif., Aug. 6--HIPPIE DISTURBANCE CLOSES DISNEYLAND--Police wearing flak jackets seal off sections of Disneyland as officials closed the famed Anaheim, Calif., amusement park tonight because of demonstrations by hippie-types, who had announced they wanted to 'liberate' Disneyland as a symbol of the establishment. There were arrests. About 29,000 people were in the park when the closing was announced."

During the summer of its fifteenth anniversary in 1970, Disneyland found itself in a unique situation where it was invaded by roughly three hundred counter culture young revolutionaries who effectively shut down the park.

The Yippie Invasion that took place Thursday August 6, 1970 was a major disturbance and a nuisance but basically it was not dangerous or violent until the end. There was some vandalism to landscaping, buildings and cars in the parking lot, some very upsetting language and filling the free Adventures Thru Inner Space attraction with dense marijuana smog.

The Yippies openly smoked joints almost everywhere in the park and some were involved with using harder drugs like acid.

While there had been some protests around the United States, Orange County in Anaheim was still highly conservative with a member of the John Birch Society, John Schmitz, representing the district in Congress. Richard Nixon was the president and a strong advocate for traditional American values.

A strict Disney Look set of guidelines for cast members including no facial hair or long hair for men was strictly enforced. An informal and unwritten dress code for guests entering the park was sporadically executed that forbid men with hair that seemed too long or wearing jeans with holes. Women who wore mini skirts that were too short or halter tops were sometimes denied entry.

While hippies were still an active part of the culture, The Youth International Party (YIP) better known as "Yippies" had become prominent in reaction to the stereotypes of the hippie movement being co-opted by main stream marketing, merchandise and the media.

Established in December 1967 by radicals Jerry Rubin and Abbie Hoffman, the movement employed street theater theatrics and pranks to advance its anti-authoritarian agenda and protests against the

Vietnam War. Their actions were intended to mock the establishment by doing silly things in public venues. The group was sometimes jokingly referred to as the Groucho Marxists.

Notices began appearing the *Los Angeles Free Press* in early July of a Yippie get-together at Disneyland for August sixth. Five hundred flyers (not the 10,000 usually cited) were distributed through the usual local underground channels like shops, newspapers and activities by Yippie leaders David Sacks and Michael Dale.

August 6, 1970 was chosen as the date for the event because it marked the 25th anniversary of the bombing of Hiroshima.

Disneyland has always been a high profile target. In this case, the Yippies saw it as representing the evils of capitalism and would be a very visible forum to publicize its protest of the ongoing war in Vietnam.

Among the Yippies' grievances was Bank of America who prominently sponsored the It's a Small World attraction in the park but also supported the Vietnam War including financially. A Bank of America near the UC Santa Barbara campus had been torched in an earlier antiwar protest.

The Disneyland protest would also include demonstrations against the supposed racist and anti-feminist values expressed in Disneyland in addition to the park's arbitrary dress code for guests that had already started to be relaxed years earlier and allowed some of the long-haired protestors to gain entry to the park.

The flyer listed the itinerary for the day:

> "Black Panther Hot Breakfast: 9am—10am at Aunt Jemima's Pancake House

> "Young Pirates League: 11am on Captain Hook's boat

> "Women's Liberation: 12 noon rally to liberate Minnie Mouse in front of Fantasyland

> "Self Defense Collective: 1pm—2pm at shooting gallery in Frontierland

> "Mid-Day Feast: 3pm barbecue of Porky Pig

> "Late in the afternoon Yippies plan to infiltrate and liberate Tom Sawyer's Island. Declaring a free state, brothers and sisters will then have a smoke-in and festival.

> "Get it on over to Disneyland, August 6. YIPPIE!"

Sacks just created the itinerary off the top of his head, trying to incorporate some of the humor that was the trademark of the group. After all, Porky Pig was not a Disney character but an icon of Warner Brothers cartoons.

Although a small handful of people (but no members of the Black Panthers) did apparently show up uneventfully for the breakfast with an occasional raised fist salute, the only listed activities that actually occurred was the boarding of the Captain Hook pirate ship in Fantasyland and the storming of Tom Sawyer's Island.

Of the 27,400 Disneyland guests who purchased admission that day, only 200 to 300 might be classified as Yippies. The *Berkeley Tribe* undergound newspaper had speculated that "up to 100,000 dope-crazed, bizarro Yippies and Yippie-symps" would descend on Disneyland.

Not even Hoffman or Rubin showed up leaving the group more or less directionless. Even the organizers themselves admitted that at least half of that number was composed of merely apolitical curiosity seekers who showed up to score some marijuana, get high at the park with some others and just have a little fun.

That small turnout was a disappointment to the organizers, the police, and the press but was still an annoyance to the families who had looked forward to a pleasant vacation day at Disneyland.

Despite fears that the group would climb the fences and walls surrounding the park to get in, all of them who entered Disneyland paid full admission and entered through the turnstiles. Some of them carried banners and banners of any kind were not allowed to be brought on to the property so they were turned away.

Those who appeared suspicious or were dressed in hippie style clothing were pulled aside at the turnstiles and their bags searched. They were advised that if they were just there to have fun like everyone else they were certainly welcome. However, if they had come to make any type of trouble, they would be asked to leave the park.

Up to that time, the Disneyland security philosophy had been to be non-confrontational and to patiently defuse all situations except in cases like extreme drunkenness where it might become a danger to other guests.

A few dozen Yippies appeared throughout the day outside the gates protesting loudly that private property should be outlawed and turned down Vice President Dick Nunis' offer of a discounted group admission of fifty cents per person to enter. Normal adult admission at that time was $3.50.

There had been a dozen meetings on the strategy to use that day especially in light of what had happened earlier in Chicago when the police overreacted to protestors.

On that Monday, three days before the event, Disneyland leaders Dick Nunis, Ron Dominguez and Jim Cora held a meeting of all park supervisors in the Mickey Mouse Theater in Fantasyland to give out assignments and to be briefed by an Anaheim police officer.

Some were given "plainsclothes" assignments to "blend in" with the crowd on Thursday and monitor any activity and report with concealed walkie-talkies in bags and wrapped packages using a special code that had been developed to call for backup.

Nunis contacted all the local newspapers, radio and television stations to ask them not to give any advance publicity to the reported event and that he would establish a media room that day in the administration building behind Main Street where they could gather. A special command and communications center was set up backstage.

Hundreds of police officers from Anaheim and Fullerton among other cities gathered backstage of Main Street starting before the park even opened. Additional staging areas were at the Disneyland Hotel and the Anaheim Convention Center.

El Toro Marine Base supplied a company of Marines with more awaiting orders to fly in by helicopter if necessary. Security patrols paced on the top of buildings. In retrospect, Disneyland may have been too overly prepared.

Everyone was expecting an overwhelming contingent of drugged out young people who were capable of doing anything. Additional cast members were required to work that day to look for possible bombs.

A small smoke bomb was found inside of It's a Small World attraction. Special courts were set up in case they had to handle mass arrests and the National Guard was told to stand ready in case things really got out of hand.

Two Bank of America security officers dressed as tourists spent the day taking photos of anyone in or near the bank.

The day started without any major incident with guests generally ignoring and avoiding the colorful young people who gathered in groups. Disneyland managers and even Nunis himself would approach groups that gathered in the park and begged them to "be cool" and to be respectful of the families who came to visit the Happiest Place on Earth that day.

There were a few minor scuffles, mostly shoving, throughout the day but never anything significant that was reported. Most of the Yippies found themselves shadowed by polite, soft-spoken Disneyland personnel who despite their efforts to be inconspicuous were easily spotted with the Yippies pointing at them and yelling, "Narc!"

In articles and editorials, Disneyland management was praised for initially taking a hands-off approach to try to prevent the potential powder keg from exploding and only resorted to a deliberate show of force when things started to get out of hand. Cast members were lauded for their patience in dealing with the unruly guests.

Dick Nunis was so reassured that Disneyland had averted a crisis and an embarrassment that he actually held a 3:20pm press briefing saying that the Yippies "weren't that different than other kids throughout the country. They may look a little different, but they are just here to have fun. Maybe we ought to listen to them a little more. "

However, as that hot summer day dragged on things became more interesting. A group of about thirty got up on the second floor deck of the Chicken of the Sea restaurant in Fantasyland that was in the shape of Captain Hook's pirate ship.

They climbed the mast, got up in the rigging, got stoned, sang, chanted and shouted obscenities but none of that prevented guests from ordering food on the first floor.

When the Disneyland Band came marching down Main Street, a group of Yippies started singing their own rendition of *Zip-a-Dee-Doo-Dah*, while running in-between the musicians to throw them off. They began singing *The Mickey Mouse March* along with *We Are Marching to Cambodia*. The band fearing that the activity might result in the marching musicians getting a horn mouthpiece to the teeth among other things retreated backstage.

About four o'clock a group met inside the Main Street Cinema and devised a plan to take over Tom Sawyer Island.

Around five o'clock, several raft loads of Yippies boarded Tom Sawyer Island and took over Fort Wilderness where they lowered the American flag and replaced it with a Viet Cong flag. They chanted "Free Charlie Manson!" and "Legalize marijuana!" while they got stoned, sang and played Frisbee. To contain the situation, the park stopped sending rafts to the island and only offered transportation off the location.

Some contemplated skinny dipping but they saw some security hiding in the bushes and decided to try it later although one security report indicated some guy running around the area naked.

Disneyland executives were concerned that the Yippies would remain on the island past the dusk curfew and perhaps hide in the rough terrain and wait for the park to close to reappear and cause chaos. However, the group got bored and someone suggested that they storm the Bank of America on Main Street which might get them more attention and publicity so they left the island.

As they marched toward Town Square, their ranks swelled with others as they sang about sex, drugs and rock 'n' roll including "LSD has a hold on me." They held hands and snaked their way down the street while the sidewalks on both sides were lined with disbelieving police.

City Hall cast members formed a chain outside of the building and locked the doors so that the Yippies could be turned away. A crowd of guests gathered on the steps of the train station and in Town Square and began singing *God Bless America*. The Yippies tried to drown them out by shouting obscenities to no avail.

When the Yippies decided to walk back up Main Street, Nunis appeared and told them it was all over and that Disneyland had gone out of its way but it was time for them to leave the park. They were no longer welcome at the Happiest Place on Earth.

Rather than exiting, some of the Yippies broke through the security line and dispersed throughout the park, forcing Nunis to call out the police contingent waiting backstage. Announcements were made that due to the behavior of some people, the park was closing early. It would officially close at 7:10pm.

The police and Disneyland cast members and executives cleared the park section by section. It took a solid two hours to do so. Those who remained on Main Street started shoving people, getting into arguments and insults and it all escalated into fights.

As David Sacks recalled in a letter to Disney historian Dave De Caro: "They got to City Hall, where they have the American flag on a flag post. And there was an empty flag post. Someone pulled out a so-called Yippie flag, red and black with a green marijuana leaf, and started to raise it on the flagpole.

"An Orange County redneck came storming up to them and said "How dare you raise that flag next to the American flag!" And someone else went to the other flagpole as this guy was trying to rip down the Yippie flag, and said 'If you rip down our flag we'll rip down your flag.'

"He started to try to untie the American flag to bring it down. At which point fisticuffs broke out and Orange County's finest appeared out from behind all the buildings of Disneyland, 800 police in brand new yellow riot gear (this was the first chance that Orange County had had to test out their new riot gear). These guys looked like something out of a comic book.

"It looked hi-tech before that was even a word. All of a sudden, the whole circle promenade was circled with these police."

Some succeeded in tearing down the red-white-and blue bunting on City Hall. When the police marched out in formation, the guests watched and cheered.

Soon after, an intimidating sheriff's helicopter from Anaheim City Hall was hovering over Main Street, as a policeman with a bullhorn ordered everyone below that Disneyland was now closed and they needed to exit. As it got dark, the helicopter remained aloft shining a light on the ground to try to find any Yippies that might be hiding.

When I interviewed Bill "Sully" Sullivan in 2007 about his time at Disneyland, he told me, "I still remember that day clearly. Flyers had been distributed so we were prepared. The police were there to keep things running smoothly.

"Dick Nunis was running the park and Roy O. Disney had told him 'Don't let them shut us down'. During the disturbance, Dick grabbed one guy by his long hair and yanked him backstage and his wig came off! He was a Secret Service agent or something in disguise who was there to keep an eye on things.

"Another time, Dick grabbed one in a headlock and pushed him toward one of the big heavy doors leading off stage. He used the guy's head to open the door. Some other guy tried to pull down the American flag on Main Street and Dick punched him right in the face."

Disneyland had a Plan B. All of the supervisors reported to their assigned perimeter positions to prevent any Yippies from trying to climb fences and re-enter the park. They were given long steel poles to bash fingers of anyone trying to climb the fence.

The police eventually herded the Yippies out of the park into the parking lot, often physically tossing out any who resisted. This action incensed the group who began swearing, chanting, spitting, and harassing the departing guests. They shouted to burn the park.

They set trash cans on fire, setting off firecrackers. Venting their frustration, they threw light bulbs and uprooted plants and flowers from landscaping by the turnstiles at the police and guests who were exiting and trying to find their cars. Some vandalized several cars in the parking lot, generally breaking off the antennas.

Some broke away and dashed to the Disneyland Hotel to try and take that over, but were intercepted by police cars. Outmatched, the Yippies scattered in all directions as the police gave chase.

Disneyland's sprinklers were turned on at night to flush out any hiding Yippies. Six Yippies who had been hiding to create more mischief once the park was closed were flushed out with sprinklers around 10pm.

Disneyland officials assured all the guests who had been forceably evicted that the price of their admission tickets would be cheerfully refunded the following morning at any ticket booth. General admission for adults was $3.50 and for juniors $2.50. Attraction tickets, of course, were always valid anytime so were not refunded.

The original news reports claimed that eighteen people were arrested but the final count was twenty-three on a variety of charges including assault, disturbing the peace, drug possession, trespassing (since they had refused to leave) and generally causing mischief. No serious injuries were reported.

By midnight it was determined that all the Yippies had been removed and the place was secure so the remaining cast members and police officers were sent home.

The next day, Disneyland security was even more diligent about screening guests to prevent any re-occurrence of the prior day's events. Many were denied entry who would have been let in weeks earlier. For several months, Disneyland strictly enforced its appearance guidelines for guests.

1971

- Attendance: 9.4 million
- Employment: 5,900
- Payroll: $33,200,000
- Candlelight Processional Narrator: John Wayne
- Disneyland Ambassador: Marva Dickson
- Highlights:
    - Indian War Canoes renamed Davy Crockett's Explorer Canoes
    - Firehouse Five Plus Two disbands
    - Roy Disney dies December 20

In 1971, all the attention and resources of the Walt Disney Company were still focused on getting Walt Disney World in Florida up and running by the first of October. No new attractions would open at the Happiest Place on Earth but a handful of things would close.

The River Belle Terrace restaurant opened in Frontierland with the Oscar Mayer Company as sponsor but it really wasn't a new restaurant. It was simply a revamping of the Aunt Jemima's Pancake House that had been there since 1955 and later called Aunt Jemima's Kitchen, and after the sponsor pulled out, for a year it was known as Magnolia Tree Terrace.

Supposedly starting in the early days of Disneyland, the restaurant invented the popular Mickey Mouse pancakes that continued for the rest of its existence.

The All-American College Band first performed at Disneyland in June 14, 1971 as part of the four day President's Holiday where the park held its lavish red-white-and-blue "I Am an American" ceremonies in Town Square. It allowed talented college musicians from across the country to perform at one of the parks for the summer season and continued for many years.

The world's biggest New Year's Eve party was celebrated with 23,000 guests on hand, the largest number in Disneyland history. The first week of February, GAF shot television commercials in the park with spokesperson Henry Fonda and GAF sent a letter stating "the cooperation was tremendous" to the maintenance, operations, security and marketing staff at Disneyland.

The Disneyland Comic Convention was held April 9-11 at the Disneyland Hotel with creator Jack Kirby drawing the cover of the program book with his escape artist character Mister Miracle being captured by Grumpy the dwarf.

Cliff Edwards, the voice of Jiminy Cricket, died on July 17. The Firehouse Five Plus Two band at Disneyland disbands after its official final performance at an auto show at the Anaheim Convention Center in 1971. Dick Nunis becomes executive vice president of Disneyland.

In Anaheim, the Southern California Visitors Council and other organizations were worried that WDW would severely impact attendance and revenue on the West Coast. In fact in 1971, attendance at Disneyland slipped to just 7.8 million guests from the previous year's ten million guests and local hotel bookings around Disneyland dropping more than ten percent from the previous year.

It was hoped that since Disneyland's attendance was primarily repeat local visitors that the impact would not be too great and that only ten percent of its guests came from east of the Mississippi since those people would be more likely to go to WDW instead of California.

One Hundred Millionth Guest

Sixteen years after Disneyland first opened it celebrated an attendance milestone. On June 17, the park welcomed its 100 millionth guest.

Valerie Suldo from New Brunswick, New Jersey was a twenty-two year old payroll clerk who was visiting the park for the first time. She was accompanied by her sister and brother-in-law, Mr. and Mrs. Stan Wyluda of San Diego who she was visiting. Miss Suldo walked through the turnstile at 11:13 a.m. and was surprised to be greeted by newsmen and flashing camera bulbs.

"I just couldn't believe it and still don't. It's by far the biggest thing that's ever happened to me," she said.

Disneyland's Director of Marketing Jack Lindquist hosted the ceremonies in front of the Town Square railroad station. Suldo received a Silver Pass to Disneyland and Walt Disney World (good for admission to both parks and all their attractions for a party of four), a hundred dollars in Bank of America traveler's checks, a United Air Lines personal credit card with a hundred dollars credit on it, a complete GAF movie camera outfit, a one year supply of Kal Kan pet food for her dog, a one year supply of coffee from Hills Brothers Coffee, a one year supply of Coca-Cola plus several Coca-Cola premium products, a selection of Pepsi-Cola/Frito products, and a symbolic plaque from Pacific Telephone and the Bell Telephone System commemorating her historic visit.

After the ceremony, she was accompanied by the Disneyland Band, Disney costumed characters and news reporters during her ride up Main Street to Sleeping Beauty Castle where she was the first signer of a special guest book prepared for the occasion. That book filled with other guest signatures collected that day was placed in the Disney Archives.

Disneyland had anticipated it would reach this goal so had already put in place the promotional theme of Festival of 100 Million Smiles.

Other Events

The usual events like Date Nite and Candlelight Ceremony still took place.

The popular Country Music Jubilee that had started in 1966 returned over several different Sundays during the summer (June 20, June 27, July 11, 18,, 25 Aug. 1, 8, 15, 22, 29) performing three times a night with popular Country Western singing stars like Conway Twitty, Buck Owens, and Tex Ritter.

This was followed by a one night Country Music Spectacular on October 16 from 8:30pm to 1:30 am. Country Western music stars performed on the Tomorrowland Stage and square dancing was featured at various locations throughout the park. It proved so popular that it continued for several years.

Some weekends were dedicated to Disney animated characters with a parade, a show and meet and greet opportunities: Snow White and the Seven Dwarfs Days (Jan. 9 -10), Dumbo Days (Jan.16-17), Peter Pan Days (Jan. 23-24), Alice in Wonderland Days (Jan. 30-31), Jungle Book Days (Feb. 6-7), Mary Poppins Days (Feb.20-21), Donald Duck Days (Feb. 27-28), Sleeping Beauty Days (March 6-7), Winnie the Pooh Days (April 17-18), Aristocats Days (April 24-25), Pinocchio Days (May 15-16), Mickey Mouse Fun Days (Oct. 24-25).

Cinderella Festival

Disneyland's Cinderella Festival took place from Wednesday through Friday March 3, 4, and 5. A special elaborate and beautiful 24-page pamphlet was produced for the event.

Why a Cinderella Festival? Cinderella Castle would be opening in Walt Disney World in about six months and Disney had just celebrated the 20th anniversary of the release of the original animated feature in 1970. In addition, Cinderella has always been one of the most fashion conscious of the Disney princesses.

The Cinderella Festival Program stated:

"A Royal Proclamation. Be it known throughout the land...To all loyal subjects...That every maid and matron entering the Happy Kingdom of Disneyland for the joyous Cinderella Festival shall be eternally a Cinderella in her own personal realm and shall be afforded all due homage and affection from her subjects.

"And be it further known that every Cinderella at this Festival named in her honor is hereby invited to attend all special events, including fashion shows and garden tours, described herein.

"She is also granted the royal privilege of bearing the Secret Palace Recipes, also published in this document.

"And finally, by royal command, every Cinderella of the realm shall, from this day forward, retain as personal possessions all the joy and merriment of the Kingdom of Disneyland...and she shall live happily ever after.

"Signed and sealed by Prince Charming of the Blood Royal."

The festivities included the following:

- Cinderella '71 Fashion Show presented by Bullock's (Tomorrowland Stage: 11 a.m., 1 p.m., 3 p.m.)

- The Way-Out Cinderella Fashion Show presented by Monsanto (Tomorrowland Terrace: 11:30 a.m., 1:30 p.m., 3:30 p.m.)

- The Casual Cinderella Fashion Show presented by Pendleton Mills (Golden Horseshoe, Frontierland: 12:30 p.m., 2:30 p.m., 4:30 p.m.)

- Cinderella's Small World of Fashions presented by Children's Wardrobes by Sears, which focused on Winnie the Pooh (Plaza Gardens, Main Street Plaza: Noon, 2 p.m., 4 p.m.)

- In Cinderella's Garden, Guided Tours of Landscape Settings (Fantasyland Theater: 11 a.m., 1 p.m., 3 p.m.)

In addition, prior to noon each day at the Main Entrance and Main Street U.S.A., every day of the Festival a female guest was crowned Princess Cinderella.

Her Royal Treasury included: Choice of five outfits from the fashion shows, $500 dollars to the organization of her choice, landscaping services for her own "castle," coronation luncheon for her and her guests and from Bullock's La Habra, a new "coiffure," and a special Polly Bergen make-up kit.

For Cinderella's Royal Feast:

"From kitchens in all parts of the Kingdom of Disneyland...from exotic places over the horizons...even from the realms of Make-Believe...have come irresistible culinary specialties to grace the banquet tables before Their Highnesses. By Command of the Palace, secrets of these delicacies are being made known to all loyal subjects and are herein published for their benefit and enjoyment.

"Since every one of these delights is served everyday throughout Disneyland, it is the expressed wish and hope of The Regal Couple that families everywhere will find some of Disneyland's happiness and joy served regularly at their tables whenever these mealtime mementos of visits to the Happiest Kingdom are served."

The pamphlet included recipes for Shrimp Tempura and Tempura Batter, Cantonese Fried Rice, and Chow Yuk (Adventureland); New Orleans Square Clam Chowder, Seafood Jambalaya, Seafood Creole, and Monte Cristo Sandwich and Batter (New Orleans Square); Spaghetti Meat Sauce (Main Street U.S.A.); and Fantasia Cheese Cake, Magic Kingdom Burger (including, interestingly enough, both a half ounce of Thousand Island dressing and an ounce of French dressing on its toasted sesame hamburger bun), and German Chocolate Cake (Fantasyland).

Guests could get a complimentary recipe book from the Carnation Company (offered at the Main Street Carnation Ice Cream Parlor and Carnation Plaza Gardens); one from Frito-Lay (at Casa de Fritos in Frontierland); one from Sunsweet Growers Inc. and Quaker Oats (at the Main Street Market House); one from the Sunkist Growers Inc. (at the Sunkist Citrus House on Main Street and the Sunkist—I Presume— in Adventureland); and, finally, one from Welch Foods Company (at the Welch's Grape Juice Bar in Fantasyland).

What was the garden tour like? Well, it met in the Fantasyland Theater and then proceeded as a walking tour using information from the book *Disneyland World of Flowers* by Morgan "Bill" Evans (originally published 1965 with a foreword by Walt Disney) and available for sale at Disneyland Park in the Main Street Flower Market.

Here is a glimpse of the tour of the Disneyland horticulture that at the time was conservatively estimated at costing three million dollars.

"His Highness, Prince Charming, has ordered the royal gardens of Disneyland opened for inspection and public tours to all who enter his kingdom during the Cinderella Festival.

"For the first time, the Disneylandscape artists—the men who pamper and nurture this botanical wonderland—will conduct the special tours, pointing out highlights of the horticulture spectacle."

Disneyland Ambassador

An actual Cinderella story was 1971 Disneyland Ambassador twenty-two year old Marva Dickson who was a former Disneyland Tour Guide.

According to Disneyland publicity, she was selected "from among hundreds of Disneyland women on the basis of attractiveness, personality, intelligence and the ability to communicate and project the congenial attitude of the entire Disneyland organization".

She was an avid mountain climber and violin player. She had attended UC Santa Barbara before transferring to USC where she graduated with a Bachelor of Arts degree in Psychology. Her parents lived in Pasadena with a fifteen year old son named David.

The ceremony was held on November 18,1970 where 1970 Disneyland Ambassador Cathy Birk and Mickey Mouse congratulated the new emissary of goodwill and friendship. Mickey presented her with a bouquet of yellow roses and the previous year's Ambassador Cathy Birk pinned the Ambassador insignia and sash on Marva.

Indian Village

The biggest closure that was needed to make way for the new Bear Country land was the Disneyland Indian Village that had been in that location since 1955.

Walt Disney had great respect and affection for Native Americans, even demonstrated in his films like the Davy Crockett series where the character was described as an "Indian fighter" but who spent much of his time helping and defending Native Americans.

Walt Disney wanted Frontierland to be representative of the wild frontier rather than a settled town. He felt that the Indian Village was a celebration of the cultural heritage of American Indians and help give guests a more accurate representation than the stereotypes seen on television and in the movies.

Walt told reporters that one of the founding principles of Disneyland was the preservation of the American heritage.

The site was filled with authentic props that had been used in the Disney live action film *Westward Ho The Wagons!* (1956). There were several teepees filled with decorations and artifacts as well as signage explaining it all.

The Chippewa Longhouse was authentic and was built by Alexander Matthews Bobidosh, President of the Ojibwe (Chippewa) Tribal Council and a member of the First Nations. The structure had "sewn" Birch & White ash roof, and frame work made of saplings laced with leather.

The village also had a facsimile of a Burial Ground, a stuffed Bison (something most Americans had never seen) and a Navajo Sand Painting exhibit.

There were demonstrations of archery in what was known as the Pawnee Arrow Game, displays and demonstrations of arts and crafts like weaving and beadwork as well as short presentations about Native American culture.

In its publications and on park postcards, Disney described it as "full blooded Indians in a peaceful and authentic village" unlike the savage war parties that burned down the settler's cabin and would occasionally attack Fort Wilderness on Tom Sawyer Island.

The main attraction was the hourly performances of ceremonial dances in a dance circle representing the sun by actual Native Americans from seventeen different tribes.

By the standards of the time, it was a respectful and authentic interpretation of Native Americans compared with other depictions in the media. However, there were other elements that were acceptable at the time but wouldn't be considered politically correct today. The restrooms were labeled "braves" (for men) and "squaws" (for women).

The Native Americans only appeared at Disneyland during weekends, summers and holidays. Starting in 1956, guests could grab an oar and climb aboard one of the Indian War Canoes captained by a real Native American at both the front and back and attempt to navigate the Rivers of America around Tom Sawyer Island.

In 1957, the Soviet Press reported that Frontierland was holding Indians in captivity to amuse "capitalist visitors", [but] Chief Riley Sunrise retorted "Captivity my eye! How many Russians make a hundred and twenty-five dollars a week?"

With the passing of Walt Disney in December 1966 and the social unrest in the late 1960s, challenges began to arise in the Indian Village. Described vaguely as "labor problems" with the Native American performers and the increasingly reduced interest in the area by guests now more interested in spacemen and aliens, Disneyland officially closed the Indian Village October 1971, the beginning of the new fiscal year.

The Indian war canoes were still popular so were renamed Davy Crockett's Explorer Canoes now piloted by frontiersmen and lasted seasonally for another twenty-five years. The site was transformed into Bear Country to showcase the new Country Bear Jamboree attraction the opened in 1972.

While the Indian Village closed in 1971, some of its spirit lived on. At the Disneyland Hotel was a miniature golf course that opened in 1961 called the Magic Kingdom Golf Course and hole number twelve was themed to the Indian Village. Ironically, it outlived the actual Indian Village by another seven years before the course was closed in 1978.

The Pacific Northwest totem poles that appeared in 1965 were relocated to Walt Disney World's Frontierland to find a new home near the train station. Though based on actual cultural designs and elements, many of these poles were crafted by artists at Oceanic Arts rather than Native American artists.

The trashcans that were cleverly designed to resemble tree stumps were relocated to WDW's Fort Wilderness Resort and Campground.

The Death of Roy O. Disney

Perhaps one of the greatest losses to Disneyland in 1971 was the passing of Roy O. Disney, the older brother of Walt Disney who took over running the Walt Disney Company after the death of his brother in December 1966.

It was Roy who kept Disneyland growing although for most of 1971 he was spending time in Florida to get WDW opened on time.

When the television special, *The Grand Opening of Walt Disney World* aired on NBC on Friday October 29, 1971, Roy sat next to his wife Edna in their Bay Hill house and began weeping.

Roy returned to California and never came back to Florida. He had planned to stay in California only until February 1st for the annual meeting and then with his wife get on a cruise ship for Australia for a few weeks and make plans for additional travel as he transitioned out of the company.

Roy had complained for some time about seeing something like a cloud over his vision but delayed going in for blood tests, assuming he just needed a new prescription for his glasses.

Roy Disney fell into a coma on Sunday, December 19, 1971 and was rushed to a hospital. He died of a cerebral hemorrhage on Monday night, December 20, 1971 in Room 421 at St. Joseph's Medical Center in Burbank, California at the age of seventy-eight. It was the same hospital where he had sobbed uncontrollably at the loss of his younger brother a half decade earlier.

Flags flew at half staff over Disneyland and Walt Disney World on that Tuesday in honor of Roy but both parks remained open for business.

"When Walt died," said Jack Lindquist, "Roy said a lot of people had come from a lot of different places that day to see Disneyland so it remained open. He felt it was the only way to do business."

Reporter Charlie Wadsworth wrote an article in the December 22, 1971, edition of The Orlando Sentinel: "It was Roy Disney's guidance and leadership that brought Walt Disney World to its opening. He was completely dedicated to building the dreams of his brother Walt. They say a little of Roy left when Walt died in 1966 of cancer. But not much could have left.

"He was the keeper of the flame and had to be the curator of the spirit that Walt Disney created. He inherited the Disney entertainment empire. It was difficult for his neighbors in Windermere to grow accustomed to the fact that the little round, balding man with the twinkling eyes and inquisitive nature was the chairman of the board. But that's the way Roy Disney wanted it. That is the way he lived…[he] was a man of great personal warmth and charm, as personable as his late brother Walt."

1972

- Attendance: 9.6 million
- Employment: 6,190
- Payroll: $37, 000,000
- Candlelight Processional Narrator: Rock Hudson
- Disneyland Ambassador: Emily Zinser
- Highlights:
  - Bear Country opens at a cost of eight million dollars
  - Main Street Electrical Parade premieres June 17
  - Winnie the Pooh for President Day
  - Rock 'n Roll Reunion sparked September entertainment with Frankie Avalon, Chuck Berry, The Drifters and The Platters.
  - Disneyland Hotel opened a $7.2 million Convention Center with a 29,000 square-foot exhibit hall and an 18,000 square-foot Grand Ballroom.

Even though Roy O. Disney passed away the previous December and had intended to retire from the company after the 1972 annual stockholder's meeting, his influence is still in evidence in the 1972 Disneyland.

Winnie the Pooh for President

Winnie the Pooh's first campaign for President began on the night of July 14, 1968 at a special Family Night at the Hollywood Bowl. A host of Disney costumed characters showed up to support Pooh.

The musical entertainment for the evening was provided by the Hollywood Bowl Orchestra and Disneyland's Kids of the Kingdom that featured the release of thousands of red, white, and blue balloons at the finale.

Pooh moved his campaigning to the Tomorrowland Stage at Disneyland to become part of the Kids of the Kingdom show *On Stage U.S.A.* that was performed twice a day. The segment was appropriately called "Winnie the Pooh for President" and sometimes included rotating celebrities like puppeteer Shari Lewis and singer Peggy Lee.

The show was performed during July and August, ending when children went back to school and attendance at Disneyland dropped.

"Pooh in '72" was the campaign slogan for a three day special Disneyland event that ran from October 21 to October 23, 1972. Each day there was a ticker tape parade down Main Street U.S.A. The Disneyland Band under the direction of Vessey Walker played "Hip-Hip-Pooh-Ray" from *Winnie the Pooh and the Blustery Day*.

Sears was having huge sales of exclusive Disney Winnie the Pooh merchandise so were eager to get on board for the promotion. The Sears stores sold some exclusive "Winnie the Pooh for President" merchandise.

Pooh, Tigger, and Eeyore did meet and greets all day at their National Campaign Headquarters in the Carnation Plaza Gardens.

Marilyn Magness, Walt Disney Imagineering Creative Entertainment Portfolio Leader for the Resort, recalled working on the event. "Pooh for President was a fun campaign. The first time Winnie the Pooh ran for president was a fun concept to put together. At that time, what a risk! But what fun to overdress Pooh in his Uncle Sam hat and his little vest and have Tigger be his campaign manager."

On October 1, 1972, at a convention held at Walt Disney World, Pooh was nominated to run for president on the Children's Party ticket. Drawings had been held at Sears, Roebuck and Co. and those stores across the nation selected delegates from each of the 50 states to be sent with their families to Walt Disney World.

Sears was having huge sales of exclusive Disney Winnie the Pooh merchandise so were eager to get on board for the promotion. The Sears stores sold some exclusive Winnie the Pooh for President merchandise like a plush figure that proved very popular.

As part of the festivities, the delegates nominated Pooh for President of the United States in the forecourt of Cinderella Castle. Two days after the Walt Disney World event, from his "West Coast retreat" at Disneyland, Pooh announced his platform and campaign strategy.

Although supposedly still recuperating from his Florida visit, Pooh took the microphone for some 30 seconds (in Sterling Holloway's offstage voice) to address a large group of personal friends and enthusiastic supporters who had gathered near Sleeping Beauty Castle.

His short speech outlined his policy platforms to put "hunny in every pot." He also mentioned his battle to "lick" the high price of ice cream cones and that there would be hot fudge sundaes every Monday and banning all spankings. The crowd cheered enthusiastically and loudly.

Pooh and his press secretary Tigger, with campaign manager Eeyore, left on a old-fashioned two week cross country, whistle-stop train campaign tour sponsored by Sears and Amtrak before setting up his official campaign headquarters in Disneyland.

The tour started on the Disneyland Railroad with plenty of photographs of Pooh surrounded by Disney characters, but eventually transferred to a special Amtrak Train that started at Los Angeles Union Station and stopped in many towns on the way to Chicago and Washington D.C.

"We went from Union Station in L.A., across country to Kansas City, Chicago and the Sears Tower, then on to Washington, D.C., then back west and up the coast to Seattle before returning to Los Angeles. We did it all in two weeks and all by train," said Gary Moore who at the time was a photographer for Disneyland who accompanied the other seven Disneyland personnel on board.

"When we got to Barstow that first night, there were several-thousand people with children all waiting to see Winnie the Pooh, Tigger and Eeyore."

A baggage car had been adapted into a traveling stage with big doors on either side that would open up, depending upon which side the audience was at a particular stop.

The show lasted roughly 10 to 15 minutes as the Pooh characters danced to a pre-recorded soundtrack. Afterward, they joined the audience for photo opportunities. The excitement of the audience was so great that the stops ran much longer than expected resulting in the train running faster between destinations.

One night, the Disney personnel were awoken in their private sleeping car at 1:30 a.m. as they approached a small town in New Mexico with a population of only 200 people.

"It turned out there were about 2,000 people waiting there to see Winnie the Pooh," Moore said. "Children were bundled up and sitting on their dads' shoulders and more, so they switched us to the siding there so we could do the show."

At the urging of his press secretary and "close personal friend" Tigger, Pooh declared, "If elected in November, I will put two tricycles in every garage, provide free candy on holidays, and make sure everyone enjoys two Saturdays a week."

Owl was in the running to be Pooh's pick for vice-president.

"According to press secretary Tigger," claimed one report, "Owl is on the inside track because of the learned bird's appeal to both the left and right wingers."

Pooh ended up picking Piglet.

"Pooh-litical" rallies in support of Pooh for President were held all over that month, with marching bands and free balloons, pictures, buttons, and posters for kids supplied by Sears.

During the three-day event in Disneyland, Pooh, Tigger, and Eeyore were available for meet and greets all day at their National Campaign Headquarters in the Carnation Plaza Gardens.

According to the California Orange County Registrar of Voters, Pooh did receive some votes in 1972, but because the records from that year were not yet computerized, the exact amount is unknown.

The popularity of the 1972 campaign guaranteed that one in 1976 would be even bigger.

Bear Country & Country Bear Jamboree

Originally the area had been an extension of Frontierland and featured the Indian Village. The huge popularity of the Country Bear Jamboree attraction in Walt Disney World prompted Disneyland to create an entire new land called Bear Country that would showcase that attraction and draw more guests around the loop of the Rivers of America. Disney spent roughly eight million dollars on the four acre spot.

Bear Country opened in 1972 with the main attraction being the Country Bear Jamboree. The Indian Trading Post remained as did the canoes but now they were themed to Davy Crockett. The Hungry Bear Restaurant appeared. The Golden Bear Lodge and Mile Long Bar also were added along with Ursus H. Bear's Wilderness Outpost.

To enhance the pathway between the Haunted Mansion and the entrance to the newly opened Bear Country, the Imagineers installed a cave on the mountainside just above eye level. The cave was identified as being the home of Rufus the bear who was in constant hibernation.

To the delight of many guests, a distinctive snore constantly emanated from the cave opening. The snore was originally recorded sometime in the mid-1930s, probably by storyman and voice artist Pinto Colvig, to be used for the dwarf Sleepy in *Snow White and the Seven Dwarfs* (1937).

It was discovered in the Disney Studios sound library decades later and incorporated into an El Dorado Hotel second floor room in Frontierland's mining town of Rainbow Ridge façade. Then the snore was moved to the opening of Rufus' cave. For awhile in Bear Country, the exterior of the men's restroom in the area was themed as Rufus' dressing room. (The female restroom was themed to Trixie.)

The famous sleeping bear was not originally part of the Country Bear Jamboree but was incorporated into the show with the holiday overlay Country Bear Christmas Special that debuted in 1984. Rufus was now the sleepy, lone stage hand in charge of fixing lights, running projections and changing backdrops.

He is constantly admonished by Zeke, Wendell or Henry for not having something working. Poor Rufus who is never seen is often heard to be out of breath as he struggles to run to different locations to fix things, sometimes resulting in something crashing to the floor in the booth behind the audience or a sudden electrical jolt.

He generally just speaks in surprised grunts. He was also incorporated into the Country Bear Vacation Hoedown show that premiered in February 1986 in a similar role.

Country Bear Jamboree was one of a small handful of Florida-only attractions that opened with the Magic Kingdom on October 1, 1971.

In a beautifully ornate proscenium theater, a variety of audio-animatronics bears and a handful of other animals like a raccoon perform a series of musical numbers with a country and western theme on multiple different stages, just like an old fashioned knee-slapping hoedown at the Grand Ol' Opry...but with lots more fur.

"Clap your hands and stomp your feet and try to keep right with 'em. One sure thing the Bear Band's got is real ol' country rhythm".

The concept art for this lively show was some of the last artwork ever seen by Walt Disney himself and it gave him a good laugh shortly before his untimely passing. Designed by Imagineer Marc Davis and Al Bertino (the physical inspiration for the "Big Al" character), the Country Bear Jamboree was originally intended to be an indoor evening attraction at the Bear Band Restaurant in Disney's planned Mineral King Ski Resort, which was to be built in California in the 1960s.

As Imagineer Wathel Rogers recalled, "After the Mineral King contract had been signed, Walt had an idea for entertainment after people had been skiing. Walt said, 'What we are going to do is have a bear band and have them perform two or three programs of entertainment. We'll say that the bears had come out of the sequoias and we trained them to be entertainers'."

The Mineral King project fell through, and with a few changes, the show premiered opening day at the Magic Kingdom in Florida, where it was so popular that a replica was built in 1972 at Disneyland in California with two theaters to accommodate the expected huge crowds. It was the first new ticketed attraction at Disneyland since the Haunted Mansion in 1969.

When it was decided that the attraction was going to be Florida-specific, it was natural that, since country music was so popular in that part of the country, when the Floridian bears came together to make music it would be country-western.

Henry and Wendell were based on a comedic musical country-western act known as Homer and Jethro. Just like Henry and Wendell, Homer played guitar and Jethro played the mandolin. Davis playfully based Wendell's appearance on fellow Imagineer Harper Goff, who played the banjo in the musical group The Firehouse Five Plus Two.

Homer and Jethro wrote *Fractured Folk Song* and *Mama Don't Whoop Little Buford*, which Henry and Wendell sing in the show.

Jethro wrote the lyrics to the song *Mama, Don't Whoop Little Buford* sung to the tune *Beautiful, Beautiful Brown Eyes*, composed by Arthur Smith in the late 1940s, but popularized by both Jimmy Wakely and Rosemary Clooney in 1951. The song's original lyrics feature the refrain "I'll never love blue eyes again" in place of the words "I think you should shoot him instead."

As the years have progressed and the world has changed, more and more things in Disney animated cartoons — from smoking to making fun of women drivers to humor in the theme park shows — were no longer considered appropriate for today's audiences. In particular, the *Mama Don't Whoop Little Buford* segment reportedly concerned some WDW guests that it was promoting child abuse. Audiences 40 years ago laughed at the idea of corporal punishment, having sometimes been the victim of it themselves by strict parents or teachers.

Since this was a Florida-only attraction when it opened, the bears all had biographies that emphasized their Southern roots. For instance, Liver Lips McGrowl was the "Miami Serenader", Trixie was known as "The Tampa Temptation" and Big Al grew up around the swamps that became Walt Disney World. When it opened in Disneyland, it was natural to change them to bears from the North Woods.

The back story for the attraction was that Ursus H. Bear, after a restful hibernation, rounded up his musically inclined kinfolk and friends to put on a down-home celebration. As guests, we've been invited to join in on the fun as the show continues to celebrate that first performance so many years ago.

Over the years, a variety of different shows with different costuming and songs have rotated through at Disneyland including a Christmas Special show (introduced in 1984) and the Vacation Hoedown (introduced in 1986) that continued to be the show until 2001.

Performances were by master of ceremonies Henry (and his raccoon hat Sammy), Gomer the piano player, The Five Bear Rugs (Zeke, Fred, Ted, Zeb, and Tennessee with Zeb's non speaking son Oscar and his teddy bear sitting on the edge of the stage), Wendell who plays the mandolin, Liver Lips McGrowl, Trixie, Terrence, The Sun Bonnets (Bunny, Bubbles and Beulah), Ernest the fiddle player, the "swinging" Teddi Barra and the unforgettable Big Albert. On the adjacent wall, the talking heads of Buff the bison, Max the deer and Melvin the bull moose often joined in the festivities.

Some of the songs in the original show were *Mama, Don't Whip Little Buford, All the Guys that Turn Me On Turn Me Down, Blood on the Saddle, and The Ballad of Davy Crockett*. The Vacation Hoedown featured *On the Road Again, California Bears Thank God I'm a Country Bear, The Great Outdoors and Rocky Top* among other songs.

Main Street Electrical Parade

"Ladies and gentlemen, boys and girls... Disneyland proudly presents our spectacular festival pageant of nighttime magic and imagination in thousands of sparkling lights and electro-syntho-magnetic musical sounds — the Main Street Electrical Parade!"

The parade was inspired by The Electrical Water Pageant that included *Baroque Hoedown* as its main musical theme and music produced by a Moog synthesizer. It premiered at Walt Disney World's Seven Seas Lagoon and Bay Lake beginning in October 1971. Rafts holding two-dimensional frames were decorated with colored Christmas bulb lights that created charming images of sea creatures.

Director of Entertainment Bob Jani along with Ron Miziker developed a dry land version for Disneyland the following year with over a half million twinkling lights on floats that were two dimensional flat frames (like the Electrical Water Pageant) on wheels designed by Bill Justice. In addition, cast members attired in lighted costumes accompanied the procession.

When the original contractor could not complete the floats in time, Disneyland itself finished building the floats (as well as using some previously existing parade floats) and installing the lights.

The new parade also used the *Baroque Hoedown* as it main musical theme interweaved with songs from Disney films produced by a Moog synthesizer that created a somewhat futuristic, other-worldly aspect to the event. Eventually, Don Dorsey used eleven synthesizers to create the soundtrack. Jack Wagner provided the synthesized vocoder voice for the intro and outro to the parade

The original parade floats included the Blue Fairy, a large drum pulled by the Casey Jr. train engine, Cinderella, a Chinese dragon and a circus calliope.

The parade did not operate during 1975 and 1976 as it was temporarily replaced by America on Parade to celebrate the American Bicentennial. During that break, the MSEP was redesigned with more dimensional floats, a longer running time and a memorable patriotic climax.

The parade units included Tinker Bell, Alice in Wonderland, Cinderella, Peter Pan, Dumbo, Snow White and the Seven Dwarfs, Pinocchio, and Pete's Dragon. Over the years units left or were added including ones for It's A Small World, Briny Deep (*Bedknobs and Broomsticks*) and 1985's *Return to Oz*.

A New Era

The year 1972 brought to a close the years when Walt or Roy would have had any direct influence on new things at Disneyland.

In the coming years, decisions about Disneyland would be made by committee under the supervision of Chief Operating Officer and President Card Walker and Chairman of the Board and Chief Executive Officer Donn Tatum. Later Ron Miller, Michael Eisner, Frank Wells and Robert Iger would control Disneyland's destiny. But those are other stories for another time.

Acknowledgements

As always, I would like to acknowledge not only the people who directly helped me with this specific book, but those who have inspired or supported me over the years. There are indeed angels in this world and I have been blessed to know so many of them.

I would like to thank all the people who have bought my Disney history books because their support has allowed this book to be published.

This book would not have been possible without the skills and encouragement of publisher Bob McLain and his Theme Park Press.

Thanks to my brothers, Michael and Chris, and their families, including their children—Amber, Keith, Autumn, and Story. Also, my grand-nieces Skylar, Shea, and Sidnee (Fairbanks) and grand nephew Max (Fairbanks) and Alex (Johansen).

Thanks to all the original Disneylanders who were so gracious and generous sharing their memories with a wet-behind-his-ears eager kid who had endless questions.

Thanks to all the historians who have written about Walt's original Disneyland including Jeff Kurtti, Todd James Pierce, Dave R. Smith, Donald Ballard, Randy Bright, Michael Broggie, Bruce Gordon, Kevin Kidney, Howard Lowery, Paula Sigman Lowery David Mumford, Sam Gennawey,

Cecil Munsey, Dave Mason, Tim O'Day, Jason Schultz, Chris Strodder, Robert Tieman, Jeff Pepper, Tom Tumbusch, and others who took the time to do the research and share it with the rest of us.

For this book in particular, I am very grateful to the following historians whose outstanding work and entertaining blog posts made me fall in love with Walt's original Disneyland all over again:

- Werner Weiss (www.yesterland.com)

- Dave De Caro (http://davelandweb.com)

- David Eppen (http://gorillasdontblog.blogspot.com)

- Patrick Jenkins (http://matterhorn1959.blogspot.com)

- and (http://vintagedisneylandtickets.blogspot.com/)

Finally, thanks to Walt Disney for having a vision and the persistence to make a dream come true for all of us and to Roy O. Disney and the others who kept it alive.

About the Author

Jim Korkis is an internationally respected Disney historian who has written hundreds of articles and thirty books about all things Disney over the last forty years. Jim grew up in Glendale, California where starting at the young age of fifteen, he was able to meet and interview some of Walt's original team of animators and Imagineers.

In 1995, he relocated to Orlando, Florida where he worked for Walt Disney World in a variety of capacities including Entertainment, Animation, Disney Institute, Disney University, College and International Programs, Disney Cruise Line, Disney Design Group, Disney Vacation Club, Disney Learning Center, Yellow Shoes Marketing and more.

Jim grew up going to Disneyland as a child with his parents and brothers, and later as a teenager and an adult. During those decades he interviewed and made friends with many people who worked at the Park. Jim has written four other books about Disneyland including The Unofficial Disney 1955 Companion that covers in extensive detail the lengthy creation and first year of operation of the Happiest Place on Earth.

His original research on Disney history has been used often by the Walt Disney Company as well as other organizations including the Disney Family Museum.

Several websites currently frequently feature Jim's articles about Disney history:

- MousePlanet.com

- AllEars.net

- CartoonResearch.com

- YourFirstVisit.net

In addition, Jim is a frequent guest on multiple podcasts as well as a consultant and keynote speaker to various businesses, schools and groups.

Jim is not currently an employee of the Disney Company.

To read more stories by Jim Korkis about Disney history, please check out his other books, all available from ThemeParkPress.com.

Other Books by Jim Korkis

- *The WDW 50th Anniversary Quiz Master Challenge (2021)*
- *The Vault of Walt: Volume 10 (2021)*
- *Hidden Treasures of Walt Disney World Resort Hotels (2021)*
- *Kungaloosh! (2021)*
- *Secret Stories of Extinct Walt Disney World (2020)*
- *Hidden Treasures of the Disney Cruise Line (2020)*
- *The Vault of Walt, Volume 9, Halloween Edition (2020)*
- *The Vault of Walt, Volume 8, Outer Space Edition (2019)*
- *Disney Never Lands (2019)*
- *Secret Stories of Extinct Disneyland (2019)*
- *The Unofficial Walt Disney World 1971 Companion (2019)*
- *The Vault of Walt: Volume 7, Christmas Edition (2018)*
- *Secret Stories of Mickey Mouse (2018)*
- *More Secret Stories of Disneyland (2018)*
- *Extra Secret Stories of Walt Disney World (2018)*
- *Call Me Walt (2017)*
- *Walt's Words (2017)*
- *Other Secret Stories of Walt Disney World (2017)*
- *Secret Stories of Disneyland (2017)*
- *The Vault of Walt: Volume 6 (2017)*
- *Gremlin Trouble (2017)*
- *Donald Duck's Daddy (2017)*
- *More Secret Stories of Walt Disney World (2016)*
- *The Vault of Walt: Volume 5 (2016)*
- *The Unofficial Disneyland 1955 Companion (2016)*
- *How to Be a Disney Historian (2016)*
- *Secret Stories of Walt Disney World (2015)*
- *The Vault of Walt: Volume 4 (2015)*
- *Everything I Know I Learned from Disney Animated Features (2015)*
- *The Vault of Walt: Volume 3 (2014)*
- *Animation Anecdotes (2014)*
- *Who's the Leader of the Club? Walt Disney's Leadership Lessons (2014)*
- *The Book of Mouse (2013)*
- *The Vault of Walt: Volume 2 (2013)*
- *Who's Afraid of the Song of the South? (2012)*
- *The Revised Vault of Walt (2012)*